EDDIE KANTAR TEACHES

# Advanced Bridge Defense

EDDIE KANTAR TEACHES

# Advanced Bridge Defense

MASTER POINT PRESS

TORONTO

**Master Point Press**
331 Douglas Avenue
Toronto, Ontario, Canada
M5M 1H2          (416)781-0351
Websites:          www.masterpointpress.com
                   www.masteringbridge.com
                   www.bridgeblogging.com
                   www.ebooksbridge.com
Email:             info@masterpointpress.com

**Canadian Cataloguing in Publication Data**

Kantar, Edwin B., 1932-
Eddie Kantar teaches advanced bridge defense

Includes index
ISBN  978-1-894154-03-1

1. Contract bridge — Defensive play.  I. Title.

GV1282.42.K36 1999      795.41'53       C98-932700-0

| | |
|---|---|
| *Editor* | Ray Lee |
| *Cover and Interior design* | Opus House |
| *Author photograph* | Shireen Mohandes |

Printed and bound in Canada

5 6 7 8 9 10        13 12 11 10 09

I know that it is customary for the author to thank the people who have helped with the book you are about to read.  I have two people I wish to thank: Ray Lee, the publisher, whose idea and patience (with me) made this book possible, and Yvonne Snyder, who read every word and told me in no uncertain terms when I wrote something that wasn't clear.  Since Yvonne plays at the level at which this book is written, I made every change she suggested.  If this book turns out to be a winner, it's because of these two people.


*Eddie Kantar*

# Introduction

Hello again. I'm assuming that you have read (survived) the first book in this series, *Eddie Kantar teaches Modern Bridge Defense*. Well, whether you have or whether you haven't, prepare yourself for some advanced defensive techniques.

The emphasis in this book will be on defensive logic. Trump promotion, card combinations, deceptive play and most of all, counting. In fact, three whole chapters are devoted to counting: counting declarer's tricks, declarer's distribution and declarer's high card points, to be specific.

Having spent a lifetime teaching intermediate players, I can say with some authority that very few can count properly. (I guess if they could count, they wouldn't be intermediate players!) Some say that when they try to count, it slows down the game too much; others says they can't play and count at the same time; others don't think they can do it, so they won't even try. I'm going to ask you to try, because if you are not counting, you are playing a different game.

A warning. Once you start counting, your game will sink a bit. It's almost inevitable. One tends to forget about everything else and make more mistakes than ever. But once you master the basic counting skills, your game will improve so much that you won't even recognize the player you once were. The players you used to think were such hot shots are now suddenly looking human. You can do some of the same stuff they can. This book is going to help you think; it's going to help you count; it's going to turn you into a competent defensive player. But you must make a commitment to hang in there. Don't let me down on this one.

*Eddie Kantar*

# Contents

# Planning the Defense at Suit Contracts

1

*Ready in defense, full of resources.*

EDMUND BURKE

The opponents are bidding their heads off; suddenly, the bidding is over and it's your lead. And just what have you been doing while the opponents were merrily sending these coded messages to each other across the table? Not daydreaming, I hope.

Defensive planning starts with the bidding and comes into clearer focus when the dummy appears. The bidding helps determine your opening lead. The dummy, partner's signals, and bridge logic help determine your follow-up plays. During the bidding you should be trying to build a picture of declarer's (and dummy's) distribution and strength. This picture also influences your opening lead. If the opponents wind up in a trump contract, you should ask yourself:

1) What kind of a trump fit do I expect from the bidding? Will it be a 6-3, 5-3, 5-4, 4-4, etc. Or are the opponents playing a misfit?
2) Did the opponents stretch to get to this contract or was it bid confidently with no invitational bids?
3) Does dummy figure to have a long side suit?
4) Has dummy preferred one of declarer's two suits to the other,

## WHAT YOU'RE GOING TO LEARN IN THIS CHAPTER:

- How to recognize what declarer's plan will be from the bidding and the dummy
- How to plan your own defensive strategy accordingly
- Some useful defensive stratagems you can apply in various common situations

particularly the second over the first, indicating shortness in the first suit?

5) Do you have four trumps, a side-suit singleton, or an honor sequence?

The answers to these questions help determine your lead. Although this chapter deals primarily with planning your defense *after* the dummy comes down, it can't hurt to review the opening-lead decision. After all, if you screw up on opening lead, it may be too late to recover no matter how clever a defender you are.

Opening leads can be categorized as: *attacking, passive* (including trump leads), *short suit,* or *honor sequence.* The last two are self-explanatory. Attacking leads are generally made in suits headed by the ace or king. They are made when you fear (or see) a long side suit in dummy or are looking for a ruff. Leading from long broken suits also falls under this category. These leads are often made when you (or partner) have four trumps and your goal is to whittle declarer's trump length down to your size or shorter. Passive leads are safe leads, leads that neither gain nor cost a trick. There is an art in knowing how and when to make passive leads. Much of this chapter will be spent going over this aspect of defensive play.

If you have an idea of how declarer will get rid of her losers, you may be able to thwart declarer's plans. Basically there are three ways declarer disposes of losers:

1) Discarding them on dummy's strong side suit.
2) Ruffing them in the short hand, usually the dummy.
3) Via endplays, elimination plays, loser on loser plays, etc.

If (1) and (2), the two common techniques, are not available, declarer is usually stuck with whatever losers she has. There is no need for the defenders to rush madly to take their aces and kings, perhaps giving up tricks by attacking new suits. Declarer's losers aren't going anywhere. *Don't panic!*

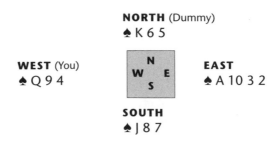

**NORTH** (Dummy)
♠ K 6 5

**WEST** (You)
♠ Q 9 4

**EAST**
♠ A 10 3 2

**SOUTH**
♠ J 8 7

This is a typical card combination where South, left to his own devices, has three losers and no winners. If the defenders get nervous and start the suit, declarer makes an undeserved trick.

If you and partner can identify these 'dangerous' suits (not always easy), these are suits to stay away from, far away. Declarer, on the other hand, is either hoping you will make a friendly play in one of these suits, or failing that, wants to force you to lead one. Thus the constant struggle between the declarer and the defenders to see who can get the other to break a dangerous suit.

# Identifying the dummy

Once the dummy appears you can usually tell if you had it right with your choice of opening leads. If not, you may have to change horses in midstream. There are three common dummy types that should hit you in the face when you see them.

### Type 1. Dummy has ruffing potential but little else

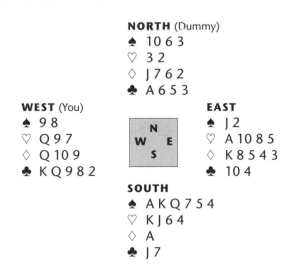

**NORTH** (Dummy)
♠ 10 6 3
♡ 3 2
◇ J 7 6 2
♣ A 6 5 3

**WEST** (You)
♠ 9 8
♡ Q 9 7
◇ Q 10 9
♣ K Q 9 8 2

**EAST**
♠ J 2
♡ A 10 8 5
◇ K 8 5 4 3
♣ 10 4

**SOUTH**
♠ A K Q 7 5 4
♡ K J 6 4
◇ A
♣ J 7

| NORTH-SOUTH VUL. DEALER SOUTH |  |  |  |
| --- | --- | --- | --- |
| **West** | **North** | **East** | **South** |
|  |  |  | 1♠ |
| pass | 2♠ | pass | 4♠ |
| all pass |  |  |  |

Opening lead: ♣K

You lead the ♣K to dummy's ace, partner's ♣10 and declarer's ♣7. You see that the dummy is pretty bleak. Furthermore, there is no possibility of long suit establishment. The only real value in this pitiful dummy is the doubleton heart.

Sure enough, declarer leads a heart to the jack and your queen at trick two. No need to cash the ♣Q, that winner isn't going away. More important is to shift to a spade at trick three. Declarer can do no better than win in her hand and lead a low heart. Either you or partner can grab this and lead a second trump. Declarer can only ruff one heart in dummy and winds up losing three hearts and one club. When the only value dummy has is a short side suit, trump leads are usually top priority.

### Type 2. Dummy has a threatening side suit

Of course, much depends upon how threatening the suit really is. For example: it may be a solid suit (very threatening); it may be a supported suit missing one honor (very threatening); you may be sitting behind the dummy with small cards in the suit so you know that if any finesses are required, they work (very threatening); or you may be sitting over the dummy with all of the missing honors and you know declarer cannot set up the suit (not threatening at all). Your defense (active or passive) depends upon your assessment of the danger of the long suit.

NORTH-SOUTH VUL. DEALER SOUTH

| West | North | East | South |
|------|-------|------|-------|
|      |       |      | 1♠    |
| pass | 2♠    | pass | 3♠    |
| pass | 4♠    | all pass |    |

Opening lead: ♡K

**NORTH** (Dummy)
♠ 10 3 2
♡ 6
◇ A Q J 10 8
♣ 8 5 4 3

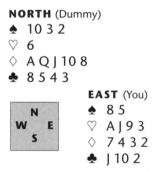

**EAST** (You)
♠ 8 5
♡ A J 9 3
◇ 7 4 3 2
♣ J 10 2

Partner leads the ♡K and dummy hits with a very threatening suit, diamonds, plus a singleton heart. A dummy with a threatening side suit calls for an attacking defense, but a dummy with a side suit singleton calls for a trump switch. What to do?

The length and strength of dummy's side suit is so overwhelming (either declarer has the ◇K or it can be finessed), that an active (attacking) defense takes precedence over a trump shift defense. Overtake the ♡K and fire the ♣J through declarer.

If the hand turns out to be something like this, you will be a real hero.

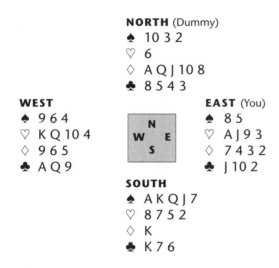

**NORTH** (Dummy)
♠ 10 3 2
♡ 6
♢ A Q J 10 8
♣ 8 5 4 3

**WEST**
♠ 9 6 4
♡ K Q 10 4
♢ 9 6 5
♣ A Q 9

**EAST** (You)
♠ 8 5
♡ A J 9 3
♢ 7 4 3 2
♣ J 10 2

**SOUTH**
♠ A K Q J 7
♡ 8 7 5 2
♢ K
♣ K 7 6

But suppose the hand had been a little different:

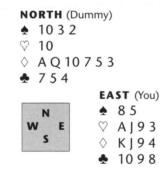

**NORTH** (Dummy)
♠ 10 3 2
♡ 10
♢ A Q 10 7 5 3
♣ 7 5 4

**EAST** (You)
♠ 8 5
♡ A J 9 3
♢ K J 9 4
♣ 10 9 8

| EAST-WEST VUL. | | DEALER EAST | |
|---|---|---|---|
| **West** | **North** | **East** | **South** |
| | | pass | 1♠ |
| pass | 2♠ | pass | 4♠ |
| all pass | | | |

Opening lead: ♡K

Partner leads the ♡K and you gaze at the dummy. This time the diamonds are not threatening, you have them locked up from here to Sunday. This dummy is good for one thing and one thing only, heart ruffs. Overtake partner's lead and shift to a trump. What about shifting to the ♣10? Club tricks cannot disappear; whatever club tricks your side has coming will come in due time. What can disappear are heart tricks. Furthermore, when you switch to a trump looking at those diamonds, you are shouting *'Partner, don't worry about the diamonds'*.

Let's take a look at a possible layout:

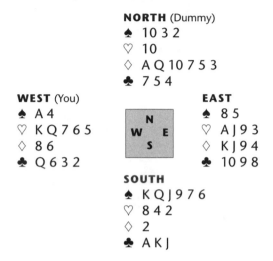

**NORTH** (Dummy)
♠ 10 3 2
♡ 10
♢ A Q 10 7 5 3
♣ 7 5 4

**WEST** (You)
♠ A 4
♡ K Q 7 6 5
♢ 8 6
♣ Q 6 3 2

**EAST**
♠ 8 5
♡ A J 9 3
♢ K J 9 4
♣ 10 9 8

**SOUTH**
♠ K Q J 9 7 6
♡ 8 4 2
♢ 2
♣ A K J

Assuming partner follows your defense and plays ace and a spade, declarer is slated to lose four tricks. Notice that declarer's ♣J isn't going anywhere, it will be a loser in due time.

If there is a strong *usable* side suit in dummy, play an attacking defense; if the long side suit in dummy is *not* usable play passively, perhaps by leading a trump to cut down dummy's ruffing power.

### Type 3. Dummy is balanced

A balanced dummy is one that has no shortness, and no side suit longer than four cards. Of course, even a four-card suit can generate winners for discards. But for our purposes, a balanced dummy is one with no ruffing potential, and no clearly establishable side suit. When a balanced dummy hits the table, think 'passive'.

Playing passively means not leading (or continuing) any suit where there is a reasonable chance of giving up a trick if any missing honors or critical spot cards are in declarer's hand. In many cases you can lose a trick by leading a suit where two honors are missing and they are divided between the two unseen hands. Deciding whether to break a new suit, or which new suit to break if forced to, is among the most difficult aspects of defensive play.

A trump lead from two, three, or four small is usually passive though at times it may eat up partner's queen (usually it can be finessed anyway). Forcing declarer to ruff is passive — as long as it doesn't set up any usable winners in dummy. A wonderful example of a passive play is leading a suit where the declaring side has all the top cards in the suit, like giving declarer ice in the winter. 'Passive' is another way of saying 'safe'.

**NORTH** (Dummy)
♠ K 8 4 3
♡ 10 8 3
◇ A 10 6
♣ K 9 6

**WEST** (You)
♠ J 9 6 5
♡ 8 7
◇ K 9 5
♣ Q 8 4 3

| BOTH VUL. | | DEALER NORTH | |
| West | North | East | South |
| --- | --- | --- | --- |
| | pass | pass | 1♡ |
| pass | 2♡ | pass | 3♡ |
| pass | 4♡ | all pass | |

The opponents have crawled painfully to game, and you don't want to give them trick ten with your opening lead. Say you start by leading a trump, noticing that dummy certainly fits the definition of 'balanced'. Not only that, but your spade holding is strong enough to remove any menace there. Clearly, it is time to get passive, and your trump lead was a good beginning. Let's look at the whole hand:

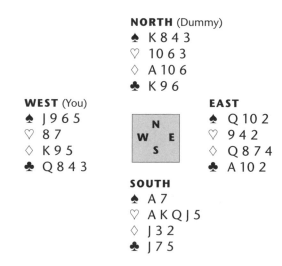

**NORTH** (Dummy)
♠ K 8 4 3
♡ 10 6 3
◇ A 10 6
♣ K 9 6

**WEST** (You)
♠ J 9 6 5
♡ 8 7
◇ K 9 5
♣ Q 8 4 3

**EAST**
♠ Q 10 2
♡ 9 4 2
◇ Q 8 7 4
♣ A 10 2

**SOUTH**
♠ A 7
♡ A K Q J 5
◇ J 3 2
♣ J 7 5

Hand repeated here for convenience.

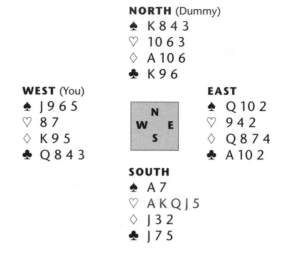

**NORTH** (Dummy)
♠ K 8 4 3
♡ 10 6 3
♢ A 10 6
♣ K 9 6

**WEST** (You)
♠ J 9 6 5
♡ 8 7
♢ K 9 5
♣ Q 8 4 3

**EAST**
♠ Q 10 2
♡ 9 4 2
♢ Q 8 7 4
♣ A 10 2

**SOUTH**
♠ A 7
♡ A K Q J 5
♢ J 3 2
♣ J 7 5

Look carefully at each minor suit. Left to her own devices declarer has two diamond and perhaps three club losers. However, if either you or your partner lead a club or a diamond, declarer has one less loser in that suit.

As it turns out, the two 'safe' suits are hearts and spades. Yes, it's much easier to detect safe suits when one can see all four hands! Nevertheless, you should know what your objective is. When you see a balanced dummy, don't do declarer's work for him, try to play a passive game.

# Other considerations

## Declarer's second suit

When declarer has a known two-suiter (assume 5-5), and a fit is uncovered in one of the two suits, defenders have three different strategies available:

1) Playing an active defense
2) Playing a forcing defense
3) Leading trumps

The trick is to know which one to use. The examples that follow are designed to show you how to answer that question.

**NORTH** (Dummy)
♠ Q 10 6 4
♡ 9 4 2
◇ K 10 9
♣ 8 4 2

**WEST**
♠ 7
♡ A Q 7 3
◇ 4 2
♣ K Q 10 9 6 3

```
      N
   W     E
      S
```

**EAST** (You)
♠ 9 5 2
♡ J 10 8 5
◇ 8 6 3
♣ A J 5

**SOUTH**
♠ A K J 8 3
♡ K 6
◇ A Q J 7 5
♣ 7

NORTH-SOUTH VUL. DEALER SOUTH

| West | North | East | South |
|------|-------|------|-------|
|      |       |      | 1♠    |
| 2♣   | 2♠    | 3♣   | 4◇[1] |
| 4♡   | 4♠    | 5♡   | 5♠    |
| all pass |   |      |       |

1) Two-suited slam try

Opening lead: ♣K

## 1)    Playing an active defense

Partner leads the ♣K. The bidding tells you that partner has a likely 6-4 pattern and declarer a likely 5-5 pattern. Say clubs are led and continued (a passive defense). Declarer ruffs, draws trumps in three rounds, discards two hearts on the fourth and fifth diamonds, concedes a heart, and *ruffs a heart in dummy*.

You could have defeated the hand by overtaking partner's lead and shifting to a heart. How could you know to do that? The tip-off is that every so often when declarer has a two-suiter declarer will be able to draw trumps and still leave at least one trump in dummy, the danger signal. If the second suit is solid, you may have to grab your tricks (active defense) at once. Given the bidding, you know only one club trick is available, so you must shift your attention to hearts. Note that it is rare for declarer to have enough trumps in dummy to pull off this little caper, but if she does, forewarned is forearmed.

## 2)   Playing a forcing defense

When either you or your partner have four trumps, the **forcing game** is a strong defense against a two-suiter. The 'forcing game' means forcing declarer, the long hand, to ruff. Assuming a typical 5-3 trump fit, one force reduces declarer to your trump length, an aggravation for the declarer. A second force is no longer an aggravation, it's a disaster. Suddenly you have more trumps than declarer; you are in control of the hand! Declarer is going to have a devil of a time taking tricks in his second suit no matter how strong it is.

| BOTH VUL. | | DEALER SOUTH | |
|-----------|-------|------|-------|
| **West** | **North** | **East** | **South** |
| | | | 1♠ |
| pass | 1NT | pass | 3♢ |
| pass | 3♠ | pass | 4♢¹ |
| pass | 4♠ | all pass | |

1) Partner might have two spades and three diamonds.

Opening lead: ♡A

**NORTH** (Dummy)
♠ J 10 9
♡ Q 4 2
♢ 9 7 6
♣ K 9 8 2

**WEST** (You)
♠ A 8 6 2
♡ A 10 7 5 3
♢ 4 2
♣ J 7

**EAST**
♠ 5
♡ K J 6
♢ 8 5 3
♣ Q 10 6 5 4 3

**SOUTH**
♠ K Q 7 4 3
♡ 9 8
♢ A K Q J 10
♣ A

With your four trumps and no strength in declarer's second suit, you decide to play the 'forcing game' and lead your longest suit, hearts. You begin with ace and a heart and are gratified to see declarer trump the third round of hearts, reducing declarer to your trump length; the first step in her ruination.

Now let's look at the hand from the declarer's point of view.

Declarer would like to draw trumps and then run diamonds, a reasonable objective, but you have other things in mind. Both dummy and declarer are void in hearts. Your goal is to force declarer to trump another heart. You can't do that as long as there is a trump in dummy. What you have to do is win the *third* round of spades, the one that voids dummy, and then play a heart forcing declarer to ruff with her last trump. Now when declarer starts playing diamonds, you ruff the third diamond and cash your fifth heart: down two.

If declarer doesn't play a third round of spades, reverting to diamonds instead, you ruff the third round of diamonds. Down one.

## 3)    Leading a trump

Another possible defense against a two-suiter, particularly when you are strong in declarer's side suit, is a trump lead to cut down dummy's ruffing power.

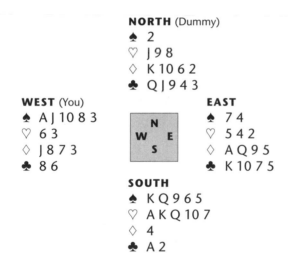

**NORTH** (Dummy)
♠ 2
♡ J 9 8
◇ K 10 6 2
♣ Q J 9 4 3

**WEST** (You)
♠ A J 10 8 3
♡ 6 3
◇ J 8 7 3
♣ 8 6

**EAST**
♠ 7 4
♡ 5 4 2
◇ A Q 9 5
♣ K 10 7 5

**SOUTH**
♠ K Q 9 6 5
♡ A K Q 10 7
◇ 4
♣ A 2

| BOTH VUL. | | DEALER SOUTH | |
| West | North | East | South |
| --- | --- | --- | --- |
| | | | 1♠ |
| pass | 1NT | pass | 3♡ |
| pass | 3NT | pass | 4♡ |
| all pass | | | |

Opening lead: ♡3

Your spade holding suggests a trump lead. Follow the play after a trump lead. Declarer wins in dummy and leads a spade to the king and your ace. You continue with a second trump. Wiggle and squirm as he will, even with the club finesse working, there are only nine tricks. Your two trump leads have done declarer in!

## Standing on your head

There will be times when the dummy will have more trump cards than the declarer. Transfer sequences produce this phenomenon:

| WEST (Opener) | EAST (Responder) |
|---|---|
| ♠ A 8 7 | ♠ 9 3 2 |
| ♡ Q 5 | ♡ J 9 7 4 3 2 |
| ◇ A K 8 7 | ◇ 4 |
| ♣ K 9 4 3 | ♣ Q 8 5 |

| West | East |
|---|---|
| 1NT | 2◇[1] |
| 2♡ | pass |

1) Transfer to hearts

In this sequence, East is going to be the dummy. Since declarer counts losers from the long hand, this can make it easier to see which suits to attack, which to avoid, and which to play to force the long hand to ruff. However, it is easier yet when the dummy has a two-suiter. Say you hold as North:

♠ — ♡ 9 3 ◇ A Q J 9 3 2 ♣ K J 9 5 4

| West | North | East | South |
|---|---|---|---|
| 1♠ | 2NT | 3♠ | 5◇ |
| all pass | | | |

Once the opening lead is made, your hand is coming down as dummy. The defenders can see the spade void plus the strength of your second suit, usually a key factor. If either defender is strong in clubs, trump leads are probably the best defense to prevent declarer from ruffing clubs in the closed hand.

NORTH VUL.     DEALER SOUTH

| West | North | East | South |
|---|---|---|---|
| 1NT | 2♣[1] | 2◇[2] | 2♠ |
| pass | 4♠ | all pass | |

1) Majors
2) Not forcing

**NORTH** (Dummy)
♠ K Q J 7 6
♡ A 9 6 4 2
◇ A 7
♣ 3

**WEST** (You)
♠ A 8 5
♡ K Q J 10
◇ 4 2
♣ K Q 10 8

**EAST**
♠ 3 2
♡ 7 5
◇ Q J 10 9 8 3
♣ J 9 7

**SOUTH**
♠ 10 9 4
♡ 8 3
◇ K 6 5
♣ A 6 5 4 2

On this hand you have so many good leads they're coming out your ears. Your partner has bid diamonds, you have a perfect sequence in hearts, you have strong clubs — what should you lead? A trump! A trump lead is a standout. Dummy is known to have a major two-suiter and South surely has more spades than hearts. What is going to happen to dummy's hearts? Declarer is going to try to trump them. Your best bet is to lead the ace and a trump in case declarer has a singleton heart. As it happens, declarer must give up a heart trick before she can trump even one heart in the closed hand. Oh no. When declarer gives up a heart, you can play a third spade. Don't look now, but because of your brilliant defense declarer has to lose three hearts and a spade.

We now enter a new realm of defensive play — reducing the long strong suit in dummy to mush. It's called:

## Killing the dummy

There are three ways to 'kill' a dummy besides shooting the poor guy. They are:

1) Giving partner an early ruff in the long suit.
2) Killing the long suit by leading it once or twice.
3) Killing the entry to a suit that will be established by ruffing.

### 1)  Giving partner an early ruff in the long suit

**NORTH** (Dummy)
♠ A K 6
♡ A 10 4
◇ 10 9
♣ Q 10 8 7 2

**WEST** (You)
♠ J 9 4
♡ 7 3
◇ K 8 2
♣ A K J 9 4

**EAST**
♠ Q 10 7 3
♡ 6 2
◇ J 7 6 5 4 3
♣ 3

**SOUTH**
♠ 8 5 2
♡ K Q J 9 8 5
◇ A Q
♣ 6 5

BOTH VUL.     DEALER NORTH

| West | North | East | South |
|------|-------|------|-------|
|      | 1♣    | pass | 1♡    |
| pass | 2♡    | pass | 4♡    |
| all pass |   |      |       |

Opening lead: ♣A

You decide to lead the ♣A and take a look around. When you see the club spots, it is clear that partner is the one with the singleton and declarer the doubleton. (If partner had two clubs, partner would have started a high-low.) If you don't do something about those clubs, declarer is eventually going to lead up to the ♣Q and establish it for a discard. What you have to do is lead a low club right now allowing partner to trump. Now the club suit is dead and declarer has to lose two more tricks: a diamond and a spade. Bravo!

## 2) Killing the long suit by leading it once or twice

One way to kill a solid side suit in dummy is to lead the suit before declarer can draw trumps; if dummy has no outside entry, and both declarer and at least one defender are void in the side suit, the suit is dead.

**NORTH** (Dummy)
♠ J 6 4 2
♡ K Q J 3
◇ 10 5 2
♣ 6 5

NORTH-SOUTH VUL. DEALER SOUTH

| West | North | East | South |
|------|-------|------|-------|
|      |       |      | 2♣    |
| pass | 2◇[1] | pass | 3♣    |
| pass | 3♡    | pass | 4NT   |
| pass | 5♣    | all pass |   |

1) Waiting

**WEST** (You)
♠ Q 10 9
♡ 9 8 7 4 2
◇ A J 9
♣ A 2

```
    N
W       E
    S
```

**EAST**
♠ 8 5 3
♡ 10 5
◇ Q 8 7 6 4 3
♣ 9 7

**SOUTH**
♠ A K 7
♡ A 6
◇ K
♣ K Q J 10 8 4 3

You decide to lead the ◇A and are pleased to see the king fall. You have the ♣A, but what about the third trick? It will have to come from spades, but what about those hearts? Declarer surely has the ♡A and the ♠AK and will discard any spade loser on hearts. Not so fast. Say you switch to the ♡9, dummy plays low, partner plays the ♡10 (count) and declarer the ♡A. When declarer leads a club, grab your ace and play a second heart.

By playing hearts twice before declarer can draw trumps, you have rendered the hearts useless. Declarer will try to discard a spade on the third heart, but partner will ruff and your ♠Q becomes the setting trick.

**3)      Killing the eventual entry to a side suit that has to be established by ruffing**

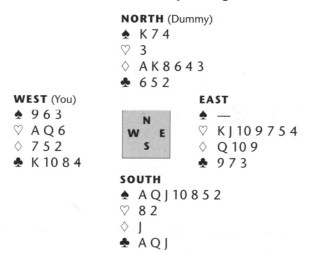

NORTH (Dummy)
♠ K 7 4
♡ 3
◊ A K 8 6 4 3
♣ 6 5 2

WEST (You)
♠ 9 6 3
♡ A Q 6
◊ 7 5 2
♣ K 10 8 4

EAST
♠ —
♡ K J 10 9 7 5 4
◊ Q 10 9
♣ 9 7 3

SOUTH
♠ A Q J 10 8 5 2
♡ 8 2
◊ J
♣ A Q J

NORTH-SOUTH VUL. DEALER EAST

| West | North | East | South |
|------|-------|------|-------|
|      |       | 3♡   | 4♠    |
| 5♡   | 6♠    | all pass |   |

Opening lead: ♡A

You lead the ♡A and partner plays the ♡7, a suit preference signal suggesting that you continue hearts. When partner's bidding shows a six-card suit or longer, and you lead that suit, partner's first play is suit preference. If partner had wished a club switch, she would have played a low heart. If partner had wanted a diamond shift, she would have played an unusually high heart, usually an honor card.

How are you going to get a club trick with those diamonds staring you in the face? First you must project the ◊Q in partner's hand. Next, you have to face reality. Declarer is going to set up the diamonds with one ruff and then draw trumps *ending in dummy,* shedding clubs and hearts on the established diamonds.

But you can prevent this. If you play a second heart and force dummy to ruff a heart prematurely, declarer can no longer set up diamonds and then draw trumps *ending in dummy.* Dummy will have only two trumps left while you will have three. After the smoke clears, the ♣K will be the setting trick.

# Practice Hands

| NEITHER VUL. | | DEALER EAST | |
|------|-------|------|-------|
| **West** | **North** | **East** | **South** |
| | | pass | 1♠ |
| pass | 1NT | pass | 3◊ |
| pass | 3♠ | pass | 4♠ |
| all pass | | | |

**Hand 1**

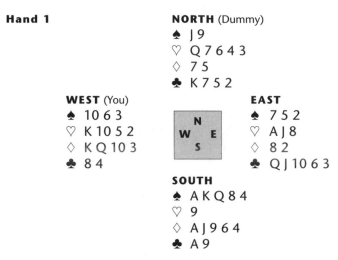

**NORTH** (Dummy)
♠ J 9
♡ Q 7 6 4 3
◊ 7 5
♣ K 7 5 2

**WEST** (You)
♠ 10 6 3
♡ K 10 5 2
◊ K Q 10 3
♣ 8 4

**EAST**
♠ 7 5 2
♡ A J 8
◊ 8 2
♣ Q J 10 6 3

**SOUTH**
♠ A K Q 8 4
♡ 9
◊ A J 9 6 4
♣ A 9

Warned by the bidding that there is likely to be diamond shortness in the dummy, your best bet to protect your diamond winners is to lead a trump. Each trump you remove from dummy is one fewer diamond declarer can ruff, one more diamond trick for you. If you lead two rounds of trumps before declarer can ruff a diamond, your side takes three diamonds and one heart. Down one.

| EAST-WEST VUL. | | DEALER SOUTH | |
|------|-------|------|-------|
| **West** | **North** | **East** | **South** |
| | | | 1♡ |
| 1♠ | 2◊ | 2♠ | pass |
| pass | 3♡ | all pass | |

Opening lead: ♠K

**Hand 2**

**NORTH** (Dummy)
♠ 7 2
♡ 6 4 2
◊ A Q 10 8 5
♣ K Q 2

**WEST**
♠ K Q 10 9 5
♡ K 7
◊ 7 6
♣ J 8 7 4

**EAST** (You)
♠ A J 3
♡ 9 5 3
◊ K J 9 4 2
♣ 10 9

**SOUTH**
♠ 8 6 4
♡ A Q J 10 8
◊ 3
♣ A 6 5 3

Partner leads the ♠K and you see at a glance that dummy's diamonds are worthless to the declarer. The main value of the dummy will be in ruffing a spade (partner figures to have five spades and declarer, three). Your play is to overtake the opening lead and return a trump in case partner has the ♡Q or ♡K. South, not playing with mirrors, will probably finesse the queen losing to partner's king. Partner, following your defense, and trusting you to have the diamonds all bottled up, returns a trump. If you and partner keep your wits about you, declarer is destined to go down one.

**Hand 3**

**NORTH** (Dummy)
♠ K 5 3
♡ 9 8 4
◇ 10 6 5 2
♣ A J 5

**WEST** (You)
♠ 6 2
♡ K Q 10 6
◇ K 9 8 7
♣ 9 7 3

**EAST**
♠ Q J 4
♡ 7 3 2
◇ A Q 3
♣ Q 6 4 2

**SOUTH**
♠ A 10 9 8 7
♡ A J 5
◇ J 4
♣ K 10 8

| EAST-WEST VUL. | | DEALER WEST | |
|---|---|---|---|
| **West** | **North** | **East** | **South** |
| pass | pass | pass | 1♠ |
| pass | 2♠ | all pass | |

Opening lead: ♡K

You lead the obvious ♡K which holds, partner playing the ♡2 denying the ace or jack.

Since declarer has both of those cards, a heart continuation is out. If the diamonds were threatening, you would switch to a club, but dummy's diamonds are not threatening. On the other hand, it may not be safe to switch to a diamond if the declarer has the AQ or AJ doubleton. What about clubs? Unless it is necessary, it is dangerous to switch to a side suit where the queen is not visible. Declarer may have a two-way guess for the queen and leading the suit obviates the guess.

By process of elimination that leaves spades. Even there you might be finessing partner out of her queen; however, declarer holding AJxxx could do that anyway. If you switch to a spade, and neither you nor partner ever leads a club unless forced to, declarer has to find the ♣Q to make 2♠.

| BOTH VUL. | | DEALER SOUTH | |
|---|---|---|---|
| **West** | **North** | **East** | **South** |
| | | | 1NT |
| pass | 2◊¹ | pass | 3♡² |
| pass | 4♡ | all pass | |

1) Transfer to hearts
2) Good hand with four hearts

Opening lead: ♠10

**Hand 4**

**NORTH** (Dummy)
- ♠ K J
- ♡ 9 8 6 5 3
- ◊ 9 8
- ♣ A Q J 6

**WEST**
- ♠ 10 9 8 3
- ♡ K 7
- ◊ Q 5 3 2
- ♣ 5 3 2

**EAST** (You)
- ♠ A 5 4
- ♡ 4 2
- ◊ A 10 6 4
- ♣ 10 9 8 4

**SOUTH**
- ♠ Q 7 6 2
- ♡ A Q J 10
- ◊ K J 7
- ♣ K 7

Partner leads the ♠10 and dummy's jack goes to your ace. Your job, looking at that dummy, is to project (imagine) some possibility to take four tricks. Clearly no more are coming in the black suits; it's going to have to come from the red ones. It is unlikely that partner can have more than one trump trick, so you must try for two diamond tricks. If partner has the ◊K, it doesn't matter which diamond you lead, but if partner has the ◊Q and declarer the ◊KJ, you must put declarer to an immediate guess before the diamonds go bye-bye on the black suits. Lead a low diamond at trick two, it's your best chance.

# Test Yourself

1)

**NORTH** (Dummy)
♠ 10 5
♡ K Q J 8 6 3
♢ A 5
♣ 8 7 5

**WEST** (You)
♠ K 4
♡ 10 9 2
♢ Q J 10 7 3
♣ K J 2

|  | NEITHER VUL. |  | DEALER SOUTH |  |
|---|---|---|---|---|
|  | **West** | **North** | **East** | **South** |
|  |  |  |  | 1♠ |
|  | pass | 2♡ | pass | 2♠ |
|  | pass | 3♠ | pass | 4♠ |
|  | all pass |  |  |  |

You lead the ♢Q to dummy's ace, partner playing the ♢2. Declarer plays the ♠10 from the table and lets it ride. What now?

***Solution on page 31***

2)

**NORTH** (Dummy)
♠ A Q J 4
♡ K
♢ Q 8 6
♣ A Q J 10 2

**EAST** (You)
♠ 9 7 2
♡ A 9 6 4
♢ A 10 4
♣ 8 5 3

|  | BOTH VUL. |  | DEALER NORTH |  |
|---|---|---|---|---|
|  | **West** | **North** | **East** | **South** |
|  |  | 1♣ | pass | 1♠ |
|  | pass | 4♠ | all pass |  |

Partner leads the ♡Q to your ace. What next?

***Solution on page 31***

3)

**NORTH** (Dummy)
♠ Q J 8 6 3
♡ 10 8 4 3
♢ K Q 5
♣ 7

**WEST** (You)
♠ A K 9 7 5
♡ K J 7
♢ 4 2
♣ J 6 3

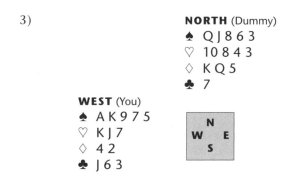

|  | NEITHER VUL. |  | DEALER EAST |  |
|---|---|---|---|---|
|  | **West** | **North** | **East** | **South** |
|  |  |  | 3♣ | 3♢ |
|  | 4♣ | 4♢ | pass | 5♢ |
|  | all pass |  |  |  |

You lead the ♠K (king from ace-king at the five-level or higher), partner plays the ♠2 and declarer the ♠4. What now?

***Solution on page 32***

4)

| EAST-WEST VUL. | | DEALER NORTH | |
|------|------|------|------|
| **West** | **North** | **East** | **South** |
| | pass | pass | 1♠ |
| pass | 3♠ | all pass | |

*Solution on page 32*

**NORTH** (Dummy)
♠ A 9 7 2
♡ K 10 6
◇ J 7 5
♣ Q 10 3

**EAST** (You)
♠ K 6
♡ J 8 5 2
◇ Q 10 3
♣ J 9 8 5

Partner leads the ♠5, and dummy plays low. After you win the trick, what are you going to do next?

5)

| NORTH-SOUTH VUL. | | DEALER NORTH | |
|------|------|------|------|
| **West** | **North** | **East** | **South** |
| | 1◇ | pass | 1♡ |
| pass | 2◇ | pass | 3♡ |
| pass | 4♡ | all pass | |

*Solution on page 33*

**NORTH** (Dummy)
♠ 7 2
♡ K J 6
◇ A K 10 9 7 6
♣ J 10

**EAST** (You)
♠ A 9 5 4
♡ 10 2
◇ Q 4 3
♣ A 9 4 3

Partner leads the ♠3 and you win the ♠A. How are you going to try to beat this hand?

6)

| EAST-WEST VUL. | | DEALER SOUTH | |
|------|------|------|------|
| **West** | **North** | **East** | **South** |
| | | | 1NT[1] |
| pass | 2♡[2] | pass | 2♠ |
| pass | 3◇ | pass | 3♠ |
| all pass | | | |

1) 15-17 HCP
2) Transfer to spades

*Solution on page 34*

**NORTH** (Dummy)
♠ K J 10 5 2
♡ A 6
◇ 8 7 5 3 2
♣ 7

**EAST** (You)
♠ 8 6 3
♡ Q J 10
◇ A K 10 9
♣ A 8 3

Partner leads the ♣Q to your ace and declarer's five. What now?

# Test Yourself — Solutions

1)

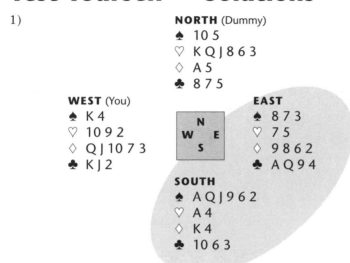

**NORTH** (Dummy)
♠ 10 5
♡ K Q J 8 6 3
♢ A 5
♣ 8 7 5

**WEST** (You)
♠ K 4
♡ 10 9 2
♢ Q J 10 7 3
♣ K J 2

**EAST**
♠ 8 7 3
♡ 7 5
♢ 9 8 6 2
♣ A Q 9 4

**SOUTH**
♠ A Q J 9 6 2
♡ A 4
♢ K 4
♣ 10 6 3

| NEITHER VUL. | | DEALER SOUTH | |
|------|-------|------|-------|
| **West** | **North** | **East** | **South** |
| | | | 1♠ |
| pass | 2♡ | pass | 2♠ |
| pass | 3♠ | pass | 4♠ |
| all pass | | | |

**Trick 1:** ♢Q ♢A ♢2 ♢4
**Trick 2:** ♠10 ♠3 ♠2 ?

Declarer has the ♢K (partner's ♢2), yet declarer 'stranded' the heart suit without a return entry. Why? He has the ♡A, that's why. If so, an active defense is called for. Win the ♠K and shift to a low club. On a good day partner has the ♣A and you score three club tricks.

2)

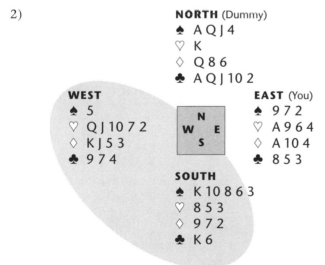

**NORTH** (Dummy)
♠ A Q J 4
♡ K
♢ Q 8 6
♣ A Q J 10 2

**WEST**
♠ 5
♡ Q J 10 7 2
♢ K J 5 3
♣ 9 7 4

**EAST** (You)
♠ 9 7 2
♡ A 9 6 4
♢ A 10 4
♣ 8 5 3

**SOUTH**
♠ K 10 8 6 3
♡ 8 5 3
♢ 9 7 2
♣ K 6

| BOTH VUL. | | DEALER NORTH | |
|------|-------|------|-------|
| **West** | **North** | **East** | **South** |
| | 1♣ | pass | 1♠ |
| pass | 4♠ | all pass | |

**Trick 1:** ♡Q ♡K ♡A ♡3
**Trick 2:** ?

If ever a dummy called for a diamond shift, this is it. Any black suit finesse works and the only real hope for *three* diamond tricks is that partner has both missing diamond honors. Go for it; switch to a low diamond at trick two.

NEITHER VUL.     DEALER EAST

| West | North | East | South |
|------|-------|------|-------|
|      |       | 3♣   | 3◇    |
| 4♣   | 4◇    | pass | 5◇    |
| all pass | | | |

**Trick 1:** ♠K ♠3 ♠2 ♠4
**Trick 2:** ?

3)

**NORTH** (Dummy)
♠ Q J 8 6 3
♡ 10 8 4 3
◇ K Q 5
♣ 7

**WEST** (You)
♠ A K 9 7 5
♡ K J 7
◇ 4 2
♣ J 6 3

**EAST**
♠ 2
♡ 9 6 5 2
◇ 9
♣ K Q 10 9 5 4 2

**SOUTH**
♠ 10 4
♡ A Q
◇ A J 10 8 7 6 3
♣ A 8

Kill the spades before they kill you! Partner is the one with the singleton spade (no high-low), so if you lead a low spade at trick two and allow partner to trump while you still retain a high spade, declarer can no longer use dummy's spades to discard a side-suit loser. Any tricks you have coming in hearts or clubs will come sooner or later. If you don't play a low spade but shift to a club instead, declarer wins, draws trumps, and leads a spade to your ace. You can now kiss your ♡K *adios*. It may take a trick on another hand, but not on this one.

EAST-WEST VUL.     DEALER NORTH

| West | North | East | South |
|------|-------|------|-------|
|      | pass  | pass | 1♠    |
| pass | 3♠    | all pass | |

**Trick 1:** ♠5 ♠2 ♠K ♠3
**Trick 2:** ?

4)

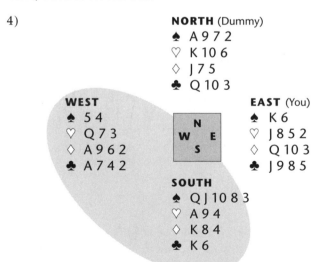

**NORTH** (Dummy)
♠ A 9 7 2
♡ K 10 6
◇ J 7 5
♣ Q 10 3

**WEST**
♠ 5 4
♡ Q 7 3
◇ A 9 6 2
♣ A 7 4 2

**EAST** (You)
♠ K 6
♡ J 8 5 2
◇ Q 10 3
♣ J 9 8 5

**SOUTH**
♠ Q J 10 8 3
♡ A 9 4
◇ K 8 4
♣ K 6

Partner's trump lead, usually suggesting broken honor strength in all suits, plus the balanced dummy suggest a passive defense. Clearly the most passive exit card you have is your remaining spade. This return, plus a continued passive defense (avoid breaking new suits), leaves declarer with four more losers.

5)

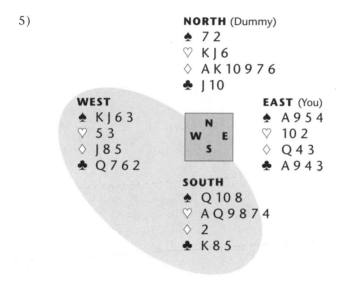

**NORTH** (Dummy)
♠ 7 2
♡ K J 6
♦ A K 10 9 7 6
♣ J 10

**WEST**
♠ K J 6 3
♡ 5 3
♦ J 8 5
♣ Q 7 6 2

**EAST** (You)
♠ A 9 5 4
♡ 10 2
♦ Q 4 3
♣ A 9 4 3

**SOUTH**
♠ Q 10 8
♡ A Q 9 8 7 4
♦ 2
♣ K 8 5

NORTH-SOUTH VUL. DEALER NORTH

| West | North | East | South |
|------|-------|------|-------|
|      | 1♦    | pass | 1♡    |
| pass | 2♦    | pass | 3♡    |
| pass | 4♡    | all pass |   |

**Trick 1:** ♠3 ♠2 ♠A ♠8
**Trick 2:** ?

If declarer has, as is likely, a singleton or doubleton diamond, the suit can easily be established via one ruff. Your side needs four black-suit tricks and this dummy calls for an active defense. You have to project the ♠K in partner's hand as well as a club honor. Shift to a *low* club. If partner has both black-suit kings, it won't matter which club you lead, but if partner has the ♣Q and declarer the ♣K, it is imperative to put declarer to an immediate club guess by leading low.

EAST-WEST VUL.   DEALER SOUTH

| West | North | East | South |
|------|-------|------|-------|
|      |       |      | 1NT[1] |
| pass | 2♡[2] | pass | 2♠ |
| pass | 3◇ | pass | 3♠ |
| all pass |   |      |       |

1) 15-17 HCP
2) Transfer to spades

**Trick 1:** ♣Q ♣7 ♣A ♣5
**Trick 2:** ?

6)

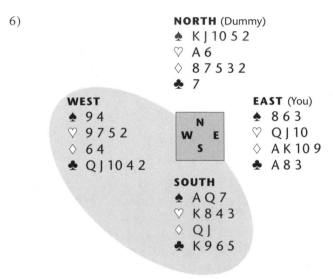

**NORTH** (Dummy)
♠ K J 10 5 2
♡ A 6
◇ 8 7 5 3 2
♣ 7

**WEST**
♠ 9 4
♡ 9 7 5 2
◇ 6 4
♣ Q J 10 4 2

**EAST** (You)
♠ 8 6 3
♡ Q J 10
◇ A K 10 9
♣ A 8 3

**SOUTH**
♠ A Q 7
♡ K 8 4 3
◇ Q J
♣ K 9 6 5

First, a few preliminaries.

1) If you add your HCP to dummy's HCP you get a grand total of 22 (14+8). That means there are 18 HCP outstanding between partner and declarer. Partner has three HCP in clubs from the lead leaving declarer with the remaining 15 to justify the 1NT opening bid.
2) Diamonds must be 2-2. If partner had a singleton he would have led it; if declarer had a singleton diamond she wouldn't have opened 1NT.

Dummy has more trumps than declarer and should be considered 'the long hand'. Since losers are usually counted from the long hand, dummy's losers appear to be all in diamonds. What can declarer do with dummy's diamonds? Surely she will try to trump one or two diamonds in the closed hand if you are in a friendly mood and never lead a trump. If you aren't a close relative of the declarer, shift to a trump at trick two and continue playing a trump each time you gain the lead in diamonds. When the smoke clears your trick pile will contain four diamonds and the ♣A. Down one.

Don't tell me I sucked you into switching to a high diamond or a high heart at trick two! For shame.

## Key ideas from Chapter 1

- Listen to the bidding before you make your opening lead.
- Re-evaluate your defensive strategy when the dummy comes down, paying particular attention to the strength of dummy's side suits.
- Defensive strategy is basically divided into two categories: active and passive. An 'active' or attacking defense means attacking side suits quickly to secure tricks before they disappear on dummy's side suit. A 'passive' or safe defense means sitting back and waiting patiently for tricks to come to you. A passive defense implies not breaking new suits that appear risky.
- If dummy has a strong usable side suit, play an active defense; go after your tricks before the mice get at them.
- If dummy's strong side suit is not usable, play a passive defense, perhaps even leading a trump to cut down dummy's ruffing power.
- If dummy's only value is side suit shortness, trump leads are usually best.
- If dummy tables with more trumps than declarer, think of the dummy as the declarer and count losers from the dummy's perspective.
- If declarer has a known two-suiter consider an active defense if her second suit is solid and she can draw trumps and remain with at least one trump in dummy. Play a forcing defense if you have four trumps or suspect partner does. Lead a trump if you are strong in declarer's side suit.
- When dummy tables with a strong side suit, there are three possible ways to kill that suit:
  1) give partner a ruff while retaining control of the suit;
  2) lead the suit once or twice *before* declarer can draw trumps. To pull this one off:
    (a) there cannot be any side suit entry to dummy;
    (b) either you or partner must be short in the suit.
  3) if the suit must be established by ruffing, attack the side suit entry that declarer must eventually use to reach the established suit.

# Learning to Think

*"I am inclined to think —," said I.*
*"I should do so," Holmes remarked impatiently.*

CONAN DOYLE

You have probably at some time had the experience of driving along and approaching a traffic light with the sun directly in your eyes. The sun is so bright that you can't actually see the signal, but you can see all the other cars around you are going through the intersection. What color do you think the light is? Green, of course.

You don't actually know for certain that the light is green (although you're probably going to find out the hard way if it isn't when you enter the intersection). What you have done is to draw an inference, or a logical conclusion, from the facts you have observed: the other cars are going through, so the light must be green.

You can apply the same logic at the bridge table, particularly on defense. For openers you have to make the assumption that both partner and declarer are playing rationally! (Yes, yes, I know what you are thinking.) If either one makes a completely irrational play, you could find yourself making an even worse one! One idiocy can easily breed another — the bridge equivalent of driving through a red light.

Say you are defending a heart contract and you lead the ♠K. You have the ♣A, and you notice that there are ten clubs between your hand and dummy. Partner overtakes your opening lead and shifts to a club. There is an overwhelming inference that partner has a singleton club. If partner lets the ♠K hold instead of overtaking and shifting to a club, there is a negative inference involved: partner is unlikely to have a singleton club.

This famous exchange is a good example of a **negative inference:**

'Is there any point to which you would wish to draw my attention?'
'To the curious incident of the dog in the night-time.'
'The dog did nothing in the night-time.'
'That was the curious incident,' remarked Sherlock Holmes.

*Silver Blaze,* Conan Doyle.

Here's another that you should have no trouble with after the last chapter. You lead a low spade against a heart contract and dummy tables with trump support plus the ♣AQ1085; you have three little clubs. Partner wins the opening lead and shifts to a trump. The inference is that partner has the clubs locked up and that you shouldn't worry about that suit. If a trump switch is possible, but partner does not shift to a trump, the negative inference is that partner does not have the clubs locked up.

Inferences are also available when dummy tables with a powerful suit such as KQJ10(x) or AQJ(x) and declarer shies away from the suit. The inference is that declarer, not partner, has the missing honor.

The following inferences related to discarding were discussed in detail in Chapter 7 of *Eddie Kantar teaches Modern Bridge Defense* but bear repeating nevertheless:

1) If dummy has something like the ◇AKJx(x) and declarer discards a small diamond from dummy, declarer cannot have the ◇Q.

2) When dummy has trump support plus side-suit shortness, yet declarer draws all of dummy's trumps or draws them after ruffing once or twice in dummy, the inference is that declarer has no more losers in that suit to ruff. The defenders can now discard that suit with impunity.

# Inferences from the lead

Say you are defending a spade contract; clubs is an unbid suit, a club is not led, and when dummy appears, you can't see the ♣A or the ♣K. The inference is that partner cannot have both of those cards (he would have led one). Either declarer has them both or they are split between the two unseen hands. To a slightly lesser degree you can take the same inference when the king and queen of a suit are not visible and not led.

Say partner bids a suit, you support the suit, and partner leads another suit. Why? There are four possible reasons. (1) Partner may have a suit headed by the AQ or the AJ and fears leading the suit in case declarer has the king. However, if you have the ace of the supported suit or dummy does, there must be another reason. (2) Partner has a sequence lead in another suit. (3) Partner has shortness with a likely trump entry and is planning on putting you on lead in the supported suit to get a ruff. (4) Partner has forgotten the bidding.

Say partner has preempted. Most preempts contain side-suit single-tons and most partners will lead a singleton without even looking at the rest of their hand. If partner preempts and doesn't lead a singleton, the inference is that partner's singleton, if she has one, is in the trump suit. Unfortunately, sharp declarers are also aware of these inferences as well as the ones coming up.

Another lead inference: say dummy has trump support with expected side-suit length, yet partner leads a trump. The inference is that partner is strong in the side suit or else partner would not be playing a passive defense. If partner leads dummy's bid and rebid suit, the inference is that partner has a singleton, otherwise the lead is too dangerous.

At notrump with no suits having been bid, partner leads the ♠2, fourth best, indicating a four-card suit. Early in the play partner turns up with a singleton diamond. The inference is that partner's original distribution was 4-4-1-4. Why? Because with a side five-card suit, partner would have probably led that suit.

Partner might well lead a strong four-card suit (KQJx, say) in preference to a broken five-card suit, but when he leads a low card, he has no honor sequence in the suit.

When partner leads from shortness at notrump, the inference is that partner's long suit(s) has been bid.

# Inferences from the Play

Many defensive inferences come from the cards played in the suit that has been led.  For example, suppose you lead the ♠5 against a heart contract and are faced with this layout:

**NORTH** (Dummy)
♠ A Q 6

**WEST** (You)
♠ K 10 8 5 3

If dummy plays the ace, the inference is that declarer has a single-ton; with two spades, the finesse is the more likely play.  Furthermore, if dummy plays the queen, there is an overwhelming inference that partner has the jack.  If declarer has the ♠J, declarer plays low from dummy.  Wouldn't you?

This diagram leads to the inevitable question any defender trying to locate a missing honor must ask himself:  if declarer has the missing honor, would declarer be playing this way?  If the answer is no, then partner has the missing honor.

Now you try it:

**NORTH** (Dummy)
♠ A 6 2

**WEST** (You)
♠ K 10 8 5 3

Again you are on lead versus a heart contract and you elect to lead a low spade.  Dummy flies with the ace; who has the  queen? Piece of cake.  Partner.  If declarer has it, declarer plays low.  Later in the hand you can even lead a low spade over to partner's queen if you need partner on lead for one reason or another.

What about this one?

**NORTH** (Dummy)
♠ 10 9 5 3

**WEST** (You)
♠ K Q 6 4

Hearts are trumps and you lead the ♠K which holds, partner playing the ♠2. What do you make of this? Partner normally encourages holding the jack or the ace when you lead the king. On the other hand, if declarer has ♠AJ, he takes the trick since the ten in the dummy ensures a quick second spade trick, not to mention the nine. Who's gone mad?

Nobody. Partner probably has ♠J2 and cannot afford to drop the jack; or she has ♠A2 or ♠AJ2 and doesn't think it is right to over-take. In any event, partner has one or both of the missing honors.

How about this?

**NORTH** (Dummy)
♠ Q 10 6

**WEST** (You)
♠ J 5

Diamonds are trumps and you lead the ♠J which rides round to declarer's ace. What do you make of this? Declarer must have the ♠K. If declarer did not have the ♠K, wouldn't declarer cover the ♠J with the ♠Q?

And this:

**NORTH** (Dummy)
♠ Q 5

**WEST** (You)
♠ J 9 6 2

You lead the ♠2 against a notrump contract, dummy plays the queen, partner the king, and declarer the ace. Who has the ♠10? Almost certainly partner. If declarer has A10x(x), declarer gets two sure spade tricks by playing low from dummy. (However, if declarer has ♠A10 doubleton, declarer might play the queen from dummy.)

And now a big league inference:

**NORTH** (Dummy)
♠ Q 5

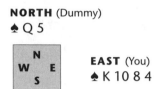

**EAST** (You)
♠ K 10 8 4

Partner leads the ♠3 against a notrump contract, no suits having been bid, and dummy plays low. What do you make of this? If declarer has ♠Ax(x) or ♠xx(x) declarer plays the ♠Q from dummy, so scratch those holdings. Declarer must have the ♠J and partner the ♠A. If declarer has ♠Jxx, declarer cannot be prevented from taking a spade trick; however if declarer has ♠Jx, you can run the entire suit if you make the proper play of the ♠K.

Partner seldom underleads aces on opening lead against a suit contract. Therefore, when partner leads a suit and you cannot see the ace, assume declarer has it and play accordingly.

**NORTH** (Dummy)
♠ K J 5 4

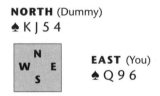

**EAST** (You)
♠ Q 9 6

Partner leads the ♠3 against a club contract. If dummy plays low, insert the ♠9. The ♠9 figures to drive out the ace. Partner should have an honor for a low card lead and that honor figures to be the ♠10. If spades are not led originally, but later in the hand partner shifts to a low spade, now there is a good chance that partner does have the ♠A.

After having led from the top of an honor sequence, your second card in the suit can lead to valuable defensive inferences.

**NORTH** (Dummy)
♠ A 7 5 4

**WEST** (You)
♠ K Q J 9

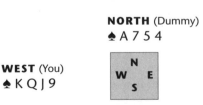

You lead the ♠K which holds. Your second play should be the lower or lowest of your remaining equals, the jack. The play of the jack shows the queen but denies the ten.

There is no calculating the number of tricks lost in the following position from players who don't play this way:

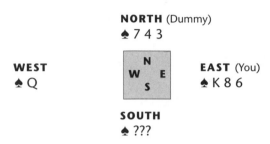

**NORTH** (Dummy)
♠ 7 4 3

**WEST**
♠ Q

**EAST** (You)
♠ K 8 6

**SOUTH**
♠ ???

Say partner leads the ♠Q against a notrump contract. You signal with the ♠8, and partner's queen takes the trick. Now partner continues with the ♠J. Which spade do you play?

Do not overtake with the king to unblock for partner; partner is unblocking for you! Partner's play of the ♠J denies the ♠10. If partner has ♠QJ10x(x), partner continues with the ♠10, not the ♠J. Partner's actual holding is ♠QJ9 and declarer's ♠A1052.

Similarly:

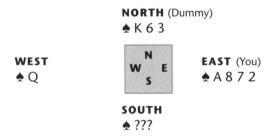

**NORTH** (Dummy)
♠ K 6 3

**WEST**
♠ Q

**EAST** (You)
♠ A 8 7 2

**SOUTH**
♠ ???

Partner leads the ♠Q against a suit contract which holds, as you signal encouragement with the ♠8. Partner continues with the ♠J, dummy covers with the ♠K, and you win the ♠A. Who has the ♠10? If partner has read this book, declarer has it. If partner has the ♠QJ10(x), partner continues with the ♠10, not the ♠J.

At notrump, the follow-up play of the jack asks partner to unblock the ten if she has it — very helpful when holding KQJ9(x).

Leading equal honors out of order (lower-higher) also leads to infer-ences. For example, if you and partner have agreed to lead the ace from AKx(x) against suit contracts, and you lead the king and then the ace (out of the normal order), the inference is that you have a doubleton. Here is another example:

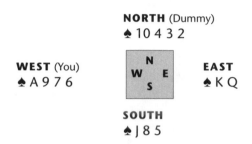

Say spades is a side suit at a trump contract and early in the hand partner shifts to the ♠Q and then continues with the ♠K. Since partner has played spades 'out of order', the inference is that part-ner has a doubleton. If there is a danger that the third spade trick can be lost, overtake and give partner a ruff.

When declarer initiates a suit, inferences also abound. The catch is to be able to pick up on them.

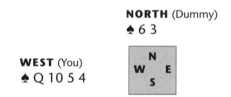

At a heart contract, dummy leads a low spade, partner plays low, and declarer's nine fetches your ten. What do you think is going on? Declarer cannot have the ♠AK and play this way, and partner cannot have the ♠AK and duck the trick. Ergo, the top spade hon-ors are divided.

If declarer has the king and partner the ace, declarer plays the king hoping to lose but one spade trick. Therefore, declarer cannot have the king: declarer has the ace and partner the king. If partner has given you count or the bidding has been revealing (say South had a chance to bid spades and didn't), you also know how the spades are dividing.

**NORTH** (Dummy)
♠ 6 4

**WEST** (You)
♠ A 8 3

Spades are trumps, dummy has side entries, and declarer leads the
♠K. The inference is that declarer has the ♠KQJ(10)x. With
KQxxx(x), declarer would lead a spade from dummy.

# Inferences from the bidding

The auction is, of course, a gold-mine of inferences, both from what
they have bid and from what they haven't. Suppose there has been
an auction where both sides have been bidding, but no-one has
mentioned hearts. Partner doesn't lead a heart; dummy shows up
with three hearts, and you have two. The eight remaining hearts
should be split 4-4 between partner and declarer: if either had five
hearts the suit would have been mentioned.

Declarer's and dummy's bidding can yield an amazing amount of
information, if you listen carefully. In the following auction

| North | South |
|-------|-------|
| 1♠ | 1NT |
| 2♠ | pass |

Unless North is a weak player, he has six spades and is unlikely to
hold four hearts. Dummy figures to have fewer than three spades.

This sequence is even more revealing:

| North | South |
|-------|-------|
| 1♠ | 2◇ |
| 2♡ | 2NT |
| 3◇ | 3NT |
| pass | |

What do you know about the two hands? To begin with, North has
a singleton club: anyone who bids two suits then supports a third
figures to have a singleton in the fourth suit. What about South,
who persists in notrump despite knowing of North's singleton club?
South is obviously well-heeled in clubs. So if you had to lead from

This topic will be covered in
much greater depth in the next
chapter

With 5-3-3-2, North should pass
1NT. Therefore, if he has no side
four-card suit, he must have six
spades.

this hand

♠ Q42  ♡ J5  ◇ A742  ♣ J542

which card would you pick?

Many experts would opt for the ♡J, a suit where partner is marked with four or five cards. If the opponents had as many as eight hearts between them, hearts would be trumps. They figure to have six or seven hearts, meaning that partner has four or five hearts. In addition, your inferior club spots plus South's insistence on notrump facing a known singleton club argue for another lead. The bidding also tells you that partner likely has a singleton diamond. A two-level response is generally made on a five-card suit and North surely has three diamonds. Although partner is likely to have four spades, spades is dummy's long suit and your spade holding also argues against that lead.

Sometimes you can draw an inference about partner's hand from the opponents' bidding, and this can lead to a spectacularly successful defense. Suppose you have ♠A5 ♡6 ◇10963 ♣QJ10652 and the auction goes:

| North | South |
|-------|-------|
| 1♠    | 2◇    |
| 3◇    | 3♠    |
| 4◇    | 4NT   |
| 5♡    | 6♠    |
| pass  |       |

See Chapter 8 for a full discussion of lead-directing doubles.

What would you lead? The bidding tells you that partner has one diamond at most (with a diamond void partner doubles 6♠ asking for an unusual lead). Holding the ace of trumps you can envision giving partner a second-round diamond ruff. What about your singleton heart? Probably the worst lead in your hand. A singleton lead against a slam contract works out great if partner has the ace of the singleton suit or the ace of trumps. But you have the ace of trumps and partner can't have the ♡A — the opponents wouldn't be in a slam off two aces after a Blackwood sequence! What about the ♣Q? That would be a reasonable choice if the diamond ruff possibility wasn't so compelling; lead a diamond.

## Distributional inferences once the dummy comes down

Once dummy tables, you can often work out the declarer's distribution by adding the number of cards dummy has in a suit to the number of cards you have in that suit and then figuring out from the bidding the distribution of the unseen hands in the suit. This little gimmick works particularly well in unbid majors.

Say partner, East, opens 1◊, South overcalls 2♣ and that ends the bidding. You lead a diamond and dummy has a doubleton heart while you have three hearts. There are eight hearts unaccounted for. If either partner or declarer had a five-card heart suit, the suit would have been mentioned. The conclusion is that hearts are 4-4.

Supported major suits may lead to simple inferences.

| Opener | Responder |
| --- | --- |
| 1♣ | 1♠ |
| 2♠ | 3NT |
| pass | |

Play responder for four spades. If responder had more than four spades, spades would be trumps. Skipping over major suits to rebid notrump also leads to distributional inferences:

| Opener | Responder |
| --- | --- |
| 1♣ | 1♡ |
| 1NT | pass |

The inference is that opener does not have four spades.

Some pairs (especially those playing a weak notrump) do not deny spades in this sequence. If in doubt, ask your opponents.

*To summarize:* One reason bridge experts *are* experts is that they have the knack of making inferences quickly from the bidding, the lead, partner's defense, and the way declarer is attacking the hand. Of course, having defended thousands upon thousands of hands doesn't hurt either. The point is that you, too, can make many of these inferences; those that have been touched upon in this chapter plus many others you will be able to work out on your own. Just don't go through too many red lights!

# Practice Hands

**Hand 1**

NORTH-SOUTH VUL. DEALER SOUTH

| West | North | East | South |
|------|-------|------|-------|
|      |       |      | 2♣    |
| pass | 2◇    | pass | 2♠    |
| pass | 4♠    | pass | 7♠    |
| all pass | | | |

Opening lead: ♡Q

**NORTH** (Dummy)
- ♠ 9 7 4 2
- ♡ 6 4
- ◇ Q J
- ♣ 9 8 7 5 3

**WEST** (You)
- ♠ 10 5
- ♡ Q J 10 8 2
- ◇ 6 4 3
- ♣ 10 6 2

**EAST**
- ♠ 6
- ♡ 9 7 5 3
- ◇ 10 9 8 7 5 2
- ♣ Q J

**SOUTH**
- ♠ A K Q J 8 3
- ♡ A K
- ◇ A K
- ♣ A K 4

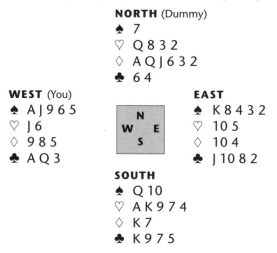

You lead the ♡Q, and South can do nothing except run off all his winners and hope someone unguards clubs. You are too shrewd for this, however: you know that if declarer had a third heart, he would have ruffed a heart in dummy after drawing trumps. So you have no problem throwing away all your hearts to keep the guarded ♣10!

**Hand 2**

NORTH-SOUTH VUL. DEALER EAST

| West | North | East | South |
|------|-------|------|-------|
|      |       | pass | 1♡    |
| 1♠   | 2◇    | 4♠   | pass  |
| pass | 5♡    | all pass | |

Your aggressive bidding has pushed the opponents to the five-level, but where are your defensive tricks coming from? Surely you have no more than one spade trick, and any club losers declarer happens to have will disappear pretty quickly on dummy's diamonds.

**NORTH** (Dummy)
- ♠ 7
- ♡ Q 8 3 2
- ◇ A Q J 6 3 2
- ♣ 6 4

**WEST** (You)
- ♠ A J 9 6 5
- ♡ J 6
- ◇ 9 8 5
- ♣ A Q 3

**EAST**
- ♠ K 8 4 3 2
- ♡ 10 5
- ◇ 10 4
- ♣ J 10 8 2

**SOUTH**
- ♠ Q 10
- ♡ A K 9 7 4
- ◇ K 7
- ♣ K 9 7 5

The bidding suggests that dummy has a strong red two-suiter, and a possible defense is to lead a low spade hoping partner has the king and can lead a club through declarer's envisioned king. Don't look now, but declarer is shaking his head in disbelief.

**Hand 3**

**NORTH** (Dummy)
♠ A Q
♡ 10 8 7
♢ K 8
♣ K J 10 9 5 2

**WEST**
♠ 10 8 7 6 2
♡ 6 4
♢ J 9 3 2
♣ A 3

**EAST** (You)
♠ K 9 5
♡ 9 3
♢ A Q 10 5
♣ 8 7 6 4

**SOUTH**
♠ J 4 3
♡ A K Q J 5 2
♢ 7 6 4
♣ Q

| | BOTH VUL. | | DEALER SOUTH |
|---|---|---|---|
| **West** | **North** | **East** | **South** |
| | | | 1♡ |
| pass | 2♣ | pass | 2♡ |
| pass | 4♡ | all pass | |

Opening lead: ♢2

Partner leads the ♢2 and you capture dummy's king with your ace. If declarer had the ♢J, he would surely have played low from dummy, so your play is to lead a low diamond to put partner in for a spade play. You must project that partner has either a club trick or a trump trick. If so, you need that spade play quickly!

Yes, declarer should have played low from dummy at trick one. Nevertheless, you must be able to take advantage of errant play.

**Hand 4**

**NORTH** (Dummy)
♠ K 8 7 2
♡ 10 7 3
♢ 9 8 6 5
♣ K 5

**WEST**
♠ Q 4
♡ A 9 8 6 5
♢ 4 3
♣ 8 7 3 2

**EAST** (You)
♠ A J 10 9 6 3
♡ Q J 4
♢ 7 2
♣ 9 4

**SOUTH**
♠ 5
♡ K 2
♢ A K Q J 10
♣ A Q J 10 6

| | NORTH-SOUTH VUL. | DEALER SOUTH | |
|---|---|---|---|
| **West** | **North** | **East** | **South** |
| | | | 1♢ |
| pass | 1♠ | 2♠[1] | 4♣ |
| pass | 4♢ | pass | 5♢ |
| all pass | | | |

1) Natural

Opening lead: ♠Q

Dummy plays low on partner's ♠Q. Declarer figures to have 10 or 11 minor-suit cards and likely a singleton spade. It seems that, if you don't attack hearts early, declarer will be able to pitch dummy's hearts on good clubs, and then ruff hearts in dummy. It may take a little courage on your part, but your play is to overtake the ♠Q and switch to the ♡Q before the mice get at those heart losers.

# Test Yourself

1)

**NORTH** (Dummy)
♠ J 6 3

**WEST** (You)
♠ K Q 10 2

**EAST**
♠ 4

**SOUTH**
♠ 5

*Solution on page 53*

Against 4♡, you lead the ♠K. Dummy plays low, partner the ♠4, and declarer the ♠5. Who has the ♠A and why?

2)

**NORTH** (Dummy)
♠ K J 6

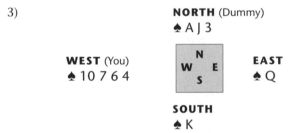

**WEST** (You)
♠ A 10 5 3

*Solution on page 53*

Diamonds are trumps, and in the middle of the hand, declarer plays the ♠K from dummy. Who has the ♠Q, and why?

3)

**NORTH** (Dummy)
♠ A J 3

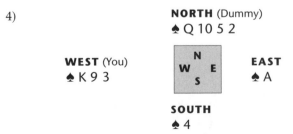

**WEST** (You)
♠ 10 7 6 4

**EAST**
♠ Q

**SOUTH**
♠ K

*Solution on page 53*

You lead the ♠4 against notrump, and the trick continues jack, queen, king. Who has the ♠9, and why?

4)

**NORTH** (Dummy)
♠ Q 10 5 2

**WEST** (You)
♠ K 9 3

**EAST**
♠ A

**SOUTH**
♠ 4

*Solution on page 53*

You lead the ♠3, dummy plays low, partner plays the ♠A and declarer the ♠4. Who has the ♠J, and why?

5)

**NORTH** (Dummy)
♠ A 8 4

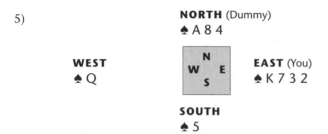

**WEST**
♠ Q

**EAST** (You)
♠ K 7 3 2

**SOUTH**
♠ 5

Partner leads the ♠Q which holds and continues with the ♠J to declarer's ace. Who has the ♠10, and why?

*Solution on page 53*

6)

**NORTH** (Dummy)
♠ 10 9 8 4

**WEST** (You)
♠ K Q J 2

**EAST**
♠ 3

**SOUTH**
♠ 5

You lead the ♠K against notrump; it holds the trick, partner playing the ♠3 and declarer the ♠5. Who has the ♠A, and why?

*Solution on page 53*

7)

**NORTH** (Dummy)
♠ K 3

**WEST** (You)
♠ Q 9 8 5 2

**EAST**
♠ 4

**SOUTH**
♠ 6

Defending against 4♡, you lead the ♠5. Dummy wins the ♠K, partner playing the ♠4 and declarer the ♠5. Who has the ♠J and why?

*Solution on page 53*

8)

**NORTH** (Dummy)
♠ K J

**WEST**
♠ 4

**EAST** (You)
♠ A 9 3

South has opened 1NT, and becomes declarer in 4♡. Partner leads the ♠4, and declarer plays the ♠K. Who has the ♠Q, and why?

*Solution on page 53*

9)

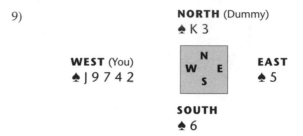

**NORTH** (Dummy)
♠ K 3

**WEST** (You)          **EAST**
♠ J 9 7 4 2          ♠ 5

**SOUTH**
♠ 6

*Solution on page 53*

You lead the ♠4 against 3NT: dummy plays the ♠K, partner the ♠5, and declarer the ♠6. Who has the ♠Q, and why?

10)

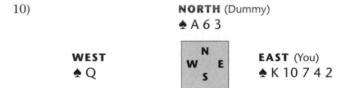

**NORTH** (Dummy)
♠ A 6 3

**WEST**          **EAST** (You)
♠ Q          ♠ K 10 7 4 2

*Solution on page 53*

After you have bid spades, partner (who has not supported you) leads the ♠Q against 3◊. Dummy plays low on this trick. Who has the ♠J, and why?

# Test Yourself — Solutions

1) *East* has the ♠A. With ♠Jxx in dummy, South would win the ace and later lead up to the ♠J for a second trick.

2) *South* has the ♠Q. Without that card he would lead up to the KJx, not away from it!

3) *Partner* figures to have the ♠9. With K9x, declarer plays *low* from dummy winning three tricks any time you have underled the queen or the ten. If you have underled the queen, partner's ten drives out the king, but declarer can lead to the jack later. If you have underled the ten, playing low forces partner to play the queen at once giving declarer an immediate three tricks.

4) *Declarer* has the ♠J. If partner has both the ace and the jack, the proper play at trick one is the jack, particularly when you have led a low card showing an honor.

5) *Declarer* has the ♠10. If partner has ♠QJ10, the proper continuation after the queen holds is the ten.

6) *East* has the ♠A, since South would have won the ace to guarantee a second stopper facing dummy's ♠10984.

7) *East* must have the ♠J, or else declarer would have let the opening lead come up to the AJx in his hand.

8) *Declarer* must have the ♠Q. Declarer knows partner is not underleading an ace into the notrump bidder. Please. If declarer had small spades, he'd surely play the ♠J from dummy, playing you for the ace and partner for the queen. Declarer's play of the ♠K from dummy shouts from the rooftops that he also has the ♠Q.

9) *South* has the ♠Q. Partner might have unblocked with ♠Qx, or else surely would have played a higher spot card holding ♠Qxx or ♠Qxxx.

10) *Partner* has the ♠J. If declarer had it, he would win the ♠A, and later lead a spade from dummy towards his jack, through your marked ♠K.

## Key ideas from Chapter 2

- Inferences can be drawn by alert defenders from the bidding, the opening lead, and the way suits are played during the hand.
- Inferences allow you to build a picture of the distribution, place missing high cards, and form a strategy for defense.
- Negative inferences can be as revealing as positive ones.
- Declarer has similar inferences available at all stages of the hand.
- Expert players 'guess right' more often than not because they are aware of all these subtle inferences and are very good at acting upon them.

# Counting Distribution

*Not everything that can be counted counts, and not everything that counts can be counted.*

ALBERT EINSTEIN

The opponents have bought the contract and you and partner are on defense. Declarer has an edge because once that dummy appears, she can see her partner's hand and make big-time plans. Your job is to try to thwart those plans (with partner's help, of course). But unless you do some counting (the dreaded word), even the best partner in the world can't save you from yourself.

There are three things you are supposed to count on defense during the play of the hand: (1) declarer's distribution, what this chapter is all about; (2) declarer's potential tricks; and (3) declarer's HCP, what the next two chapters are all about.

The quicker you get a read on declarer's distribution, the easier it is to defend a hand without making mistakes. Players who don't count make many more defensive errors than players who do. That's a given.

It all boils down to this: declarer has thirteen cards just like you do. Those cards have to be divided into some distributional pattern just as yours are. Your job is to try to figure out what that pattern is before the hand is over. But how do you do it?

Counting is not nearly as difficult as some make it out to be. There are times when declarer's bidding is so revealing that you will be able to zero in on declarer's distribution before the opening lead is made!

# Major-suit openings

Throughout this chapter we're going to assume 'standard' bidding methods. Obviously, to some extent your exact inferences depend on what system your opponents are using. Whatever their system and agreements are, inferences are available; the opponents know what they are — make sure you do too by asking the right questions.

Sequences that begin with an opening bid of 1♡ or 1♠ and wind up with the opening bidder being the declarer are usually the easiest to count.

| Opener | Responder |
|--------|-----------|
| 1♠ | 2♢ |
| 2♡ | 2NT |
| 3♢ | 3♠ |
| 4♠ | pass |

First things first. Assume an opening bid of 1♠ or 1♡ shows a 5-card suit unless it is rebid, when you can assume six. Assume a second-bid suit shows four cards unless it is rebid; if it is, assume five. Assume delayed support (opener's 3♢ bid) shows three cards.

Of course, if your opponents play 'four-card majors', you have to make allowances. Also, third-seat opening bids of 1♠ or 1♡ may be made with a four-card major. However, some players won't open a four-card major even at gunpoint; assume that a 1♠ or 1♡ opening bid shows a five-card suit.

Using this as a guide, opener in our example auction figures to have a 5-4-3-1 hand pattern (starting with spades, then hearts, then diamonds, etc.) This has to help you on defense. It has to.

When you count declarer's hand, you only need a count on three suits, not four. Once you know three, you know all four.

In the example sequence, declarer bid three suits, so counting her hand was a piece of cake. Sometimes declarer bids only two suits.

| Opener | Responder |
|--------|-----------|
| 1♠     | 1NT       |
| 2◇     | 3◇        |
| pass   |           |

Assume opener has five spades and four diamonds. Say the opening lead is the ♣A followed by the ♣K which declarer ruffs. You now have a count on the third suit, clubs, and declarer's likely distribution is 5-3-4-1. 'Can't declarer have five diamonds?' you may ask. Of course, but until you learn otherwise, assume four.

## Revising your count

Maybe the diamonds in the above auction are divided like this:

**NORTH** (Dummy)
◇ A 10 4 3

**WEST** (You)
◇ J 6

**EAST**
◇ Q 9

**SOUTH**
◇ K 8 7 5 2

South is declarer in 3◇, and plays the ◇K and a diamond to the ace, felling your jack and partner's queen simultaneously. Clearly each of you has played your last diamond so declarer must have five, not four diamonds. Time to revise your estimate of declarer's distribution. The revised count is 5-2-5-1. You must remain 'count flexible' in the face of new evidence.

The fall of the cards in a side suit may also offer a chance for a 'count revision'.

BOTH VUL.     DEALER SOUTH

| West | North | East | South |
|------|-------|------|-------|
|      |       |      | 1♠ |
| pass | 2♣ | pass | 2♡ |
| pass | 2NT | pass | 3♡ |
| pass | 4♡ | all pass | |

**NORTH** (Dummy)
♠ 2
♡ K J 3
◇ Q J 8 6
♣ K J 10 5 4

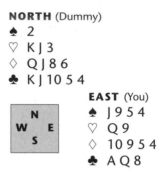

**EAST** (You)
♠ J 9 5 4
♡ Q 9
◇ 10 9 5 4
♣ A Q 8

You go into battle figuring declarer has 5-5 in the majors. Say partner leads the ◇A which declarer ruffs. Your provisional 'count estimate' should be 5-5-0-3. Say declarer continues by playing the ace and a low spade ruffing in dummy, partner playing the ♠K on the second lead. Partner's play of the ♠K is supposed to deny the queen (defenders follow suit with the lower of equals). Since partner has two spades, declarer has six. The new revised count reads 6-5-0-2.

This is declarer's hand:

♠ AQ10763  ♡ A8542  ◇ —  ♣ 73.

Say declarer, instead of cashing the ♠A, makes the stronger play at trick two of a club to the jack, partner playing the ♣2, a count signal. If partner has three clubs, declarer has two clubs. Given this information, again you have to revise your count and should play declarer for 6-5 or possibly 5-6 in the majors. Opener, with six hearts and five spades, may not have been strong enough to open 1♡ and reverse into spades.

On a bad day declarer only bids one suit, but even that suit may be 'count revealing'.

| Opener | Responder |
|--------|-----------|
| 2♠[1] | 4♠ |
| pass | |

1) Weak

You start by assuming declarer has six spades. Your job is to zero in on two other suits. Help may be just around the corner. Say the defense begins with three high hearts, and declarer ruffs the third round. Good. That's two suits you know about. Declarer has six spades and two hearts. Now declarer attacks clubs. You and partner will probably be giving each other a count signal in clubs, something coming up again later in this chapter. Say you can tell from partner's count signal that declarer started with two clubs. The count is complete. Declarer's distribution should be 6-2-3-2.

It can't be emphasized too strongly how important it is to become familiar with these hand patterns you see sprinkled all over this chapter. An easy aid to remembering patterns is to look at your own and try to absorb it. Another is to have a friend give you three numbers such as '5-2-2', and you fill in the missing number ('4') to complete the distribution. You can even test yourself out loud that way. Only do it when you are alone or else they may cart you off somewhere.

So what exactly are your counting crutches?

1) The bidding: yours, theirs and what isn't bid (the biggie!)
2) Spot card leads and cards returned in those suits.
3) Count signals.
4) When anyone shows out of a suit.
5) Common sense, including what partner does and doesn't lead. For example, spades are trumps, partner makes an opening lead, and you see ten clubs between your hand and dummy. If partner has a singleton club, partner will presumably lead it looking for a ruff. If partner doesn't lead a club, play declarer for a singleton or a void in clubs.

Just to show you can count with the best of 'em, here's an example. Don't let me down.

**NORTH** (Dummy)
♠ J 4
♡ 9 8 4
♢ Q 10 9 4 2
♣ K J 5

**WEST** (You)
♠ 10 9 8 2
♡ K Q 10 2
♢ 5 3
♣ A 8 6

```
  N
W   E
  S
```

| EAST-WEST VUL. | | DEALER SOUTH | |
| **West** | **North** | **East** | **South** |
| --- | --- | --- | --- |
| | | | 1♠ |
| pass | 1NT[1] | pass | 2♢ |
| pass | 3♢ | all pass | |

1) Not forcing

You lead the ♡K and partner signals encouragement. You lead a low heart to partner's ace, and partner returns a third heart which declarer ruffs. What do you make of declarer's distribution? Declarer should be 5-2-4-2. Consequently, if declarer leads a low club, play low and hope declarer misguesses. However, if declarer follows to a third round of hearts implying that declarer has a 5-3-4-1 hand pattern, grab your ♣A if declarer leads a club, or if you lead the suit, lead the ace. A possible defense in that case is to cash the ♣A and exit with a spade. If declarer started with

♠ AKxxx ♡ xxx ◇ AJxx ♣ x,

declarer will not be able to get to dummy to take the diamond finesse. If declarer tries to ruff a third round of spades, partner overruffs.

Now try these sequences and see what you come up with:

| Opener | Responder |
| --- | --- |
| 1♠ | 1NT |
| 2♠ | 2NT |
| 3♡ | 3♠ |
| pass | |

Play declarer for six spades and four hearts. Once you get a count on either minor, the puzzle is solved.

| Opener | Responder |
| --- | --- |
| 1♠ | 2♣ |
| 2♡ | 2NT |
| 3♠ | 4♠ |
| pass | |

Again opener shows six spades and four hearts. The difference between this sequence and the last is that bidding a second suit and then returning to the first shows a stronger 6-4 hand.

| Opener | Responder |
| --- | --- |
| 1♡ | 1♠ |
| 2◇ | 2NT |
| 3◇ | pass |

Opener figures to be 5-5 in the reds with fewer than three spades. With three-card spade support, opener is supposed to show that support sooner or later. Yes, opener might have six hearts and five diamonds or even five hearts and six diamonds with a hand not strong enough to reverse (10-13 HCP). Nevertheless, play opener for the most likely distribution until you learn otherwise.

| Opener | Responder |
|--------|-----------|
| 1♠ | 2♡ |
| 2NT | 3NT |
| pass | |

Opener should have a balanced hand without any singletons. Opener's most likely distribution is some 5-3-3-2 pattern. In fact, once you discover opener's doubleton, you should assume 3-3 in the two other suits. There is a further inference that declarer's doubleton is in hearts. The 2♡ response shows a five-card suit so if opener has three hearts, he tends to raise. Start by assuming that opener is 5-2-3-3, keeping 'revision time' open.

What other patterns fit this auction? Declarer may be 5-2-4-2 and not be strong enough to introduce diamonds at the three-level. Opener may even be 5-1-3-4 with a singleton honor in hearts; the opening lead may tell you that declarer started with four clubs. 'Revision time' has arrived.

What about when declarer jump shifts? Unless opener rebids the second suit, assume for the moment that it is a four-card suit.

| Opener | Responder |
|--------|-----------|
| 1♡ | 1♠ |
| 3◊ | 3♡ |
| 3NT | pass |

Opener figures to have 5-4 in the reds with fewer than three spades. Play opener for 1-5-4-3 or 2-5-4-2.

When opener rebids a major the assumption is a six-card suit, but there are exceptions.

| Opener | Responder | | Opener | Responder |
|--------|-----------|---|--------|-----------|
| 1♡ | 1♠ | | 1♠ | 1NT |
| 2♡ | pass | | 2♠ | pass |

In each of these sequences opener has skipped over *three* possible rebids to rebid the original suit. Whenever opener skips over three possible rebids, assume a six-card suit (whether the suit is a minor or a major). Of course, we are referring to openers who know how to bid, not those that rebid a five-card minor just to show their partners that it wasn't a short club or a short diamond!

Be wary of sequences like:

| Opener | Responder |
|--------|-----------|
| 1♡ | 1♠ |
| 3♣ | 3◊ |
| 3♡ | 4♡ |
| pass | |

3♣ may have been bid on a three-card suit to create a game force. Opener could have:

♠ Ax  ♡ AQJxxx  ◊ xx  ♣ AKx

The more suits the opener skips over to rebid the original suit, the more likely it is to be a six-card suit.

| Opener | Responder | Opener | Responder |
|--------|-----------|--------|-----------|
| 1♡ | 2◇ | 1♠ | 2♡ |
| 2♡ | 4♡ | 2♠ | 4♠ |
| pass | | pass | |

When the original response is made in the suit directly *beneath* the opener's suit in rank, opener may have a second suit and not be strong enough to introduce it at the next level, which constitutes a reverse. The inference of a six-card suit has shrunk from nearly 100% to something like 60%.

Jump rebids show six- or seven-card suits; double-jump rebids tend to show seven-card suits, or possibly six-card suits if partner has bid notrump and indicated a balanced hand.

| Opener | Responder | Opener | Responder |
|--------|-----------|--------|-----------|
| 1♡ | 1♠ | 1♡ | 1NT |
| 3♡ | 4♡ | 4♡ | |
| pass | | pass | |

Either of these jumps can show a six- or seven-card suit, but the jump to 4♡ is more likely to contain a seven-card suit because the 1NT response does *not* show a balanced hand.

# Notrump openings

Players are more likely to open 1NT with a five-card major at matchpoints, where playing in notrump can result in a much higher score. On the other hand, it is relatively common for players to open 2NT with a five-card major.

An opening bid of 1NT, 2NT, or 3NT is presumed to show one of three possible distributions: any 4-3-3-3, any 4-4-3-2 or some 5-3-3-2 patterns. If opener has a five-card suit, it is more likely that suit is a minor. Some players won't open 1NT with a five-card major, others will, while others will pick and choose. This is something you have to ask about. Knowing your opponents' bidding tendencies is important when trying to count a hand; very important.

Your job is to figure out which of these three distributions declarer has as quickly as possible. The bidding, especially when Stayman enters the picture, simplifies the problem. Here's an easy one:

| South | North |
|-------|-------|
| 1NT | 2♣ |
| 2♡ | 3NT |
| 4♠ | pass |

South must have four hearts and four spades. Once you discover how many clubs or diamonds South has, South's distribution is known.

Now look at this sequence:

| South | North |
|-------|-------|
| 1NT | 2♣ |
| 2♡ | 3NT |
| pass | |

South has four hearts but fewer than four spades. With four spades South bids 4♠ over 3NT because North has promised four spades.

| South | North |
|-------|-------|
| 1NT | 3NT |
| pass | |

The worst; South can have any of the three distributions. Help may be on the way, however. Say partner leads the ◇2, showing four; dummy tables with ◇K6, and your diamonds, regrettably, are the ◇95. Right off the bat you know declarer has five diamonds and some 5-3-3-2 pattern. You also know that partner has made an unfortunate lead smack into declarer's five-card suit. What else is new? Once you discover declarer's doubleton, at least you will have a 'read' on the hand — though it may be too late!

| South | North |
|-------|-------|
| 2NT | 3♣ |
| 3◇ | 3♡ |
| 3NT | pass |

Say North's 3♡ bid systemically shows five hearts and four spades. If so, South, who has denied a four-card major, shows two hearts and three spades with his 3NT rebid. Your partner's expected minor-suit lead may clarify declarer's exact distribution.

Transfer sequences can also lead to distributional inferences.

| South | North |
|-------|-------|
| 1NT | 2◇[1] |
| 2♡ | 2NT |
| pass | |

1) Transfer to hearts

With three hearts and a minimum hand, South would convert to 3♡.

South's pass of 2NT typically denies three hearts, so start by playing South for a doubleton heart; not much to go on. However, if South turns up with five clubs, play South to be 3-2-3-5. If South turns up with four clubs, South is either 4-2-3-4 or 3-2-4-4.

| South | North |
|-------|-------|
| 1NT   | 2♡[1] |
| 3♠    | 4♠    |
| pass  |       |

1) Transfer to spades

South loves spades, and the way most people play, the jump shows four spades.

# Minor-suit openings

Clearly it is easier to count declarer's hand after a major-suit opening bid because you can assume a five-card suit and usually be right. A minor-suit opening bid can be made with as few as three cards in the suit, however. It might be a good idea to dismiss some myths right away. There is a large group out there that thinks every time partner opens 1♣ or 1♢, it is likely to be a 'short club' or a 'short diamond'. Not true.

Let's start with the 1♣ opening bid. Say you pick up

♠ A943  ♡ A754  ♢ KQ2  ♣ 65.

Another restricting factor is that with the same distribution and more high cards, you would open 1NT.

Playing five-card majors, you have no choice but to open 1♢. This, by the way, is the *only* distribution where you are supposed to open 1♢ with a three-card diamond suit. Do you have any idea how often this happens? Less than 5% of the time! In other words, when partner opens 1♢, chances are partner has four or more diamonds 95+% of the time. To turn this figure around: when defending against a declarer who opens 1♢ and turns up with three diamonds, assume a 4-4-3-2 pattern.

What about those who play 'better minor' and open 1♢ with

♠ AQ4  ♡ J875  ♢ AQ4  ♣ 987?

Even including this aberration (my feeling), an opening bid of 1♢ with a three-card diamond suit is unlikely.

What about a 'short club'? How often can you expect a 1♣ opening to be made with exactly three clubs? Less than 15% of the time. To turn this figure around: if partner opens 1♣ you can expect to find four or more clubs in partner's hand at least 85% of the time. If more players realized what these numbers were, they would support minor-suit opening bids more often.

Let's look at sequences that begin with 1♣ or 1◊.

| Opener | Responder |
| --- | --- |
| 1♣ | 1◊ |
| 2♣ | pass |

This is an easy one. Opener has skipped over three possible rebids, 1♡, 1♠, and 1NT. Opener has at least six clubs and does not figure to have a four-card major.

This sequence brings us to the topic of opener skipping over one or two major suits to rebid a minor suit. When this happens, the inference is that the opener does not have four cards in a 'skipped-over' major. Once again, nothing is written in stone. Opener may have:

♠K4 ♡ 8653 ◊ 2 ♣ AKQ1087

and feel it is more descriptive to rebid 2♣ rather than 1♡ over a 1◊ response.

| Opener | Responder |
| --- | --- |
| 1♣ | 1◊ |
| 1♠ | 1NT |
| 2◊ | pass |

Several inferences available: (1) opener has skipped over 1♡ to rebid 1♠ so opener does not have four hearts; (2) opener has bid two suits and supported a third. When this happens, assume five cards in the first suit, four in the second, and three in the third. Play opener for 4-1-3-5. Notice a 'short club' is not even a ballpark thought when three suits are bid. Many players would be better off if they had never heard of a short club or a short diamond when trying to work out declarer's distribution. The frequency is too low. On the preceding sequence, opener might have

♠ AK87 ♡ 2 ◊ AJ5 ♣ Q10874.

1NT and 2NT rebids are supposed to show balanced hands:

| Opener | Responder |
| --- | --- |
| 1♣ | 1♡ |
| 1NT | 2NT |
| pass | |

This one is not as easy as it looks. A possible distribution is 3-2-3-5. Opener should not rebid a five-card minor suit in preference to rebidding 1NT with a balanced hand. Another possibility is 3-2-4-4; however, some players always open 1◇ with 4-4 in the minors, others always open 1♣. You can save yourself mucho counting headaches if you ask your opponents about their agreements concerning opening the bidding with 4-4 in the minors.

Continuing with this sequence: has opener denied four spades? It would appear so. However, there is an auxiliary problem with an opener who opens a short club with 4-3-3-3 distribution.

♠ Q843   ♡ AJ3   ◇ K104   ♣ QJ5

Is opener better served to rebid 1♠ or 1NT with this distribution? Suffice it to say that many top players rebid 1♠ while many others rebid 1NT. You should ask whether opener has denied four spades before making your opening lead. Also, you and your partner should decide how you plan to rebid such hands yourselves.

When opener makes a jump rebid, showing at least a six-card suit, and then bids the suit again, assume a seven-bagger.

| Opener | Responder |
| --- | --- |
| 1♣ | 1◇ |
| 3♣ | 3♡ |
| 4♣ | 5♣ |
| pass | |

Play opener for seven clubs and no spade stopper.

When opener reverses, assume five cards in the first suit and four in the second, and go from there.

| Opener | Responder |
| --- | --- |
| 1♣ | 1♠ |
| 2♡ | 3♡ |
| 4♡ | pass |

Play opener for five clubs and four hearts. Don't even think about a short club in reversing sequences.

When opener makes a jump rebid of 2NT and responder raises to 3NT, you don't know much.

| Opener | Responder |
|--------|-----------|
| 1◇ | 1♠ |
| 2NT | 3NT |
| pass | |

This one is a toughie. Opener can have many possible distributions including some with up to six diamonds! This one requires your antennae to be up, way up. For starters, opener cannot have a short diamond: with 4-4-3-2 distribution, opener raises spades.

However, when opener makes a jump rebid of 2NT and responder bids a second suit, things begin to clear up.

| Opener | Responder |
|--------|-----------|
| 1◇ | 1♠ |
| 2NT | 3♡ |
| 3NT | pass |

Responder figures to have five spades and four hearts. Opener should have fewer than three spades and cannot have four hearts. Opener's most likely distributions are 2-3-4-4, 2-3-5-3, 2-2-6-3 and 2-3-6-2.

A jump rebid of 2NT after a minor-suit opening bid can conceal a six-card suit.

# When responder becomes declarer

In the previous examples opener always wound up being the declarer. Let's not discriminate. Responder is quite apt to become the declarer, particularly if opener supports one of responder's suits, if responder has a long, strong suit, or if responder bids notrump and plays there.

The rules stay in place. If responder bids two suits, assume 5-4; if responder rebids the same suit, assume a six-card suit; if the initial response is a natural 2NT or 3NT (not 1NT) assume one of the three balanced-hand distributions.

| Opener | Responder |
|--------|-----------|
| 1♣ | 1♡ |
| 1♠ | 2♡ |
| pass | |

The assumption is that responder has six hearts and fewer than four spades. Had responder jumped to 3♡ over 1♠, the assumption would still be a six-card suit. However, had responder leaped to 4♡ over 1♠, not knowing of any heart support, seven hearts is more likely than six.

| Opener | Responder |
|--------|-----------|
| 1♣ | 1♠ |
| 2♠ | 2NT |
| 3♠ | pass |

Responder has four spades and denies four hearts. With 4-4 in the majors, the normal response is 1♡. What about diamonds? Has responder denied four diamonds by skipping over that suit too? No. In the modern game the emphasis is on bidding major suits as quickly as possible before competition, particularly preemptive competition, may cause you to 'lose the suit'. With strong hands, hands approaching opening-bid strength, responder can afford to go slowly and bid 1◇ (especially with strong diamonds) and then bid the major next, but with weaker hands, the major suit is normally bid first.

As usual, you should realize that not everyone plays this way. Ask!

| Opener | Responder |
|--------|-----------|
| 1♣ | 1♠ |
| 2♠ | 4♠ |
| pass | |

This one is also a bit tricky. If opener 'promises' four spades with that raise (as some play), then responder can leap to game with a four-card spade suit. However, if opener can have three spades, as most play, then the leap to 4♠ shows at least five spades. Ask.

| Opener | Responder |
|--------|-----------|
| 1◇ | 1♠ |
| 2◇ | 2♡ |
| 2NT | 3♡ |
| 4♡ | pass |

Play responder for 5-5 in the majors.

| Opener | Responder |
|--------|-----------|
| 1♢ | 1♡ |
| 2♢ | 2♠ |
| 2NT | 3♠ |
| 4♡ | pass |

Play responder for five spades and six hearts. With 5-5, regardless of strength, the first response is in spades, the higher-ranking suit, not hearts.

| Opener | Responder |
|--------|-----------|
| 1♢ | 1♠ |
| 2♠ | 3NT |
| pass | |

Responder has exactly four spades and denies four hearts. Opener apparently has three spades. With four spades, opener usually returns to 4♠ on this sequence. However, if opener has promised four spades with the raise, opener may pass 3NT.

Distributional inferences change dramatically when the original response is 2NT as opposed to an original suit response followed by a 2NT rebid.

| Opener | Responder |
|--------|-----------|
| 1♢ | 2NT |
| 3♣ | 3♡ |
| 3NT | pass |

Responder is balanced and does not figure to have a four-card major. The 3♡ bid says, 'my hearts are much stronger than my spades, so don't bid 3NT unless you have a spade honor or spade length'. Perhaps responder has

♠ Q54 ♡ AKJ ♢ 1076 ♣ K532.

Now compare the previous sequence to this one:

| Opener | Responder |
|--------|-----------|
| 1♢ | 2♣ |
| 2♠ | 2NT |
| 3NT | pass |

The 2NT *rebid* does not necessarily promise a balanced hand; responder might be 3-4-1-5 or even 3-3-1-6.

Be wary of a 1NT response, particularly to a major-suit opening bid.

| Opener | Responder |
|--------|-----------|
| 1♠ | 1NT |
| 3NT | pass |

Responder does not necessarily have a balanced hand. He may have a wildly distributional hand that is not strong enough to respond at the two level. To give you an idea of what responder could have:

♠ —  ♡ J8743  ◇ K43  ♣ Q10874

Sometimes a 1NT responder has a chance to show a six-card minor.

| Opener | Responder |
|--------|-----------|
| 1♡ | 1NT |
| 2NT | 3◇ |
| pass | |

Play responder for at least six diamonds, fewer than three hearts, and fewer than four spades.

# When partner joins the party

In the previous sequences only the opponents were bidding. It was almost as if your side had a case of terminal lockjaw. On most hands the defenders join in, and many of the bids your partner makes show a specific number of cards in a particular suit. For example, if your partner opens 2♡, weak, you know partner has six hearts. If the opponents play the hand, you will know the moment the dummy comes down how many hearts declarer has. (Of course declarer also knows how many hearts you have.)

The more bidding your side does, the easier it is to count declarer's hand. Try this one from the East chair:

NORTH-SOUTH VUL. DEALER SOUTH

| West | North | East | South |
|------|-------|------|-------|
| | | | 1♡ |
| 2♠[1] | dbl[2] | pass | 2NT |
| pass | 3NT | all pass | |

1) Weak
2) Negative

**NORTH** (Dummy)
♠ A 9 3
♡ 9 6
◇ K Q 9 6
♣ A 9 7 5

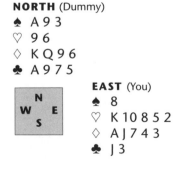

**EAST** (You)
♠ 8
♡ K 10 8 5 2
◇ A J 7 4 3
♣ J 3

Partner leads the ♣2, fourth best. What is declarer's distribution? You can do it! Just go back to the bidding and the opening lead.

There are three clues: declarer's 1♡ bid, partner's 2♠ bid, and the lead of the ♣2. Declarer figures to have five hearts (did not rebid hearts); partner should have six spades, leaving declarer three; the lead of the ♣2 usually shows four, so declarer has three clubs. Putting it all together, declarer should have a 3-5-2-3 hand pattern.

Defenders can also take inferences from what partner does *not* bid. For example:

| West | North | East | South |
|------|-------|------|-------|
| (You) | | | |
| | | 1♡ | 1♠ |
| 2♡ | 2♠ | all pass | |

Partner's pass of 2♠ denies six hearts. With six hearts partner is supposed to compete to 3♡. Knowing partner has only five hearts tells you how many hearts declarer has (when dummy comes down). Similarly your raise to 2♡ normally shows three hearts. Holding four hearts you are supposed to compete to 3♡ yourself. The rule is not to let the opponents play at the two-level if your side has a nine-card fit. Important.

This concept is called the **Law of Total Tricks**. U.S. expert Larry Cohen has written several books on the Law and its applications in competitive auctions.

# When someone preempts

When either side makes a preemptive bid, counting becomes easier for everybody, particularly when the preemptive bidder becomes the declarer. Why? Because when declarer is known to have a long suit there are fewer 'other' cards to count!

**NORTH** (Dummy)
♠ K 5
♡ 8 7 6
◇ K J 10 9
♣ J 9 7 6

**WEST** (You)
♠ 8 2
♡ K Q 4
◇ A 7 5 3
♣ A 5 4 3

| BOTH VUL. | | DEALER SOUTH | |
|------|-------|------|-------|
| **West** | **North** | **East** | **South** |
| | | | 3♠ |
| all pass | | | |

Declarer's hand is:

♠ AQJ10xxx
♡ xxx
♢ xx
♣ K

You lead the ♡K, partner encourages with the ♡9, and you continue with the ♡Q and a heart to partner's jack, declarer following. Partner switches to the ♣2, declarer plays the king, you win and return the ♣3 (showing four); dummy plays the ♣9, partner the ♣10, and declarer ruffs. Are you counting? Declarer exits with a low diamond. What do you do?

*Play low.* The clues are all there. The bidding tells you that South has seven spades. The play in hearts indicates declarer started with three hearts and declarer is known to have a singleton club. Declarer must be 7-3-2-1, so you want to give declarer a guess in diamonds by playing low.

One further point. Let's go back to the heart suit:

**NORTH** (Dummy)
♡ 8 7 6

**WEST** (You)
♡ K Q 4

**EAST** (Loving partner)
♡ A J 9 3

**SOUTH**
♡ 10 5 2

When partner wins the third round of hearts with the ♡J, you know partner still has the ♡A. However, if partner is careless and wins the third round of hearts with the ♡A, partner *denies* the ♡J. Now you have a miscount on the hearts which is why it is mega-important for defenders to take a trick with the *lower* or *lowest* equal.

If partner wins the third heart with the ace, and declarer eventually leads a diamond, you should fly with your ace playing declarer for a 7-4-1-1 pattern. Can you see now why good players make so many more mistakes when not playing with other good players? Their partners screw them up!

# The opening lead

The most readable count card is the opening lead of a deuce versus notrump (or the opening leader's known lowest card), indicating a four-card suit (playing fourth-best leads). That clue, coupled with the bidding, may be all third hand needs to get a complete count!

**NORTH** (Dummy)
♠ 6 2
♡ 7 3
◇ A J 5 4
♣ K Q J 4 2

**EAST** (You)
♠ J 7 3
♡ A 10 6 4
◇ 9 3
♣ A 10 9 6

| BOTH VUL. | | DEALER SOUTH | |
| **West** | **North** | **East** | **South** |
|---|---|---|---|
| | | | 1♠ |
| pass | 2♣ | pass | 2◇ |
| pass | 3◇ | pass | 3NT |
| all pass | | | |

Partner leads the ♡2. What does everybody have? You can do it!

Declarer has shown five spades and four diamonds. Partner's lead shows four hearts leaving declarer with three hearts. Voilà, declarer has a 5-3-4-1 hand pattern. When you return the ♡4, your lowest from three remaining cards in partner's suit, partner also has a complete count on the hand.

One can make some remarkable plays with an early count.

**NORTH** (Dummy)
♠ 10 7 6 4 3
♡ K J
◇ A Q 9 3
♣ 8 6

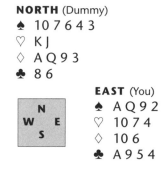

**EAST** (You)
♠ A Q 9 2
♡ 10 7 4
◇ 10 6
♣ A 9 5 4

| BOTH VUL. | | DEALER SOUTH | |
| **West** | **North** | **East** | **South** |
|---|---|---|---|
| | | | 1♡ |
| pass | 1♠ | pass | 2◇ |
| pass | 3◇ | pass | 3NT |
| all pass | | | |

Partner leads the ♣2. What is declarer's distribution, and how do you plan to defend?

Declarer figures to be 5-4 in the reds, and the lead pinpoints three clubs in declarer's hand, ergo declarer has a singleton spade! Regardless of what that spade is, your side has four spade tricks if you play the ace and another spade next. Declarer's hand:

♠ K ♡ AQ982 ♢ KJ54 ♣ KJ7.

If you woodenly return a club, declarer races off with the next ten tricks.

When partner leads high in a suit you have bid but he has not supported, then assume partner has a doubleton. At notrump a high-low lead in an unbid suit generally shows a five-card suit. But what about a suit contract? Does it show two or five cards? How can you tell? The answer to most distributional ambiguities can be found by going back to the bidding.

| BOTH VUL. | | DEALER SOUTH | |
|---|---|---|---|
| **West** | **North** | **East** | **South** |
| | | | 3♠ |
| pass | 4♠ | all pass | |

**NORTH** (Dummy)
♠ A Q 8
♡ J 7 6
♢ A K J 10 8
♣ J 10

**EAST** (You)
♠ 3 2
♡ A K 9
♢ 9 4 3 2
♣ A 9 8 5

Partner leads the ♡3 to your king and declarer's four. When you play the ♡A, partner plays the ♡2 and declarer the five. How do you read the hearts, and what now?

Partner has either two or five hearts. Whenever partner can have one of two distributions, assume the shorter, work out how many that gives declarer, and ask yourself if that is a reasonable possibility. If it isn't, assume partner has the larger number. In this case, if partner has two hearts, declarer has five. This is not reasonable given the bidding. Play partner for five hearts, declarer for two, and shift to a low club. Why a low club?

With those diamonds staring you in the face, you must try for *two* quick club tricks to defeat the contract. If partner has the ♣K, it doesn't matter which club you lead, but if partner has the ♣Q, and declarer the ♣K, you must put declarer to an immediate guess by leading low.

Declarer's hand:

♠ KJ109754  ♡ 54  ◇ 65  ♣ K7.

Playing fourth-best leads, the lead of a low card at a suit contract can also be ambiguous. For example, the three is led from Q73, Q743, and singleton three. Although it may be difficult to distinguish three-card length from four-card length, the bidding usually makes a singleton lead an 'easy read'.

**NORTH** (Dummy)
♠ K 8 6 5
♡ K 10 8
◇ J
♣ J 10 8 7 3

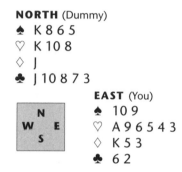

**EAST** (You)
♠ 10 9
♡ A 9 6 5 4 3
◇ K 5 3
♣ 6 2

A modern popular method, especially against suit contracts, is to lead low from an odd number of cards, and high-low to show an even number. Playing this, you lead the 4 from K642, and the 2 from K62 or K6542.

| EAST-WEST VUL. | | DEALER WEST | |
|---|---|---|---|
| **West** | **North** | **East** | **South** |
| pass | pass | pass | 1♠ |
| 1NT[1] | 3♠ | pass | 4♠ |
| all pass | | | |

1) Unusual for the minors

Partner leads the ♡2, dummy plays low, you win the ace, and declarer plays the ♡J. Partner's lead is either a singleton or low from three to the queen. Which is it? Go back to the bidding.

Partner's 1NT overcall by a *passed* hand is 'unusual' describing a hand with at least 5-5 in the minors. If partner has led from ♡Q72 partner is void in spades, giving declarer seven. Doubtful. The more likely possibility is that partner is 2-1-5-5 and is looking for a ruff or two. Might as well oblige. Return the ♡9, a suit preference play asking for the higher-ranking side suit, diamonds. As it happens, partner ruffs, underleads his ◇A to your king and you give partner a second heart ruff. Down one. Cheers.

Declarer's hand:  ♠ AQJ42  ♡ QJ7  ◇ Q1092  ♣ A
Partner's hand:  ♠ 73  ♡ 2  ◇ A8764  ♣ KQ954

# The count signal

The final nail in declarer's coffin is the count signal that you and partner give to tell each other how many cards you have in any suit declarer or dummy leads first. However, remember that if the count in one of these suits is already known from the bidding, it is no longer necessary to give count. In fact, it is counterproductive. Why tell partner how many cards you have in a suit when partner already knows? Declarer may be eavesdropping!

Let's take a look at a side suit in a spade contract.

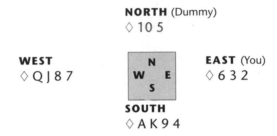

**NORTH** (Dummy)
◇ 10 5

**WEST**
◇ Q J 8 7

**EAST** (You)
◇ 6 3 2

**SOUTH**
◇ A K 9 4

Diamonds is an unbid suit and South begins with two top diamonds with the intention of ruffing a third. West begins a count signal by playing the 8-7, high-low, showing an even number of diamonds; East plays the 2-3, low-high to show an odd number of diamonds. After South ruffs a diamond in dummy, both East and West know that South has another diamond.

But let's say diamonds is declarer's second-bid suit. Now both defenders can be reasonably sure declarer has four diamonds and neither should give count.

The count signal is used most often (and most effectively) when declarer leads up to a suit in dummy, particularly one lacking the ace.

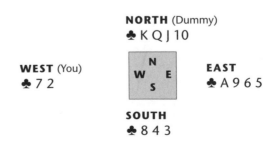

**NORTH** (Dummy)
♣ K Q J 10

**WEST** (You)
♣ 7 2

**EAST**
♣ A 9 6 5

**SOUTH**
♣ 8 4 3

Say South has shown a balanced hand during the bidding and eventually leads a club towards dummy. West plays the ♣7 starting a high-low to show an even number of clubs. The trouble is that from East's point of view West also plays the ♣7 from the ♣8742, once again starting a high-low to show four clubs. How can East tell?

The key, as ever, lies in the bidding. Since South has shown a balanced hand, West can't have four because that would place South with a singleton club. No, West has two clubs and South has three. However, if South is marked with club shortness, then East should play West for four clubs and South for a singleton.

Another point about count signals. When the opponents lead a suit first, the only thing the defenders can do is give count. You *can't* give attitude, so don't bother trying. For example:

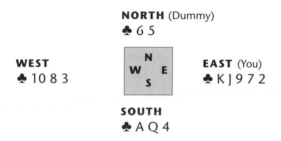

**NORTH** (Dummy)
♣ 6 5

**WEST**
♣ 10 8 3

**EAST** (You)
♣ K J 9 7 2

**SOUTH**
♣ A Q 4

Clubs is a side suit in a heart contract and declarer leads a low club from dummy. Play the ♣2, count. Don't play something like the ♣7 and then the ♣2 thinking you are echoing to show that you have club strength. Your high-low in clubs shows an even number of clubs and partner is likely to miscount the hand; it's on your head if he does and goes wrong later in the play.

What about trying to screw declarer up (assuming he is even watching) by giving false count? Giving false count is a two-edged sword. Declarer may be misled, but then again, so may partner. If partner goes wrong in the endgame because you gave false count in an important suit, it's on your head again. The best time to give false count is when you have *all* of your side's high card strength and partner, holding zilch, is not going to be involved. Partner, however, the one with zilch, gives honest count to help the stronger hand out. *The strong hand lies (occasionally), the weak hand tells the truth.*

Let's see if you are ready for prime-time, sitting East.

| NEITHER VUL. | | DEALER SOUTH | |
|---|---|---|---|
| **West** | **North** | **East** | **South** |
| | | | 3◇ |
| 4♠ | 5◇ | all pass | |

Opening lead: ♠A

**NORTH** (Dummy)
♠ 10 3 2
♡ A K Q 10
◇ A Q 4
♣ 4 3 2

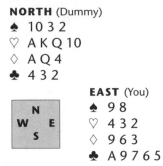

**EAST** (You)
♠ 9 8
♡ 4 3 2
◇ 9 6 3
♣ A 9 7 6 5

Partner starts with the ♠AK, declarer ruffing the second round. Tricks three, four, and five are top diamonds, partner discarding three spades. Declarer continues by playing the ♡AKQ, discarding the ♣J on the third round of hearts. Next comes a low club from dummy. Which club do you play, and worse, why?

If you are counting, you know that declarer started with a 1-2-7-3 hand pattern and remains with *two* clubs. There is no danger of losing your ♣A if you make the proper prime-time play of a low club (without hesitating or trembling or sweating). You are hoping declarer remains with the ♣K10 and guesses wrong; if partner has the ♣K, it doesn't matter which club you play.

Declarer's hand:

♠ 7  ♡ 85  ◇ KJ108752  ♣ KJ10

# The wrap-up

So there you have it, all these weapons in your counting arsenal: the bidding, the leads, the showouts, the count signals, plus a little common sense, all helping you to get an early or an eventual count on declarer's hand. Of course, once you have the count you have to know what do with it! Hey, nobody ever said this was an easy game.

# Practice Hands

**Hand 1**

**NORTH** (Dummy)
♠ J 9 8 7 6 5
♡ Q 2
♢ A Q 3
♣ 8 4

**WEST**
♠ A 3
♡ 9 8 7
♢ 8 6 5 4
♣ J 10 6 3

N
W E
S

**EAST** (You)
♠ K Q 10 4
♡ 10 4 3
♢ 10 9
♣ A 9 5 2

**SOUTH**
♠ 2
♡ A K J 6 5
♢ K J 7 2
♣ K Q 7

| NONE VUL. | | DEALER SOUTH | |
|---|---|---|---|
| **West** | **North** | **East** | **South** |
| | | | 1♡ |
| pass | 1♠ | pass | 2♢ |
| pass | 2♡ | pass | 2NT |
| pass | 3NT | all pass | |

Opening lead: ♣3

Partner leads the ♣3. The bidding tells you that South has five hearts and four diamonds; the opening lead tells you that South has three clubs and therefore a singleton spade. Your best chance is to shift to a low spade at trick two. If partner has ♠Ax, you take an immediate four spade tricks; if declarer has the singleton ace, you still beat the hand if partner has a heart entry. Returning a club at trick two only nets you four tricks at most; your side needs five.

**Hand 2**

**NORTH** (Dummy)
♠ K 4
♡ K 6 3
♢ J 10 7
♣ K J 10 4 2

**WEST** (You)
♠ 8 5 3 2
♡ 4 2
♢ K Q 8 6 2
♣ A 7

N
W E
S

**EAST**
♠ 10 9
♡ Q J 5
♢ A 9 4
♣ Q 9 8 5 3

**SOUTH**
♠ A Q J 7 6
♡ A 10 9 8 7
♢ 5 3
♣ 6

| EAST-WEST VUL. | | DEALER SOUTH | |
|---|---|---|---|
| **West** | **North** | **East** | **South** |
| | | | 1♠ |
| pass | 2♣ | pass | 2♡ |
| pass | 2NT | pass | 3♡ |
| pass | 4♡ | all pass | |

Opening lead: ♢K

You lead the ♢K, and partner encourages with the ♢9. You continue with a diamond to partner's ace and declarer ruffs partner's diamond return.  At trick three declarer leads a low club.  Up or down, Mrs. Brown?

*Up.*  Declarer's bidding has described a hand with at least 5-5 in the majors.  Declarer has turned up with two diamonds so that club that is staring you in the face must be a singleton.  Hop up with the ♣A and hope partner has a major-suit trick.

| BOTH VUL. | | DEALER SOUTH | |
|-----------|-------|------|-------|
| **West** | **North** | **East** | **South** |
| | | | 1♠ |
| pass | 2♣ | pass | 2♡ |
| pass | 2NT | pass | 3♡ |
| pass | 4♡ | all pass | |

Opening lead: ◇A

**Hand 3**

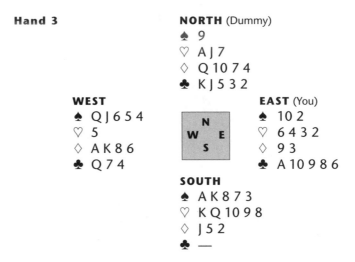

**NORTH** (Dummy)
♠ 9
♡ A J 7
◇ Q 10 7 4
♣ K J 5 3 2

**WEST**
♠ Q J 6 5 4
♡ 5
◇ A K 8 6
♣ Q 7 4

**EAST** (You)
♠ 10 2
♡ 6 4 3 2
◇ 9 3
♣ A 10 9 8 6

**SOUTH**
♠ A K 8 7 3
♡ K Q 10 9 8
◇ J 5 2
♣ —

Partner leads the ◇A and you start an echo with the ◇9.  Partner continues with the king and a diamond and you ruff the third round, declarer following with the two, the five and the jack.

The count is complete.  Declarer has shown 5-5 in the majors and has turned up with three diamonds.  Declarer has a club void! Don't even think of playing that ♣A — it is not the setting trick! Instead, shift to a trump.  Partner has five spades  and declarer may have to trump three spades in dummy.  If you take one of those trumps out of dummy, declarer could wind up a trick short.  On this layout, a trump return is the only one that defeats the contract.

**Hand 4**

**NORTH** (Dummy)
- ♠ K 5 3 2
- ♡ Q J 10 2
- ◇ K 8 3
- ♣ 8 6

**WEST**
- ♠ A 10 8
- ♡ 9 4
- ◇ Q 10 5 2
- ♣ A 9 7 2

**EAST** (You)
- ♠ 7 6
- ♡ A 8 6 3
- ◇ J 9 7 4
- ♣ 10 5 3

**SOUTH**
- ♠ Q J 9 4
- ♡ K 7 5
- ◇ A 6
- ♣ K Q J 4

| NEITHER VUL. | | DEALER WEST | |
| West | North | East | South |
| --- | --- | --- | --- |
| pass | pass | pass | 1NT |
| pass | 2♣ | pass | 2♠ |
| pass | 3♠ | pass | 4♠ |
| all pass | | | |

Opening lead: ♡9

Partner leads the ♡9, almost certainly a short suit — but is it a singleton or a doubleton? You have no side entries, so if it's a singleton you have to win this trick and return a heart. If it's a doubleton, you have to duck, so partner can reach your hand when she gets in with her presumed trump entry. What did you decide? The auction tells you the answer — if partner has a singleton, then South has four hearts, which he has denied by bidding 2♠ over his partner's Stayman enquiry. So play the encouraging ♡8, and when partner gets in with the ♠A, she will play another heart to your ace, and get her ruff for down one.

Most partnerships bid 2♡ holding 4-4 in the majors over Stayman. However, some bid their better major first. Ask!

# Test Yourself

*Solutions on page 85*

1) In each of the following auctions, what would you assume North's major-suit distribution to be?

a)

| North | South |
|-------|-------|
| 1♠ | 2◇ |
| 2♡ | 3◇ |
| 3♠ | 4♠ |
| pass | |

b)

| North | South |
|-------|-------|
| 1♠ | 2♣ |
| 2♠ | 2NT |
| 3♡ | 4♡ |
| pass | |

c)

| North | South |
|-------|-------|
| 1♠ | 2◇ |
| 2♡ | 3♠ |
| 3NT | pass |

d)

| North | South |
|-------|-------|
| 1♠ | 2♡ |
| 2NT | 3NT |
| pass | |

e)

| North | South |
|-------|-------|
| 1♡ | 1NT |
| 2♠ | 2NT |
| 3♠ | 4♠ |
| pass | |

f)

| North | South |
|-------|-------|
| 1♡ | 1NT |
| 2♠ | 2NT |
| 3♡ | 4♡ |
| pass | |

g)

| North | South |
|-------|-------|
| 1♣ | 1◇ |
| 1♡ | 2NT |
| 3♠ | 4♠ |
| pass | |

h)

| North | South |
|-------|-------|
| 2NT | 3♣ |
| 3◇ | 3♠[1] |
| 3NT | pass |

1) 5 spades and 4 hearts

2)

**NORTH** (Dummy)
♡ K Q 7

**WEST** (You)
a) ♡ 6 5 2
b) ♡ 9 6 5 2
c) ♡ 9 8 6 5 2
d) ♡ 10 9 5 2
e) ♡ 9 2

*Solution on page 85*

You are defending a spade contract, and South leads a low heart towards dummy. Assuming hearts is an unbid suit and you wish to give partner count, which heart do you play in each case?

3)

**NORTH** (Dummy)
♠ 6

**WEST**
♠ Q 10 8 4

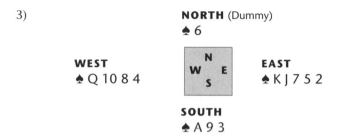

**EAST**
♠ K J 7 5 2

**SOUTH**
♠ A 9 3

Diamonds are trumps and declarer plans to ruff both losing spades in the dummy. Declarer begins by playing the ace and then trumping the ♠3, If the defenders wish to give each other count, in what order do they play their spades?

*Solution on page 85*

4)

**NORTH** (Dummy)
♠ A 7 2
♡ J 10 6 5
♢ K Q 10 8 6
♣ 9

**EAST** (You)
♠ J 9 5 4
♡ A Q 8 2
♢ 4
♣ Q 8 6 5

| EAST-WEST VUL. | | DEALER NORTH | |
| West | North | East | South |
| --- | --- | --- | --- |
| | pass | pass | 1♢ |
| 1♠ | 3♢ | 4♠ | 4NT |
| pass | 5♢ | pass | 6♢ |
| all pass | | | |

Partner leads the ♠K, dummy wins, and a spade is ruffed at trick two. A diamond is led to dummy, partner producing the jack, and another spade is ruffed. Declarer continues with the ace, king and four of clubs, ruffing in dummy, partner playing the two, three, and seven in that order. What is declarer's original distribution, and which heart do you play when the jack is led from dummy?

*Solution on page 86*

BOTH VUL.     DEALER NORTH

| West | North | East | South |
|------|-------|------|-------|
|  | pass | pass | 1♡ |
| pass | 3♡ | pass | 4♡ |
| all pass | | | |

5)

**NORTH** (Dummy)
♠ 4 3 2
♡ Q J 10 2
♢ K 6 5
♣ K Q 4

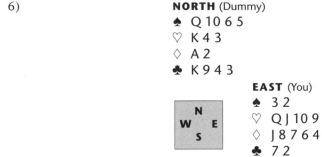

**EAST** (You)
♠ A K 7 6
♡ 4 3
♢ 9 8 2
♣ 10 7 6 5

*Solution on page 86*

Partner leads the ♢Q which dummy wins with the ♢K. Dummy's ♡Q loses to partner's ace and partner exits with the ♢10 taken by declarer's ace. Declarer crosses to dummy with a heart, partner playing the ♡9, and ruffs a diamond in the closed hand. Next, South continues by playing the ace and a club to dummy's queen, discarding spade on the ♣K. Hello, are you still there? A low spade is led from dummy. Which spade do you play?

BOTH VUL.     DEALER NORTH

| West | North | East | South |
|------|-------|------|-------|
|  | 1♣ | pass | 1♠ |
| pass | 2♠ | pass | 6♠(!) |
| all pass | | | |

6)

**NORTH** (Dummy)
♠ Q 10 6 5
♡ K 4 3
♢ A 2
♣ K 9 4 3

**EAST** (You)
♠ 3 2
♡ Q J 10 9
♢ J 8 7 6 4
♣ 7 2

*Solution on page 87*

Partner leads the ♢K to dummy's ace. A spade is led to declarer's ace, and then a spade back to the queen in dummy, partner following. Declarer continues by ruffing a diamond in the closed hand, finally exiting with the ace-king and a low heart to your jack, partner following to all three hearts. What now?

# Test Yourself — Solutions

*Problem 1*

a) Six spades and four hearts.

b) Six spades and four hearts.

   The difference between this and (a) is that North is showing a weaker hand here by rebidding 2♠ immediately and bidding the heart suit later.

c) Five spades and four hearts.

   Apparently North has weak spades and a fitting honor in diamonds, plus a club stopper or two.

d) Five spades and two hearts.

   With three hearts, North tends to raise hearts. He might even have a singleton heart honor, but not, of course, a heart void!

e) Six hearts and five spades.

   The spade rebid promises five, and if North has only five hearts the proper opening bid is 1♠.

f) Six hearts and four spades.

   North already showed five hearts and four spades with the first two bids; the heart rebid shows six but denies five spades — see the answer to part (e).

g) Four hearts and four spades.

   North should be 4-4-1-4 or 4-4-0-5.

h) Two spades and three hearts.

   South shows five spades and four hearts. With three spades North normally raises to 4♠.

*Problem 2*

a) ♡2  Low from odd.

b) ♡6  Second highest from four.

c) ♡2  Low from odd.

d) ♡5  Third-highest from four in this case, since the ♡9 may be an important spot.

e) ♡9  High-low from a doubleton.

*Problem 3*

West plays the 8-4, high-low to show an even number of spades. Even though one tries to play second highest with four if possible, care must be taken if the second-highest card has trick-taking potential, particularly when dummy has four or five cards in the suit. Don't waste a potential trick to give count. Period. East plays 2-5, low high to show an odd number of cards.

| EAST-WEST VUL. | | DEALER NORTH | |
|---|---|---|---|
| **West** | **North** | **East** | **South** |
| | pass | pass | 1◇ |
| 1♠ | 3◇ | 4♠ | 4NT |
| pass | 5◇ | pass | 6◇ |
| all pass | | | |

**Trick 1:** ♠K ♠A ♠9 ♠3
**Trick 2:** ♠2 ♣4 ◇2 ♠6
**Trick 3:** ◇3 ◇J ◇K ◇4
**Trick 4:** ♠7 ♠5 ◇5 ♠10
**Trick 5:** ♣A ♣2 ♠9 ♣6
**Trick 6:** ♣K ♣3 ♡5 ♣5
**Trick 7:** ♣4 ♣7 ◇6 ♣8
**Trick 8:** ♡J

If you need *three* heart tricks to defeat the contract (against 5◇, say), play partner for ♡Kx and duck the ♡J to keep the suit fluid.

4)

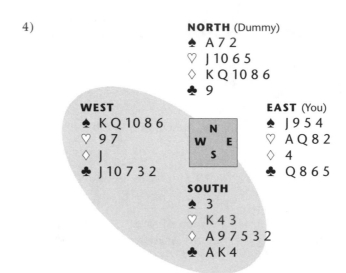

**NORTH** (Dummy)
♠ A 7 2
♡ J 10 6 5
◇ K Q 10 8 6
♣ 9

**WEST**
♠ K Q 10 8 6
♡ 9 7
◇ J
♣ J 10 7 3 2

**EAST** (You)
♠ J 9 5 4
♡ A Q 8 2
◇ 4
♣ Q 8 6 5

**SOUTH**
♠ 3
♡ K 4 3
◇ A 9 7 5 3 2
♣ A K 4

The count is known. Declarer has a singleton spade, six diamonds, and judging from partner's count signal, three clubs. Declarer has three hearts and your job is to get two heart tricks if declarer has the king. The bottom line is that you must play partner for ♡9x and cover the jack with the queen. When declarer takes the ♡K, partner must unblock the ♡9. If she does, you have two heart tricks coming with your ♡A8 sitting over dummy's guarded ♡10. If partner fails to unblock, declarer can duck the ♡9 leaving partner on lead. As partner has no more hearts, partner must lead a black card giving declarer a ruff and a sluff. Goodbye second heart trick.

| BOTH VUL. | | DEALER NORTH | |
|---|---|---|---|
| **West** | **North** | **East** | **South** |
| | pass | pass | 1♡ |
| pass | 3♡ | pass | 4♡ |
| all pass | | | |

**Trick 1:** ◇Q ◇K ◇2 ◇7
**Trick 2:** ♡Q ♡3 ♡5 ♡A
**Trick 3:** ◇10 ◇5 ◇8 ◇A
**Trick 4:** ♡6 ♡9 ♡10 ♡4
**Trick 5:** ◇6 ◇9 ♡7 ◇3
**Trick 6:** ♣A ♣3 ♣4 ♣6
**Trick 7:** ♣J ♣2 ♣Q ♣5
**Trick 8:** ♣K ♣7 ♠5 ♣8
**Trick 9:** ♠2 ?

5)

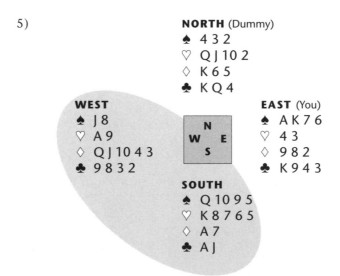

**NORTH** (Dummy)
♠ 4 3 2
♡ Q J 10 2
◇ K 6 5
♣ K Q 4

**WEST**
♠ J 8
♡ A 9
◇ Q J 10 4 3
♣ 9 8 3 2

**EAST** (You)
♠ A K 7 6
♡ 4 3
◇ 9 8 2
♣ K 9 4 3

**SOUTH**
♠ Q 10 9 5
♡ K 8 7 6 5
◇ A 7
♣ A J

Declarer's hand counts out to 4-5-2-2 distribution meaning declarer still has *three* spades left.  Play a low spade and hope partner has a doubleton honor, it's your only chance.  Notice that if partner has Qx and you mistakenly play your king, you can no longer take three spade tricks even if you lead a low spade next.  Partner is out of spades and has to concede a ruff and a sluff.

6)

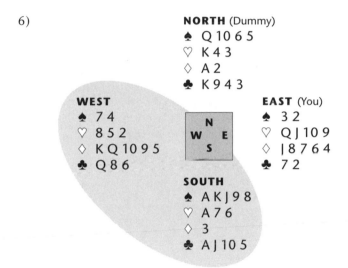

**NORTH** (Dummy)
♠ Q 10 6 5
♡ K 4 3
◇ A 2
♣ K 9 4 3

**WEST**
♠ 7 4
♡ 8 5 2
◇ K Q 10 9 5
♣ Q 8 6

**EAST** (You)
♠ 3 2
♡ Q J 10 9
◇ J 8 7 6 4
♣ 7 2

**SOUTH**
♠ A K J 9 8
♡ A 7 6
◇ 3
♣ A J 10 5

| BOTH VUL. | | DEALER NORTH | |
| **West** | **North** | **East** | **South** |
| --- | --- | --- | --- |
| | 1♣ | pass | 1♠ |
| pass | 2♠ | pass | 6♠(!) |
| all pass | | | |

**Trick 1:** ◇K  ◇A  ◇8  ◇3
**Trick 2:** ♠5  ♠2  ♠A  ♠4
**Trick 3:** ♠8  ♠7  ♠Q  ♠3
**Trick 4:** ◇2  ◇6  ♠9  ◇5
**Trick 5:** ♡A  ♡2  ♡3  ♡9
**Trick 6:** ♡6  ♡5  ♡K  ♡10
**Trick 7:** ♡4  ♡J  ♡7  ♡8
**Trick 8:** ?

South is known to hold five spades, three hearts, one diamond, and therefore, four clubs.  It would be a mistake to shift to a club because North and South each still have four clubs.  A ruff and a sluff won't help declarer.  You are hoping partner has the ♣Q and that declarer eventually misguesses after you lead a diamond (or a heart) giving South that useless ruff and sluff.  If you return a club, you make a friend of South for life; if you return a red card, partner will cherish your counting skills.

## Key ideas from Chapter 3

- The answer to most defensive problems, particularly count problems, lies in the bidding: yours, theirs, and what isn't bid!
- At times you must ask your opponents about their methods to help you with the count. (Will they raise a major suit response with three trumps or do they require four? Which suit do they open with 4-4 in the minors? Etcetera.)
- The opening lead frequently plays a vital role in counting.
- Giving each other count in 'mystery suits' (not suits declarer has bid or where the count is known), completes or helps complete the count picture in many a hand.
- If you make a real commitment to try to count each hand, you may find yourself playing worse for the first few months — too much to do, not enough time to do it. Not to worry, *everyone* goes through that phase. However, once you climb the hurdle, you will be playing at a completely different level. Trust me.

# Counting Tricks

*They don't ask how, just how many*

OLD GOLF SAYING

4

It is inescapable.

Bridge is a game of counting. Once you make a 'counting commitment' you are on the way to becoming a much better player. In the previous chapter you zeroed in on counting declarer's distribution. In this chapter you will zero in on counting tricks — yours and declarer's. After all is said and done, bridge is a game of tricks. You bid for tricks, you take as many tricks as you can in the play, and on defense you try to prevent the opponents from taking enough tricks to make their contract.

# Clues from the bidding

Obviously it is easier to count tricks after you see the dummy. For example, when defending a notrump contract, if dummy arrives with ♣AKQJx and you have ♣xxx, count five club tricks for declarer. However, if you are looking at ♣10xxxx, count only four.

Sometimes the bidding will tip you off that there is going to be a powerful suit in one or both of the opponent's hands. This information influences your choice of opening leads. Say you are West and you hold:

♠ Q10853 ♡ AK5 ◇ 963 ♣ 32.

| West | North | East | South |
|------|-------|------|-------|
| (You) | | | |
| | | | 1NT |
| pass | 2NT | pass | 3NT |
| all pass | | | |

You have no reason to believe that either player has a long, strong, suit so you make your normal lead of the ♠5 hoping eventually to set up your spades. But say this is the bidding:

| West | North | East | South |
|------|-------|------|-------|
| (You) | | | |
| | | | 1♣ |
| pass | 1◇ | pass | 3♣ |
| pass | 3◇ | pass | 3NT |
| all pass | | | |

This is a different ball game. South surely has a long, powerful club suit, and North might have the same in diamonds. You are not going to have time to set up your spades. You must make an attacking lead looking for quick tricks. Lead the ♡K hoping to hit partner with something like ♡Qxxxx or ♡Jxxxx (and declarer ♡Qx).

This difference in strategy — (1) establishing a long suit perhaps giving up the lead once or twice to do it, or simply sitting back and waiting for your tricks by leading a suit in which the opponents have the top tricks (a passive defense), or (2) taking your tricks as quickly as possible before giving up the lead (active defense) — is the key to most defensive thinking. And this decision is based largely upon your assessment of how many tricks declarer has available. This chapter will give you the tools to help you solve this problem.

# Clues from the dummy

**NORTH** (Dummy)
♠ 6 4
♡ A K 3
◇ 7 4
♣ K Q J 10 7 4

**WEST** (You)
♠ Q J 10 9 8
♡ 8 6 4
◇ A J 9 2
♣ A

| BOTH VUL. | | DEALER WEST | |
|-----------|-------|-------------|----------|
| **West** | **North** | **East** | **South** |
| 1♠ | 2♣ | pass | 2NT |
| pass | 3NT | all pass | |

You lead the ♠Q, partner plays the ♠2, and declarer wins the ♠K. Already you know that declarer has two spade tricks from partner's discouraging signal at trick one. At trick two declarer leads the ♣9, you win the ace, and partner plays the ♣5. Suddenly declarer has a bushel basket of tricks staring you in the face. Count. You know of two spade tricks and now you see five more club tricks plus the ♡AK for a grand total of nine. This is not even counting a likely ♡Q in declarer's hand. No matter; you have arrived at a point that comes up often during the defense of many a contract:

*When declarer has enough tricks in three suits to make the contract, switch to the fourth suit. Just do it!*

Many players in this spot automatically continue with a spade to drive out declarer's ace while retaining the ◇A as an entry to the established spades. That may be the right play on some hands with some other dummy, but it not the right play on this hand with this dummy. *Declarer has too many tricks staring you in the face for you to give up the lead and go quietly.* What you have to do is shift to a low diamond. This is the diamond layout you are hoping for:

**NORTH** (Dummy)
◇ 7 4

**WEST** (You)
◇ A J 9 2

**EAST** (Partner)
◇ K 10 3

**SOUTH**
◇ Q 8 6 5

If your projection is right (you have to project minimum honor card strength in partner's hand when desperation sets in), and partner makes the standard third-hand play of the ◇K followed by the ◇10, your side collects four diamond tricks. If partner doesn't have the ◇K the contract could never be beaten, but at least you tried.

As an aside, the above hand was one I used many years ago in an ill-fated television show that never saw the light of day. The format was to have one celebrity, usually a well-known movie star who supposedly played bridge, plus three other local players on the set. After I interviewed the movie star, and talked for a moment or two to each of the other players, they would all adjourn to the bridge table and play one lesson-type hand that I had set up — a hand they had never seen before.

Many famous entertainers have been bridge players. The late comedian George Burns was an active player even at age 100! Lucy Lawless (*Xena, Warrior Princess*) is also reputed to be a bridge fan.

Complications soon arose. It was apparent that many of these movie stars hadn't played bridge for eons. One of them had never played at all; she had only watched her mother play! One guest was Steven Allen's wife, Jane Meadows. She insisted on being photographed from one angle only. At first I was more nervous than anyone because I was not confident about my interviewing skills. When I mentioned this to Jane, she told me not to worry. She said, 'Just ask me any question and you won't have to say another word.' She was right. She saved me from myself.

Back to the hand. For this hand the celebrity was the late Jim Backus, who was the movie voice of 'Mr. Magoo' for many years. He was the nicest guy, but he hadn't played bridge for decades and was afraid he would make a fool of himself. It had been agreed that we would never make the celebrity be the dummy, so I put Jim in the East seat. He was so nervous that I told him privately 'If your partner ever leads a diamond, play the king; and then play the ten.' I know I wasn't supposed to do that, but if you had seen him, you would have done the same. He even wrote himself a little note about how to play those diamonds.

Well, the cameras started rolling (this was a one-shot deal — no second takes) with me off-camera as the commentator. The bidding went as I had hoped. The lead was the ♠Q; declarer won this and led a club to West's ace. Now West started to think as Jim glanced at the little note he had written. Finally, to my horror, West laid down the ◇A! Jim, of course, played the ◇K, and then led the ◇10 out of turn. Talk about ill-fated TV shows.

# Clues from the lead and the play to the first trick

On the last hand you were able to count declarer's spade tricks from partner's discouraging signal. Here is another example — again you are leading an honor card:

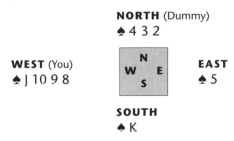

**NORTH** (Dummy)
♠ 4 3 2

**WEST** (You)
♠ J 10 9 8

**EAST**
♠ 5

**SOUTH**
♠ K

You are leading against a notrump contract and start with the ♠J. This is greeted by the ♠5 from partner and the ♠K from declarer. What is going on?

When you lead an honor against notrump, partner is expected to: signal encouragement with honor third or honor fourth in your suit (the 7 from Q7x or Q7xx), overtake with a doubleton honor (Qx, Kx, or Ax) or play low without an honor. Here, partner's ♠5 can be read as her lowest spade and you should play partner to be 'honorless'. Declarer should have the ♠AKQ. Furthermore, if you use the lead convention 'jack denies', partner will never have a problem counting declarer's tricks anytime you lead a jack.

This book recommends that you adopt the convention that the lead of a jack denies holding a higher honor in the suit, while the lead of a 10 or a 9 promises 0 or 2 higher honors.

This position is a little trickier:

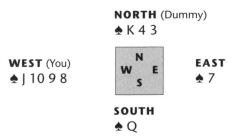

**NORTH** (Dummy)
♠ K 4 3

**WEST** (You)
♠ J 10 9 8

**EAST**
♠ 7

**SOUTH**
♠ Q

Defending 3NT, you lead the ♠J, dummy plays low, partner the ♠7, and declarer the ♠Q. Play partner for the ♠A7x(x), not a doubleton.

At notrump encouraging signals are generally reserved for honor cards, not shortness; assume declarer has one spade trick. If partner plays a discouraging spade, play declarer for three spade tricks.

When an honor card is led, both players have a pretty good idea of how many tricks declarer can take in that suit. However, when a spot card is led, it is usually the opening leader who is in a better position to count declarer's tricks.

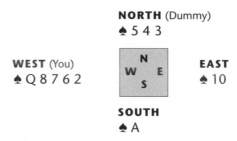

**NORTH** (Dummy)
♠ 5 4 3

**WEST** (You)
♠ Q 8 7 6 2

**EAST**
♠ 10

**SOUTH**
♠ A

Defending a notrump contract, you lead the ♠6 to the ♠10 and ♠A. How many spade tricks does declarer have coming? Two. Partner must have the ♠J, or else declarer would have taken the trick with that card. Partner cannot have the ♠K. He would have played it with KJ10(x) in case you had led from the ace. Also, the play of the ♠10 denies the ♠9. Declarer has the ♠AK9, partner ♠J10 doubleton.

Say declarer wins the opening lead with the ♠J, not the ace. Now what is going on? Declarer must have the ♠AKJ9, and partner the singleton ♠10. At notrump you have run into a hornet's nest; in a suit contract, you can start giving partner spade ruffs.

Partner's normal play of third hand high, but the lower of equals, is very helpful in counting declarer's tricks. Also, if partner wins the trick in the suit you have led and returns the suit, the card partner returns is usually all you need to get a complete 'read' on the suit.

**NORTH** (Dummy)
♠ 5 4

**WEST** (You)
♠ A 10 8 3 2

**EAST**
♠ K 9 7

**SOUTH**
♠ Q J 6

During the bidding South has denied holding four spades and winds up in notrump. You lead the ♠3 to the king and six. When partner returns the ♠9 (higher of two remaining cards), you know declarer has the ♠QJ blank left. It is usually right to allow declarer to win the second round of the suit, keeping a spade in partner's hand to return to you in case partner has an outside entry.

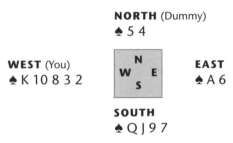

**NORTH** (Dummy)
♠ 5 4

**WEST** (You)          **EAST**
♠ K 10 8 3 2          ♠ A 6

**SOUTH**
♠ Q J 9 7

Say the bidding has not been revealing and you lead the ♠3 against notrump. Partner wins the ace and returns her lowest card, the ♠6, showing an original holding of *two or four* cards. Most of the time the bidding resolves these ambiguities; some of the time it doesn't!

In the above diagram, partner started with two spades and it will cost you a trick to play the king on declarer's queen and return the suit. But suppose the spades were distributed like this:

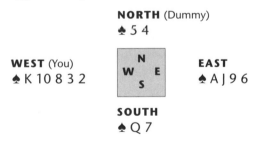

**NORTH** (Dummy)
♠ 5 4

**WEST** (You)          **EAST**
♠ K 10 8 3 2          ♠ A J 9 6

**SOUTH**
♠ Q 7

Again partner wins the ace and returns the six. Again declarer plays the queen. This time your side has five spade tricks available and you had better win the king and play back a low spade or you'll never hear the end of it. Not to worry, nine times out of ten the bidding and/or the strength of the dummy tells you how many spades declarer (or partner) has. Sometimes you have to play your partner for length to have any chance of defeating the contract.

When declarer wins your long-suit opening lead in dummy with the *queen* or a lower card, partner is supposed to give count, not attitude. You already know partner's attitude; he couldn't beat dummy's card.

**NORTH** (Dummy)
♠ Q J 6

**WEST** (You)
♠ K 10 8 2

**EAST**
♠ 9

**SOUTH**
♠ 4

Either against a suit or notrump you start with the ♠2, dummy plays the ♠J and partner contributes the ♠9. What's going on? Partner figures to have ♠9x (with ♠9753, partner plays the ♠7, second highest from four), and declarer, ♠Axxx. Assuming declarer has the wherewithal to lead up to dummy's ♠Q, credit declarer with three spade tricks. If, instead of the ♠9, partner plays the ♠3, also a count card, showing a likely ♠xxx, credit declarer with ♠Axx and two spade tricks.

**NORTH** (Dummy)
♠ A K 6

**WEST** (You)
♠ J 9 3 2

**EAST**
♠ 4

**SOUTH**
♠ 5

You lead a low spade against a suit or notrump; dummy plays the king, partner the ♠4, and declarer the ♠5. What's up?

When dummy has the king, the ace, or the AK, and an honor is played from dummy, third hand signals attitude, not count. The play of the ♠4 denies the ♠Q (unless partner has ♠Q4 doubleton). Count declarer for three spade tricks. P. S. You can also infer that declarer does not have ♠Q10xx; with that holding a low card is normally played from dummy.

Sometimes partner's play at trick one coupled with a revealing discard can be all you need to get a 'trick-taking' count.

**NORTH** (Dummy)
♠ K Q 10
♡ 8 7 6
♢ 9 2
♣ K J 10 9 4

**WEST** (You)
♠ 9
♡ K J 5 4
♢ Q 10 8 4 3
♣ A 6 2

```
      N
   W     E
      S
```

| NEITHER VUL. | | DEALER SOUTH | |
|---|---|---|---|
| **West** | **North** | **East** | **South** |
| | | | 1NT |
| pass | 3NT | all pass | |

You elect to lead the ♢4 in preference to the ♡4 and partner's ♢J loses to the king. At trick two a low club is led to the jack, partner following. When declarer continues with the ♣10 from dummy, partner discards the ♠2. What now? Think like this: 'I know declarer has two diamond tricks from the play to trick one. Furthermore, because the ♢9 is in dummy I can establish my diamonds using the king of hearts as my entry to get in and cash my diamonds'. That's one way to look at this problem, but it's the wrong way. It only takes into account your *eventual* tricks; it does not take into account declarer's *immediate* tricks, tricks that can be taken the next time declarer has the lead.

Declarer has two diamond tricks, and now four club tricks for a total of six. The discard of the ♠2 tells you that declarer has the ♠A. This, in turn, means you can add at least three tricks to your previous total of declarer's 'immediate tricks' giving declarer nine or ten tricks 'on the ready' (they can be taken the next time declarer has the lead).

Players who are not counting declarer's tricks will continue with a high diamond upon winning the ♣A. Happily you are no longer a card-carrying member of that union. Your play is to shift to a low heart upon winning the ♣A. You must find partner with the ♡Axx(x) to defeat this contract. These are the unseen hands:

Declarer's hand:     ♠ A3  ♡ Q109  ♢ AK76  ♣ Q753
Partner's hand:     ♠ J876542  ♡ A32  ♢ J5  ♣ 8

If partner wins the ♡A and returns a heart, your side takes four heart tricks and defeats the contract. But what if partner wins the ♡A and returns a *diamond*? Horrors! Now declarer has nine tricks.

'Relatively' in this sense means that if you switch to, say, a six in your second suit, and the 2,3,4 and 5 are all visible, the six is a 'relatively' low card. In fact, it is a *very* low card! Conversely if you switch to a six and none of the lower cards are visible, that six should be considered a 'relatively' high card.

How does partner know to return a diamond, your first suit, or a heart, your second suit? It goes by the *relative* size of the card you lead in the second suit. If you lead a *relatively* low card in your second suit, you are asking partner to return your second suit; if you lead a *relatively* high card in your second suit, you are asking partner to return the first suit. Got it?

This 'rule of switching' is consistent with the lead of a low card showing strength and the lead of a high card denying strength. You just have to educate your partner on how to deal with your magnificent switches. If you had wanted partner to return a diamond because you couldn't safely lead one yourself, you would have switched to a high heart. Say your hearts were something like ♡J8x(x) or ♡108x(x). With those holdings switch to the ♡8.

Most important is that you realize why you are shifting to a second suit when you can so easily set up your first suit. *You don't have time to set up your first suit*! Now try this one:

| EAST-WEST VUL. | | DEALER SOUTH | |
|---|---|---|---|
| **West** | **North** | **East** | **South** |
| | | | 1NT |
| pass | 2♣ | pass | 2♢ |
| pass | 3NT | all pass | |

**NORTH** (Dummy)
♠ K 4 3 2
♡ K Q J
♢ 6 5
♣ J 10 6 3

**WEST** (You)
♠ Q J 10 9 7
♡ 9 2
♢ A J 9 3
♣ K 5

Blessed with a beautiful spade sequence you lead the ♠Q, captured by dummy's ♠K. The ♣J is led from dummy, partner plays the ♣2, count, and you win the ♣K. How many tricks does declarer have ready to roll?

You know declarer has two spade tricks, and at most three heart tricks (South has denied a four-card major, remember?) for a total of five. What about clubs? Partner's ♣2 shows an odd number of clubs, clearly three, which means declarer started with four clubs and has three club tricks established for a grand total of eight. There is no need to panic and shift to a diamond. Bide your time;

drive out declarer's ♠A, and sit back and wait for declarer who eventually will have to lead a diamond. When she does, you will be ready.

For the curious:

Declarer's hand:      ♠ A85  ♡ A86  ◊ K107  ♣ AQ87
Partner's hand:       ♠ 6  ♡ 107543  ◊ Q842  ♣ 942

Bridge is a strange game. If partner had played the ♣9 at trick two, showing a doubleton, declarer's immediate trick count after you won the ♣K would have been nine, not eight (four clubs, two spades and three hearts). Now the right play is to shift to a low diamond hoping partner has ◊Kx or ◊Kxx to defeat the contract.

The Rule of Eleven helps third hand count declarer's tricks in the suit that has been led:

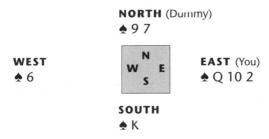

**NORTH** (Dummy)
♠ 9 7

**WEST**
♠ 6

**EAST** (You)
♠ Q 10 2

**SOUTH**
♠ K

Assume South opens 1NT, denies a four-card major, and winds up in 3NT. Partner leads the ♠6 and your ♠Q loses to the ♠K. What can you deduce using the Rule ?

The Rule of Eleven (subtracting the card partner has led from 11) tells you that there are five spades higher than the ♠6 in the three remaining hands: dummy's, yours, and declarer's. You can see four higher spades (two in your hand, two in the dummy) so declarer has started life with only one spade higher than the ♠6, the ♠K.

The implications are clear. Partner has started with ♠AJ8xx(x) and the spades are ready to rumble. Do not let declarer steal a trick from you in another suit by playing second hand low with a side-suit winner when your side has the setting tricks ready to be taken.

Speaking of 'stealing', defenders live by the rule

***Thou shalt not steal the contract-fulfilling trick from under me.***

BOTH VUL.     DEALER NORTH

| West | North | East | South |
|------|-------|------|-------|
|      | 1◇    | pass | 2NT[1] |
| pass | 3NT   | all pass | |

1) 13-15 HCP

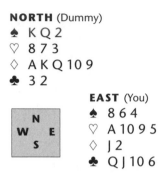

**NORTH** (Dummy)
♠ K Q 2
♡ 8 7 3
◇ A K Q 10 9
♣ 3 2

**EAST** (You)
♠ 8 6 4
♡ A 10 9 5
◇ J 2
♣ Q J 10 6

Partner leads the ♠J, taken by dummy's queen. At trick two a low heart is led. This is how you have to train yourself to think: 'The opening lead tells me that declarer has three spade tricks; the dummy tells me that declarer has five diamond tricks for a total of eight tricks. In order to defeat this contract, my partner must have the ♣A'. Using this reasoning, rising with the ♡A and shifting to the ♣Q is a must play.

 Declarer's hand:  ♠ A53 ♡ KQJ ◇ 7654 ♣ K54
 Partner's hand:  ♠ J1097 ♡ 642 ◇ 83 ♣ A987

Declarer was trying to stealing a ninth trick from you early in the play, but you were counting tricks!

EAST-WEST VUL.     DEALER EAST

| West | North | East | South |
|------|-------|------|-------|
|      |       | pass | 1◇ |
| pass | 1♡    | pass | 1NT |
| pass | 3NT   | all pass | |

**NORTH** (Dummy)
♠ 6 5 3
♡ A K Q 9 2
◇ Q J 10
♣ 7 6

**WEST** (You)
♠ A Q 4
♡ J 10
◇ A 6 4
♣ J 9 4 3 2

You lead the ♣3, partner plays the ♣10, and declarer the ♣K. At trick two a low diamond is led. Any thoughts?

Declarer is marked with the ♣AKQ from partner's play at trick one. In addition, you can see five winning heart tricks in the dummy for a total of eight. If declarer has the ◇K, which is quite likely, you cannot afford to play low. You would be giving declarer her ninth trick! A better play is to go up with the ◇A and switch to the ace-queen of spades! If declarer has the ◇K, not only does partner need the ♠K to defeat the contract, but he is also marked with that card. With the ♣AKQ and two more kings, South would have opened 1NT. What if partner has the ◇K and declarer the ♠K? Then you could be looking very silly, couldn't you?

| Declarer's hand: | ♠ J108  ♡ 543  ◇ K832  ♣ AKQ |
| Partner's hand: | ♠ K972  ♡ 876  ◇ 975  ♣ 1085 |

Even if partner has the ◇K, and declarer the ♠K, you still can't beat the hand if declarer has ♠K10x or ♠KJx even if partner is clairvoyant enough to return a spade instead of a club. Winning the ◇A and shifting to a high spade is your percentage action.

## When a 'conventional' lead is made

If the opening lead is a conventional card such as a jack (jack denies) or a 9 or 10 (zero or two higher), third hand can often direct the course of the defense more accurately. Of course, this assumes you are using these lead conventions.

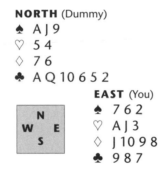

**NORTH** (Dummy)
♠ A J 9
♡ 5 4
◇ 7 6
♣ A Q 10 6 5 2

**EAST** (You)
♠ 7 6 2
♡ A J 3
◇ J 10 9 8
♣ 9 8 7

| EAST-WEST VUL. | | DEALER NORTH | |
|---|---|---|---|
| **West** | **North** | **East** | **South** |
| | 1♣ | pass | 2NT[1] |
| pass | 3NT | all pass | |

1) 13-15 HCP

(1) How do you defend if partner leads the ♡10 (0 or 2 higher)?
(2) How do you defend if partner leads the ♡9 (0 or 2 higher)?

If partner leads a conventional ♡10 and you are looking at the ♡J, partner must be leading top of a sequence, giving declarer the ♡KQ. That in itself isn't so terrible, but that plus the dummy you are looking at, is. You don't have time to develop partner's hearts with eight or nine black-suit tricks staring you in the face. Your play is to rise with the ♡A and shift to the ◇J hoping partner has ◇AQxx.

However, if partner leads a conventional ♡9, partner figures to be leading from the ♡K109xx or ♡Q109xx. It would be nice to know which, but your best shot is to win the ♡A and return the ♡J hoping (praying) partner has led from the ♡K109xx. Playing partner for one card, the ♡K, is better than playing partner for two cards, the ◇AQ.

| BOTH VUL. | | DEALER NORTH | |
|---|---|---|---|
| **West** | **North** | **East** | **South** |
| | 1◇ | pass | 1♡ |
| pass | 2◇ | pass | 3NT |
| all pass | | | |

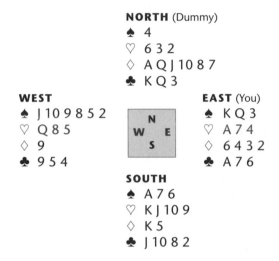

**NORTH** (Dummy)
♠ 4
♡ 6 3 2
◇ A Q J 10 8 7
♣ K Q 3

**WEST**
♠ J 10 9 8 5 2
♡ Q 8 5
◇ 9
♣ 9 5 4

**EAST** (You)
♠ K Q 3
♡ A 7 4
◇ 6 4 3 2
♣ A 7 6

**SOUTH**
♠ A 7 6
♡ K J 10 9
◇ K 5
♣ J 10 8 2

Partner leads the ♠J (jack denies) and you begin an unblock by playing the ♠Q which holds. You continue with the ♠K which also holds. Should you play a third spade to drive out the ace?

Count tricks. Declarer has the ♠A, six diamond tricks (whoever has the ◇K), and surely several club tricks once your ace is driven out. And how are you going to get partner in to score those established spades if you do play a third spade?

If partner has the ♡K, you can underlead your ♡A after you get in with the ♣A and all will be rosy. But what if declarer has the ♡K? When you lead a low heart he will surely play it to prevent partner from getting in. Actually, all you need in partner's hand to defeat this contract is the ♡Q, not the ♡K.

Simply switch to a low heart at trick three *before* your ♣A has been driven out. Even if declarer plays the ♡K, you have five tricks ready to be taken once you get in with the ♣A: two spades, the ♣A, and two hearts. Counting your tricks and their tricks was once again the answer.

## When partner leads an obvious singleton

**NORTH** (Dummy)
♠ K 10 9 5
♡ Q 10
♢ K Q 10 7 6
♣ A K

**WEST**
♠ 6 3
♡ K J 4 3 2
♢ 4
♣ Q 8 7 3 2

**EAST** (You)
♠ A 8 4
♡ 9 6 5
♢ A 9 3 2
♣ 10 9 5

**SOUTH**
♠ Q J 7 2
♡ A 8 7
♢ J 8 5
♣ J 6 4

| BOTH VUL. | | DEALER WEST | |
| **West** | **North** | **East** | **South** |
| pass | 1♢ | pass | 1♠ |
| pass | 3♠ | pass | 4♠ |
| all pass | | | |

Partner leads the ♢4, an obvious singleton. Of course the first impulse is to win the ace and give partner a diamond ruff. However, first impulses are not always right. A better impulse is to count *your* tricks. You need four tricks to defeat this contract and you can see three: the ♢A, the ♠A and a diamond ruff. Furthermore, you know you can give partner that diamond ruff later when a trump is played because partner figures to have two spades (partner is unlikely to have two singletons and be silent throughout the entire auction). A far better play at trick two is a heart, trying to build up your fourth defensive trick there before declarer's hearts go away on the established diamonds.

## Opening leader's play with 'remaining equals'

Wondering what that means? Consider this diagram:

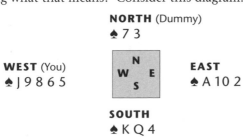

**NORTH** (Dummy)
♠ 7 3

**WEST** (You)
♠ J 9 8 6 5

**EAST**
♠ A 10 2

**SOUTH**
♠ K Q 4

You lead the ♠6, partner wins the ♠A and returns the ♠10 to declarer's king. At this point you remain with the ♠J983. The ♠J98 are *all* equals and you can give partner that information by playing the jack, your highest equal, under the king.

Now partner can place declarer with the ♠Q.

For those who dig rules, this is the rule:

***When either declarer or partner is winning the second round of the suit you have led, and you remain with equals, following suit with your highest equal (here the jack) denies a higher card.***

Playing the highest equal on the second lead of a suit can save partner many a headache:

| NEITHER VUL. | | DEALER SOUTH | |
|---|---|---|---|
| **West** | **North** | **East** | **South** |
| | | | 3◇ |
| pass | 5◇ | all pass | |

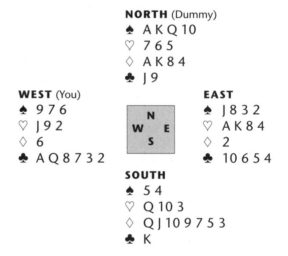

**NORTH** (Dummy)
♠ A K Q 10
♡ 7 6 5
◇ A K 8 4
♣ J 9

**WEST** (You)
♠ 9 7 6
♡ J 9 2
◇ 6
♣ A Q 8 7 3 2

**EAST**
♠ J 8 3 2
♡ A K 8 4
◇ 2
♣ 10 6 5 4

**SOUTH**
♠ 5 4
♡ Q 10 3
◇ Q J 10 9 7 5 3
♣ K

You elect to lead the ♡2, thrilling partner no end. Partner plays the ♡K and ♡A. On the second heart lead, declarer plays the ♡10, telling you that declarer still has the ♡Q. Unfortunately partner is not privy to that information unless you play the ♡J under the ♡A, denying the ♡Q. Once partner knows you don't have the ♡Q, partner will shift to a club defeating the contract one trick.

Looks easy, but if you don't play the ♡J, a good partner will play you for the ♡Q92 and continue with a third heart, in which case you can kiss your ♣A *adios*.

## Discarding honors from equals

Those seemingly spectacular plays of playing honor cards to deny higher honor cards come in handy when discarding. This is a topic that was covered in the chapter on discarding in *Eddie Kantar teaches Modern Bridge Defense*, but it is apropos here as well. Briefly, the discard of an ace, king, queen or jack shows the lower equals, but denies a higher honor.

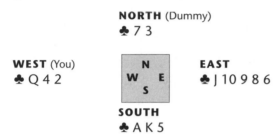

**NORTH** (Dummy)
♣ 7 3

**WEST** (You)        **EAST**
♣ Q 4 2        ♣ J 10 9 8 6

**SOUTH**
♣ A K 5

At notrump you lead another suit, and you see two little clubs in the dummy. From your point of view it is a bit difficult to work out the number of tricks declarer has available in clubs. However, if early in the play partner discards the ♣J, you can place declarer with the ♣AK, or two tricks in the suit.

# Counting tricks in dummy's strong suit

The stronger the suit in dummy, the easier (and more discouraging) it is to determine how many tricks declarer has available — or will have available. At times one defender has a clearer count than the other.

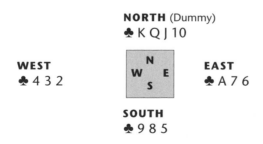

**NORTH** (Dummy)
♣ K Q J 10

**WEST**        **EAST**
♣ 4 3 2        ♣ A 7 6

**SOUTH**
♣ 9 8 5

This is notrump and there are side entries to the dummy. From West's point of view, declarer has either three or four club tricks depending upon who has the ace. East, on the other hand, *knows* that declarer soon will have three club tricks available.

For the sake of discussion, exchange the East and South clubs. Now neither defender can see the ♣A. However, if declarer does not try to drive out the ♣A, a play that is almost automatic with a suit of this strength in the dummy, the inference is that declarer has the ♣A and both defenders should count declarer for four club tricks.

At times looks can be deceiving:

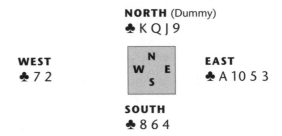

**NORTH** (Dummy)
♣ K Q J 9

**WEST**
♣ 7 2

**EAST**
♣ A 10 5 3

**SOUTH**
♣ 8 6 4

This time West can't be sure how many club tricks declarer has, but East knows that declarer has only two club tricks coming. If East's ♣10 is a smaller club, East counts three club tricks as the ten is likely to fall under the KQJ unless declarer started with a small singleton.

Strong suits in the dummy missing the king lend themselves to easy trick counting:

**NORTH** (Dummy)
♣ A Q J 10

When you see a suit like this and declarer doesn't attack this suit, play declarer for the king. If declarer takes the finesse and it loses, play declarer for three tricks. If you (West) have the king, and the finesse can be repeated as many times as necessary, count four tricks.

When you do have honor cards in dummy's long suit, the relationship of your honors to dummy's honors is critical. First, the good news: when your honors are sitting 'over' dummy's honors (you play after dummy).

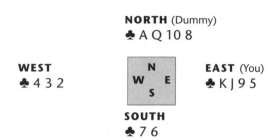

**NORTH** (Dummy)
♣ A Q 10 8

**WEST**
♣ 4 3 2

**EAST** (You)
♣ K J 9 5

**SOUTH**
♣ 7 6

West cannot tell how many club tricks declarer has available, but *you* know that declarer can only take one measly club trick. Now let's turn the East-West clubs around; the bad news:

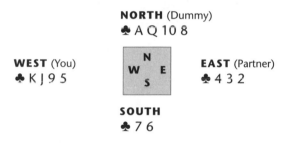

**NORTH** (Dummy)
♣ A Q 10 8

**WEST** (You)
♣ K J 9 5

**EAST** (Partner)
♣ 4 3 2

**SOUTH**
♣ 7 6

You can see that all finesses in clubs are working and that declarer can probably take three club tricks by making the normal play of low to the ten first. Partner sees that whatever finesse(s) necessary in clubs are working, and will count declarer for four club tricks.

The relationship of the defender's honor cards to dummy's honor cards can tell the defenders just how good their chances are.

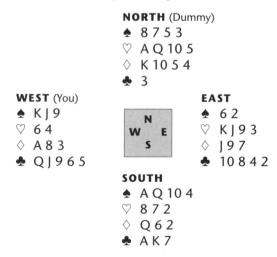

**NORTH** (Dummy)
♠ 8 7 5 3
♡ A Q 10 5
♢ K 10 5 4
♣ 3

**WEST** (You)
♠ K J 9
♡ 6 4
♢ A 8 3
♣ Q J 9 6 5

**EAST**
♠ 6 2
♡ K J 9 3
♢ J 9 7
♣ 10 8 4 2

**SOUTH**
♠ A Q 10 4
♡ 8 7 2
♢ Q 6 2
♣ A K 7

Say that South opens 1NT and after a Stayman sequence winds up in 4♠. South doesn't know it, but this hand is stacked against her. Both spade finesses lose, both heart finesses lose and the ◊J is sitting over the ◊10. South is doomed to go down. However, if you reverse the East-West hands, South can make a slam! Both spade finesses work, both heart finesses work, and the finesse of the ◊10 works.

The point is that it isn't how many honor cards you hold, but rather where they are in relation to the opponents' honor cards. Given the original diagram, both East and West know that the hand is not lying well for the declarer. Reverse the East-West hands and both defenders know they are dead ducks.

Frequently the trick count is dependent upon which of the two unseen hands holds the one missing honor.

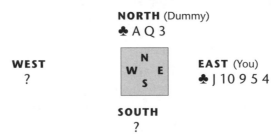

From your point of view if declarer has the ♣K she has three club tricks; if partner has it, declarer has two club tricks. Sometimes the bidding tells you who has it, sometimes it doesn't.

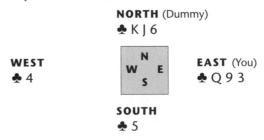

At notrump declarer leads the ♣5 to dummy's ♣J as partner plays the ♣4. There are several possibilities. If partner has ♣xxx, then declarer has ♣Axxx and three club tricks available after you take your queen. If partner has ♣42 doubleton, then declarer has ♣A10xxx and has four club tricks coming. Finally, if partner has ♣Axx, declarer has ♣10xxx and declarer has two club tricks coming *eventually.* Fortunately, the bidding usually helps you sort this out, particularly in the major suits.

Another awkward trick-counting scenario occurs when both you and dummy have small cards in the same side suit.

**NORTH** (Dummy)
♣ 9 4 3 2

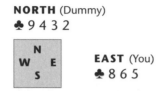

**EAST** (You)
♣ 8 6 5

At a suit contract partner leads another suit. Immediately you can deduce that partner doesn't have an honor sequence in clubs. It's still not clear what's going on. You do know that if declarer needs a club finesse or two it isn't going to work. On the other hand, if declarer shies away from clubs you can also deduce that declarer doesn't have something like ♣KQJ or ♣AQJ. With a powerful holding like that, the suit is usually attacked early. A likely scenario is declarer holding ♣Kx(x) or ♣AQ(x) hoping your partner will eventually be forced to lead the suit.

# Counting tricks in declarer's suits (suits you can't see)

It is ever so much easier to count tricks in long suits you can see as opposed to long suits you can't see. Clever observation, Kantar. When declarer attacks one of her own side suits (as opposed to the trump suit), and you are last to play to the trick, you do have this going for you: (1) partner's count signal (2) the fall of the cards (3) partner's playing an honor from known length showing the *top* of an honor sequence.

**NORTH** (Dummy)
♣ 3 2

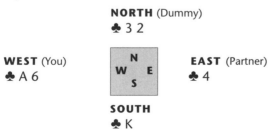

**WEST** (You)
♣ A 6

**EAST** (Partner)
♣ 4

**SOUTH**
♣ K

**NORTH** (Dummy)
♣ 3 2

**WEST** (You)          **EAST**
♣ A 6                      ♣ 4

**SOUTH**
♣ K

***Case 1.*** South bids and rebids clubs, winds up playing in notrump, and early in the hand leads a club from dummy. Partner contributes the ♣4, and declarer, the ♣K. Now you have to try to work out what is going on.

If partner is giving count, partner has three clubs and declarer, six. Of course you can't see those six clubs. Furthermore, partner may have four clubs and might not have been able to spare a higher club to show you an even number. If so, declarer has five clubs. Nevertheless it is almost a certainty that declarer's clubs are headed by the KQ. If so, it is usually right to duck the first club (declarer can't see that your ace is doubleton), particularly with a doubleton club in the dummy. If declarer's clubs are headed by the KQ10, you force declarer to enter the dummy and lead another club. If declarer misguesses and plays the queen, partner's jack becomes a winner. Even if declarer has ♣KQJxxx, winning the second round of clubs may make it difficult for declarer to re-enter her hand to cash her remaining clubs.

***Case 2.*** South has never bid clubs and leads a club from dummy at notrump, East and South playing the same cards as before. What is going on? It appears that partner has five clubs and declarer four (unless declarer has an unbid six-card club suit!). Again, with a doubleton in dummy, it is usually wise to duck the first round.

In neither case can you tell for sure how many tricks declarer has coming in the suit. However, by ducking and seeing what happens on the second round of the suit, you will have a better idea. For example, if declarer enters dummy to lead the suit again, you can infer that declarer does not have a KQJ10 combination. With that holding, declarer continues the suit from her hand.

Counting tricks in a long suit that is concealed in the closed hand is easier when there is an honor card (or two) in the dummy.

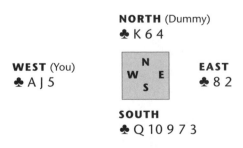

**NORTH** (Dummy)
♣ K 6 4

**WEST** (You)          **EAST**
♣ A J 5                    ♣ 8 2

**SOUTH**
♣ Q 10 9 7 3

Say declarer leads a low club to the king and a club to the ten. If partner plays high-low, you will have a good reading on the suit. Credit declarer with an eventual three club tricks.

When partner plays an honor card in second seat, it is easy to count declarer's tricks. All you need is an agreement that the play of an honor card from known length shows a sequence. In effect, partner plays the same card he would have led had he been on lead. Not everyone plays this way, but it is simple and recommended.

This topic was covered in more detail in *Eddie Kantar teaches Modern Bridge Defense*, Chapter 6.

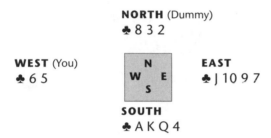

**NORTH** (Dummy)
♣ 8 3 2

**WEST** (You)
♣ 6 5

**EAST**
♣ J 10 9 7

**SOUTH**
♣ A K Q 4

When a club is led from dummy, partner plays the ♣J (the same club he would have led) telling you that declarer has the ♣AKQ.

When declarer plays a high card and partner follows suit with the highest missing card, assume partner has played his last card in the suit.

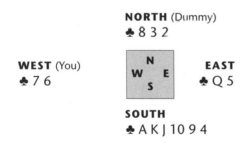

**NORTH** (Dummy)
♣ 8 3 2

**WEST** (You)
♣ 7 6

**EAST**
♣ Q 5

**SOUTH**
♣ A K J 10 9 4

Clubs are trumps and declarer bangs down the ♣AK. When partner plays the queen, assume partner has played his last club and does *not* have the jack.

In other words, declarer has six club tricks coming. If partner actually has the ♣QJ5, partner plays the five and the jack, not the five and the queen.

# Counting declarer's trump tricks

Now you're really playing with the big boys. When defending a trump suit contract, there are new trick-counting variables to deal with (aren't you thrilled to hear that?):

1. *Counting how many trumps declarer has.* Clearly it is easier to count declarer's trump tricks when you have an idea of how many trumps are in the closed hand.

2. *You must keep in mind that when declarer trumps in the long hand, she does not gain an extra trick, but when she trumps in the short hand she does.*

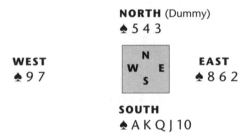

**NORTH** (Dummy)
♠ 5 4 3

**WEST**        **EAST**
♠ 9 7           ♠ 8 6 2

**SOUTH**
♠ A K Q J 10

Spades are trumps. If South draws trumps, South is entitled to five trump tricks. If the defenders force declarer to trump twice in the closed hand, declarer takes the same five trump tricks. However, each time declarer trumps in the North hand, it adds one trump trick to declarer's trick count.

3. *Counting tricks if declarer crossruffs.*

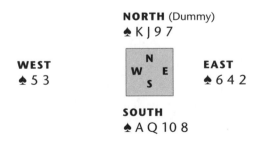

**NORTH** (Dummy)
♠ K J 9 7

**WEST**        **EAST**
♠ 5 3           ♠ 6 4 2

**SOUTH**
♠ A Q 10 8

Spades are trumps, a trump is *not* led, and there is a short side suit in each hand. If declarer can manage to use all of her trumps separately, she can take eight trump tricks, four in each hand. If you (or partner) lead a spade before the crossruff begins, declarer is limited to seven trump tricks: six separately plus the trick taken when you led a spade. Similarly, if you can lead trumps twice, declarer can take no more than six trump tricks: four separately plus the two tricks taken when you led the suit.

Finally, if your side leads trumps three times, you limit declarer to *five* trump tricks; the three tricks taken when your side led a trump, plus the remaining two trumps that almost always can be used separately.

*4. The danger of the lurking hidden side suit.*

If declarer can draw trumps and remain with trumps in both hands, a new danger exists. If declarer has a strong second suit hiding back there, she can run that suit and shorten dummy in another side suit, eventually trumping a loser or two in the shortened suit. Very discouraging.

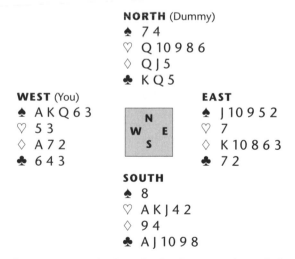

**NORTH** (Dummy)
♠ 7 4
♡ Q 10 9 8 6
◇ Q J 5
♣ K Q 5

**WEST** (You)
♠ A K Q 6 3
♡ 5 3
◇ A 7 2
♣ 6 4 3

**EAST**
♠ J 10 9 5 2
♡ 7
◇ K 10 8 6 3
♣ 7 2

**SOUTH**
♠ 8
♡ A K J 4 2
◇ 9 4
♣ A J 10 9 8

| NEITHER VUL. | | DEALER EAST | |
| **West** | **North** | **East** | **South** |
| --- | --- | --- | --- |
| | | pass | 1♡ |
| 1♠ | 2♠[1] | 4♠ | 5♡ |
| all pass | | | |

1) Strong heart raise

If you and partner are playing the lead convention of the Q from the AKQ asking for count (recommended), you have a better chance to defeat this contract.

Most defenders, not seeing any danger, would begin with two high spades. Declarer ruffs, draws trumps, discards *two* diamonds from dummy on the clubs, concedes a diamond, and finally ruffs a diamond in the dummy. Making five.

However, if the ♠Q is led and partner plays the ♠2, count, you can figure partner for five spades. This in turn, tells you that declarer will ruff the second round of spades. That in itself is no big deal. However, if declarer has a hidden club suit and can discard two diamonds on the fourth and fifth clubs, it is a big deal. Looking at this dummy, that is really what you have to fear. Your right play at this point is the ◇A hoping partner has the ◇K. You would hate to see one of your diamond winners vanish.

Thus far we have considered four trick-counting variables when defending a suit contract. Here are the final two:

*5. Does dummy have a long strong, side suit? If so, how many tricks can declarer take from that suit?*

*6. Can declarer set up a long suit in dummy by ruffing? If so, how many tricks can declarer take from that suit?*

When declarer has a long, strong, side suit in dummy it sort of hits you in the face. Once you know exactly how many winners (tricks) are available, you can plan your defense accordingly.

If dummy had the ◇KJx, your play at trick two holding the same hand should be a low diamond forcing declarer to guess the diamond position.

| BOTH VUL. | | DEALER SOUTH | |
|------|-------|------|-------|
| **West** | **North** | **East** | **South** |
| | | | 2♡[1] |
| pass | 4♡ | all pass | |

1) Weak

**NORTH** (Dummy)
♠ A K Q 10 9 2
♡ A J 4
◇ 6
♣ 8 6 4

**EAST** (You)
♠ J 5 3
♡ 8 6
◇ A 10 8 7 5
♣ J 7 2

Partner leads the ◇K and you see this humungous spade suit ready to rain down winners upon you. Clearly you must take your minor-suit winners as quickly as possible.

You need four minor-suit tricks to defeat the contract, and only one is available in diamonds so *three* must come from the club suit. Partner wouldn't lead the ◇K holding the ♣AK, so you must project the ♣AQ10 in partner's hand. Overtake the opening lead and pound back the ♣J. What a player you are!

Declarer's hand:  ♠ 8  ♡ KQ10953  ◇ J92  ♣ K95
Partner's hand:  ♠ 764  ♡ 72  ◇ KQ43  ♣ AQ103

At times the bidding plus the looks of the dummy tell you that the defensive tricks must come from going for a ruff in *dummy's* long suit, a suit you seldom attack! Keep an open mind.

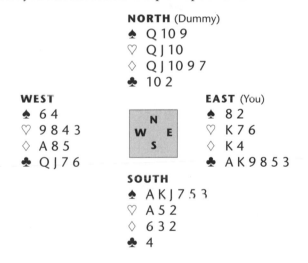

**NORTH** (Dummy)
♠ Q 10 9
♡ Q J 10
◇ Q J 10 9 7
♣ 10 2

**WEST**
♠ 6 4
♡ 9 8 4 3
◇ A 8 5
♣ Q J 7 6

**EAST** (You)
♠ 8 2
♡ K 7 6
◇ K 4
♣ A K 9 8 5 3

**SOUTH**
♠ A K J 7 5 3
♡ A 5 2
◇ 6 3 2
♣ 4

| BOTH VUL. | | DEALER WEST | |
| **West** | **North** | **East** | **South** |
| pass | pass | 1♣ | 1♠ |
| 2♣ | 2♠ | 3♣ | 4♠ |
| all pass | | | |

Partner leads the ♣Q and you survey the landscape.

Partner should have at least four clubs for a minor-suit raise, placing declarer with a singleton. Furthermore, partner must have an outside ace or king to justify the raise. That outside trick might be in the trump suit or might be a red-suit ace. If partner has a trump trick, then declarer has both red-suit aces, and you are one dead duck because both red-suit finesses work.

If partner has the ♡A, only two heart tricks are available — not enough. However, if partner has the ◇A and declarer has three diamonds, you can secure a diamond ruff and defeat the contract. Overtake the ♣K and switch to the ◇K. How else are you going to take *three* more tricks?

The following hand was defended by the late Jim Jacoby, East, in the 1972 World Bridge Olympiad. It gives you an idea of how quickly and deeply experts think when it comes to counting tricks.

NORTH-SOUTH VUL.  DEALER WEST

| West | North | East | South |
|------|-------|------|-------|
|      |       |      | 2NT[1] |
| pass | 3♣[2] | pass | 3♠ |
| pass | 4♣[3] | pass | 5♣[4] |
| pass | 6♠ | all pass | |

1) 20-21 HCP
2) Stayman
3) Gerber for key cards
4) 3 aces or 2 aces and the ♠K

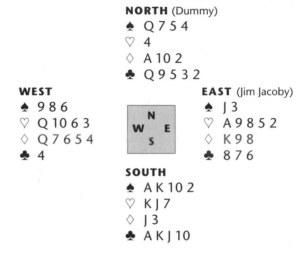

**NORTH** (Dummy)
♠ Q 7 5 4
♡ 4
◊ A 10 2
♣ Q 9 5 3 2

**WEST**
♠ 9 8 6
♡ Q 10 6 3
◊ Q 7 6 5 4
♣ 4

**EAST** (Jim Jacoby)
♠ J 3
♡ A 9 8 5 2
◊ K 9 8
♣ 8 7 6

**SOUTH**
♠ A K 10 2
♡ K J 7
◊ J 3
♣ A K J 10

West led the ◊5, taken by dummy's ace.

Declarer drew three rounds of trumps and then played five rounds of clubs discarding his remaining diamond.  West discarded the ◊4 on the second club indicating a five-card suit, then discarded a heart and two more diamonds.

Finally the singleton heart was led from dummy and Jim Jacoby played low like a flash!  Why?  Because he counted declarer's tricks!

He counted five spade tricks (three rounds were played plus one trump remained in each hand that could be made separately), five club tricks and the ◊A for eleven.  He knew that the declarer had the ♡K, but he hoped that declarer had ♡KJx and would misguess if he played low.

Sure enough that's what happened, and declarer never could get that elusive twelfth trick; down one.

# When declarer can establish dummy's long suit by ruffing

When declarer sets up winners in the dummy by ruffing a long suit, the established cards can be counted as tricks. However, there is a catch. There has to be an entry to cash those established winners *after* trumps have been drawn. Declarer has two ways to get to a suit that has been established by ruffing: (1) Draw trumps ending in dummy. This option must be used if there are no other side-suit entries to dummy. (2) Draw trumps, and then enter dummy with a side-suit winner.

What are your countermeasures? You either have to cash all of your tricks quickly before they go off on dummy's established winners, or you have to kill the eventual entry to dummy before the suit is established. If you can do that, you can sit back and wait for all your tricks in the other suits. Oh, how they hate it when you do that. First let's try counting tricks in side suits that can be established without your being able to attack dummy's side-suit or trump entry. Assume diamonds is a side suit at a spade contract.

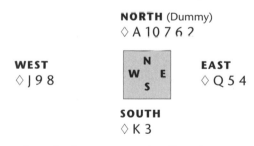

**NORTH** (Dummy)
◇ A 10 7 6 2

**WEST**
◇ J 9 8

**EAST**
◇ Q 5 4

**SOUTH**
◇ K 3

If declarer plays the king, ace, and ruffs a diamond, the suit breaks 3-3 and the two remaining diamonds in dummy are high. Credit declarer with four diamond tricks.

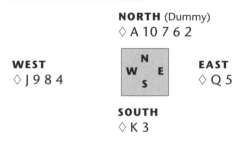

**NORTH** (Dummy)
◇ A 10 7 6 2

**WEST**
◇ J 9 8 4

**EAST**
◇ Q 5

**SOUTH**
◇ K 3

This time the suit does not break so well for declarer, but given enough dummy entries declarer can still establish dummy's fifth diamond by ruffing two diamonds and returning to dummy to use the established winner. If declarer has the wherewithal to do all of this, the defenders must count declarer for three diamond tricks.

That necessary return entry to dummy that declarer needs so badly to use the established suit may lie in the trump suit. If so, declarer must draw trumps *ending* in the dummy. However, clever defenders may be able to prevent that by forcing dummy to ruff prematurely. Take a good look at the following example:

| EAST-WEST VUL. | | DEALER NORTH | |
|---|---|---|---|
| **West** | **North** | **East** | **South** |
| | 1♠ | pass | 2♦ |
| pass | 2♠ | pass | 3♣ |
| pass | 4♦ | pass | 5♦ |
| all pass | | | |

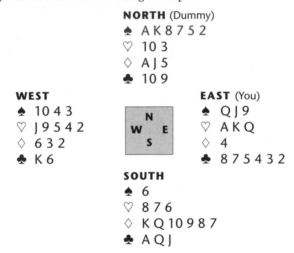

**NORTH** (Dummy)
♠ A K 8 7 5 2
♡ 10 3
◇ A J 5
♣ 10 9

**WEST**
♠ 10 4 3
♡ J 9 5 4 2
◇ 6 3 2
♣ K 6

**EAST** (You)
♠ Q J 9
♡ A K Q
◇ 4
♣ 8 7 5 4 3 2

**SOUTH**
♠ 6
♡ 8 7 6
◇ K Q 10 9 8 7
♣ A Q J

If ever a bidding sequence screamed for a heart lead, this is it. Accordingly, partner leads the ♡4 to your queen. When you cash the ♡A, partner plays the ♡2 confirming a five-card suit. If partner has five hearts, declarer has three. Playing a third heart immediately, forcing dummy to ruff, kills the spade suit establishment. Why? Partner figures to have three diamonds so declarer will not be able to ruff a spade and draw trumps *ending in the dummy* to use the established spades.

Had you switched to a club at trick three, declarer makes the hand easily by rising with the ♣A, setting up the spades, and drawing three rounds of trumps *ending in the dummy*. When the third diamond is removed prematurely, so is the contract.

The bottom line is that your heart play is eventually going to force declarer to take a losing club finesse. Follow the play after dummy ruffs the third spade. Declarer plays the ♠AK, discarding a club, ruffs a spade, and then plays two high diamonds ending in dummy hoping they break 2-2. When they don't, declarer is reduced to a losing club finesse. Down one.

# Practice Hands

**Hand 1**

**NORTH** (Dummy)
- ♠ 6 3
- ♡ A Q J
- ◇ 4 2
- ♣ K Q 10 7 6 3

**WEST** (You)
- ♠ A J 9 2
- ♡ 9 8 7 3
- ◇ 8 6 5
- ♣ J 2

```
      N
   W     E
      S
```

**EAST**
- ♠ K 8 5
- ♡ 10 6 4
- ◇ A 10 9 7 3
- ♣ 8 4

**SOUTH**
- ♠ Q 10 7 4
- ♡ K 5 2
- ◇ K Q J
- ♣ A 9 5

| BOTH VUL. | | DEALER NORTH | |
|---|---|---|---|
| **West** | **North** | **East** | **South** |
| | 1♣ | pass | 3NT[1] |
| all pass | | | |

1) 16-17 balanced

You lead the ♠2; partner wins the king and returns the ♠8 to the ♠10 and your ♠J. Partner's return indicates three spades which means declarer remains with the guarded queen. You have to find an entry in partner's hand to lead another spade. If you do, you will take five tricks: four spades and partner's entry. Looking at the dummy, you decide that partner must have a minor suit ace or the ♡K to have a chance, but which?

If partner has the ♣A, there is no rush to lead a club as declarer will surely have to lead a club early on in order to establish such a powerful suit. The real choice is between diamonds and hearts. If partner has the ♡K, then declarer must have the ◇AKQ plus the ♣A to justify the opening one notrump bid (coming up in the next chapter on counting declarer's points) and is not about to take a heart finesse with at least ten tricks off the top.

The most realistic shot is to play partner for the ◇A. Switch to the ◇8, your highest diamond, showing weakness, and hope partner has read this chapter. If so, she will win the ace and return a spade, not a diamond. Success!

| BOTH VUL. | | DEALER NORTH | |
|---|---|---|---|
| **West** | **North** | **East** | **South** |
| | 1♣ | 1♠ | 1NT |
| pass | 3NT | all pass | |

**Hand 2**

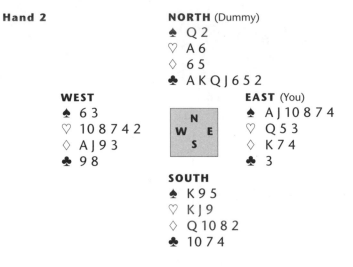

**NORTH** (Dummy)
♠ Q 2
♡ A 6
◇ 6 5
♣ A K Q J 6 5 2

**WEST**
♠ 6 3
♡ 10 8 7 4 2
◇ A J 9 3
♣ 9 8

**EAST** (You)
♠ A J 10 8 7 4
♡ Q 5 3
◇ K 7 4
♣ 3

**SOUTH**
♠ K 9 5
♡ K J 9
◇ Q 10 8 2
♣ 10 7 4

Partner leads the ♠6 and dummy plays low. Normally with this holding you play the ♠10 to drive out the king and establish your remaining spades. But this isn't 'normally'. This dummy is positively scary! You can see seven solid club tricks, plus the ♡A for eight tricks, and if you let declarer win the opening lead with the ♠K, you have just given up all hope of defeating this contract. Win the ♠A and shift to a low diamond. You have to 'project' partner with the ◇AQ9x or ◇AJ9x. In either case, four tricks are available. No other defense is worth talking about.

| BOTH VUL. | | DEALER SOUTH | |
|---|---|---|---|
| **West** | **North** | **East** | **South** |
| | | | 1♡ |
| pass | 1♠ | pass | 2♡ |
| pass | 4♡ | all pass | |

**Hand 3**

**NORTH** (Dummy)
♠ A K 6 5 2
♡ J 5
◇ 7 6 5
♣ A 6 5

**WEST** (You)
♠ J 7
♡ K 9 3
◇ K J 4 2
♣ Q J 10 7

**EAST**
♠ 10 9 8 4
♡ 4 2
◇ A 8 3
♣ 9 8 3 2

**SOUTH**
♠ Q 3
♡ A Q 10 8 7 6
◇ Q 10 9
♣ K 4

You lead the ♣Q which is captured in dummy with the ♣A, partner playing the ♣2. At trick two declarer leads the ♡J from dummy to your king. Your thinking should go like this: 'Declarer figures to have at *least* six hearts (has skipped over three other bids to rebid hearts) and partner would have covered the ♡J with a doubleton honor so declarer remains with five winning hearts, minimum. In addition, declarer is known to have two club tricks and at least two spade tricks for a grand total of nine. If declarer has the ◇A, there is no chance, so play partner for that card and switch to a low diamond.' As it happens, partner wins the ace and returns a diamond allowing you to defeat the contract one trick. Even if your diamond lead goes smack into the AQ, all you will have done is present declarer with an overtrick; not the end of the world.

**Hand 4**

**NORTH** (Dummy)
- ♠ A 2
- ♡ 7 6 3
- ◇ K J 7 6 5
- ♣ A Q 10

**WEST**
- ♠ K 9 8 7 4
- ♡ 8 5 2
- ◇ —
- ♣ 8 7 5 3 2

**EAST** (You)
- ♠ J 10 5
- ♡ Q J 10 9
- ◇ A Q 4 3
- ♣ 6 4

**SOUTH**
- ♠ Q 6 3
- ♡ A K 4
- ◇ 10 9 8 2
- ♣ K J 9

BOTH VUL.     DEALER NORTH

| West | North | East | South |
|------|-------|------|-------|
|      | 1◇    | pass | 2NT[1] |
| pass | 3NT   | all pass | |

1) 13-15 HCP

Partner leads the ♠7, dummy plays low, and your ♠10 drives out declarer's ♠Q. At trick two, declarer leads the ◇10, partner discarding the ♣2. The Rule of Eleven tells you that declarer has only one more spade stopper, the ace. Furthermore partner, with a diamond void, figures to have five spades. Win the ◇Q, exit with the ♠J, and when you get in with the ◇A, return your remaining spade. Your side will take three spade tricks and two diamond tricks before declarer can establish her diamond suit. What about that tempting heart shift at trick three? It doesn't add up. Declarer needs the ♡AK to justify the 2NT bid and five tricks are available with the spade continuation. Go for it.

# Test Yourself

1)

| BOTH VUL. | | DEALER SOUTH | |
|---|---|---|---|
| **West** | **North** | **East** | **South** |
| | | | pass |
| pass | 1♠ | pass | 2NT[1] |
| all pass | | | |

1) 11-12 HCP

*Solution on page 124*

**NORTH** (Dummy)
- ♠ K Q 10 8 7
- ♡ A Q 2
- ◊ 9 8
- ♣ Q 8 7

**WEST** (You)
- ♠ A 5 4
- ♡ J 7 6
- ◊ J 10 7 3 2
- ♣ K 4

You lead the ◊3 to the queen and king. At trick two declarer leads the ♠J which you duck, partner playing the ♠2. When he continues with the ♠9 you win the ace, partner playing the ♠3. What now?

2)

| BOTH VUL. | | DEALER SOUTH | |
|---|---|---|---|
| **West** | **North** | **East** | **South** |
| | | | 2NT[1] |
| pass | 3♣ | pass | 3◊ |
| pass | 3NT | all pass | |

1) 20-21 HCP

*Solution on page 125*

**NORTH** (Dummy)
- ♠ 7 6 5
- ♡ J 10 9 8
- ◊ J 9
- ♣ K Q J 10

**EAST** (You)
- ♠ Q 8 2
- ♡ A 7 6
- ◊ 10 4
- ♣ 8 6 5 3 2

West leads the ◊8, won by dummy's jack and declarer calls for the ♡J. What do you do?

3)

| BOTH VUL. | | DEALER NORTH | |
|---|---|---|---|
| **West** | **North** | **East** | **South** |
| | 1♡ | pass | 1♠ |
| pass | 2♠ | pass | 4♠ |
| all pass | | | |

*Solution on page 125*

**NORTH** (Dummy)
- ♠ Q J 5
- ♡ K Q 10 8 5
- ◊ A J 3
- ♣ 7 3

**EAST** (You)
- ♠ 9 3
- ♡ 9 7 4 2
- ◊ K 10 2
- ♣ A 9 8 5

Partner leads the ♣Q. What is your plan to secure four tricks? Project!

4)

**NORTH** (Dummy)
♠ 6
♡ A Q 4
◇ K Q J 10 9 5
♣ 9 8 2

**EAST** (You)
♠ 10 9 3
♡ J 7 6 5
◇ 8 7 2
♣ A 10 6

| BOTH VUL. | | DEALER WEST | |
|---|---|---|---|
| **West** | **North** | **East** | **South** |
| 1♠ | 2◇ | pass | 2NT |
| pass | 3NT | all pass | |

*Solution on page 126*

Partner leads the ♠5 to your nine and declarer's queen. Declarer leads a diamond to the king, then the ◇Q to partner's ace. How do you play 1) if partner returns the ♣3? 2) if partner returns the ♣7?

5)

**NORTH** (Dummy)
♠ 9 6 4
♡ A K Q 6
◇ 9 8 6
♣ Q J 5

**WEST** (You)
♠ A J 7 3
♡ 10 7
◇ Q J 10 7 3
♣ K 9

| BOTH VUL. | | DEALER SOUTH | |
|---|---|---|---|
| **West** | **North** | **East** | **South** |
| | | | 1♣ |
| 1◇ | 1♡ | pass | 1NT |
| pass | 3NT | all pass | |

*Solution on page 126*

You lead the ◇Q to the deuce and king. Declarer crosses to the ♡A (♡2 from partner, count) and leads the ♣Q, ducked to your king. How do you continue if partner plays 1) the ♣2? 2) the ♣7?

6)

**NORTH** (Dummy)
♠ J 8 7 6 4
♡ J 2
◇ A Q J 10
♣ 3 2

**WEST** (You)
♠ K Q 10 9 5 2
♡ A 8
◇ 9 6
♣ Q 10 9

| BOTH VUL. | | DEALER SOUTH | |
|---|---|---|---|
| **West** | **North** | **East** | **South** |
| | | | 1♣ |
| 1♠ | 1NT | 2♡ | 5♣ (!) |
| dbl | all pass | | |

*Solution on page 127*

Enough is enough. You are not going to let them push you around! You lead the ♠K and declarer ruffs. Declarer continues with the ♣AK and a club to your queen, partner following to the first club, then discarding the ◇2 and the ♡5. Now what?

# Test Yourself — Solutions

BOTH VUL.　　DEALER SOUTH

| West | North | East | South |
|------|-------|------|-------|
| | | | pass |
| pass | 1♠ | pass | 2NT[1] |
| all pass | | | |

1) 11-12 HCP

**Trick 1:**  ◇3  ◇8  ◇Q  ◇K
**Trick 2:**  ♠J  ♠4  ♠5  ♠2
**Trick 3:**  ♠9  ♠A  ♠8  ♠3
**Trick 4:**  ?

This topic was discussed at length in Chapter 3 of *Eddie Kantar teaches Modern Bridge Defense.*

1)

**NORTH** (Dummy)
♠ K Q 10 8 7
♡ A Q 2
◇ 9 8
♣ Q 8 7

**WEST** (You)
♠ A 5 4
♡ J 7 6
◇ J 10 7 3 2
♣ K 4

**EAST**
♠ 6 3 2
♡ 9 8 3
◇ Q 5
♣ A J 6 3 2

**SOUTH**
♠ J 9
♡ K 10 5 4
◇ A K 6 4
♣ 10 9 5

Oddly enough, this is an easier hand to defeat in a contract of 2NT than it would be in a contract of 3NT! Against a contract of 3NT you must allow for partner playing the ◇Q from ◇AQx, in which case you can take four diamond tricks and defeat the contract. However, in a contract of 2NT four diamond tricks is not enough.

If partner does have the ◇AQx, declarer will surely have the ♡K and the ♣A to justify the 2NT response. If declarer has these cards, he has the rest of the tricks after you cash your four diamonds. You have to think of something else.

What about setting up your diamonds by driving out declarer's likely ◇A and waiting to get in with the ♣K? No good. Declarer must have the ♡K or the ♣A to go along with the ◇AK to justify the 2NT response. Either of those cards brings declarer's trick count to at least eight tricks after he wins your diamond return.

What you really need is five *quick* tricks. The only way to get them is to project the ♣AJxxx in partner's hand and shift to the ♣K! It's your only hope. Won't everyone be impressed.

2)

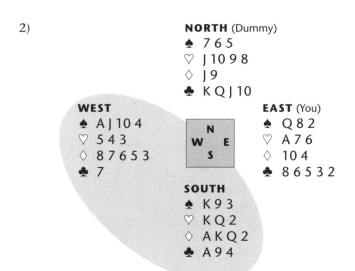

**NORTH** (Dummy)
♠ 7 6 5
♡ J 10 9 8
◇ J 9
♣ K Q J 10

**WEST**
♠ A J 10 4
♡ 5 4 3
◇ 8 7 6 5 3
♣ 7

**EAST** (You)
♠ Q 8 2
♡ A 7 6
◇ 10 4
♣ 8 6 5 3 2

**SOUTH**
♠ K 9 3
♡ K Q 2
◇ A K Q 2
♣ A 9 4

| BOTH VUL. | | DEALER SOUTH | |
| West | North | East | South |
| --- | --- | --- | --- |
| | | | 2NT[1] |
| pass | 3♣ | pass | 3◇ |
| pass | 3NT | all pass | |

1) 20-21 HCP

**Trick 1:** ◇8 ◇J ◇4 ◇2
**Trick 2:** ♡J ?

No stealing! Partner's lead marks declarer with the ◇AKQx and dummy's clubs tell you of four more tricks coming in that suit. In order to defeat this contract, partner needs very good spades. Win the ♡A and shift to the ♠Q playing partner for ♠AJ10x. In any case, don't duck the heart, it is declarer's ninth trick and you know it!

3)

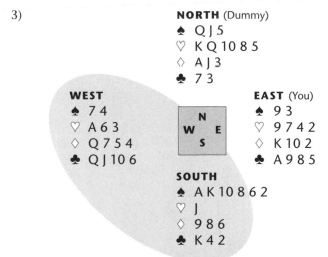

**NORTH** (Dummy)
♠ Q J 5
♡ K Q 10 8 5
◇ A J 3
♣ 7 3

**WEST**
♠ 7 4
♡ A 6 3
◇ Q 7 5 4
♣ Q J 10 6

**EAST** (You)
♠ 9 3
♡ 9 7 4 2
◇ K 10 2
♣ A 9 8 5

**SOUTH**
♠ A K 10 8 6 2
♡ J
◇ 9 8 6
♣ K 4 2

| BOTH VUL. | | DEALER NORTH | |
| West | North | East | South |
| --- | --- | --- | --- |
| | 1♡ | pass | 1♠ |
| pass | 2♠ | pass | 4♠ |
| all pass | | | |

Opening lead: ♣Q

Win the ♣A and shift to a low diamond projecting the ◇Q in partner's hand along with the ♡A or a trump trick. It is your only chance to build up two diamond tricks before everything goes away on the hearts. This trick-taking dummy calls for an aggressive defense.

BOTH VUL.          DEALER WEST

| West | North | East | South |
|------|-------|------|-------|
| 1♠ | 2◇ | pass | 2NT |
| pass | 3NT | all pass | |

**Trick 1:** ♠5 ♠6 ♠9 ♠Q
**Trick 2:** ◇4 ◇3 ◇K ◇2
**Trick 3:** ◇Q ◇7 ◇6 ◇A
**Trick 4:** ♣3 ?

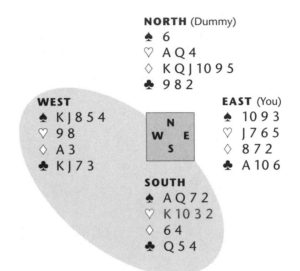

**NORTH** (Dummy)
♠ 6
♡ A Q 4
◇ K Q J 10 9 5
♣ 9 8 2

**WEST**
♠ K J 8 5 4
♡ 9 8
◇ A 3
♣ K J 7 3

**EAST** (You)
♠ 10 9 3
♡ J 7 6 5
◇ 8 7 2
♣ A 10 6

**SOUTH**
♠ A Q 7 2
♡ K 10 3 2
◇ 6 4
♣ Q 5 4

Partner's switch to a low club shows strength and asks for a club return.  Win the ♣A and return the ♣10.  Had partner switched to the ♣7, a relatively high club (you can see the 8, 9, and 10), showing weakness, win the ♣A and return the ♠10, partner's first suit. What you need to defeat the contract with a spade return is to find partner with ♠AQ8xx or ♠AJ8xx.

BOTH VUL.          DEALER SOUTH

| West | North | East | South |
|------|-------|------|-------|
| | | | 1♣ |
| 1◇ | 1♡ | pass | 1NT |
| pass | 3NT | all pass | |

**Trick 1:** ◇Q ◇6 ◇2 ◇K
**Trick 2:** ♡5 ♡7 ♡A ♡2
**Trick 3:** ♣Q ♣2 ♣4 ♣K
**Trick 4:** ?

5)

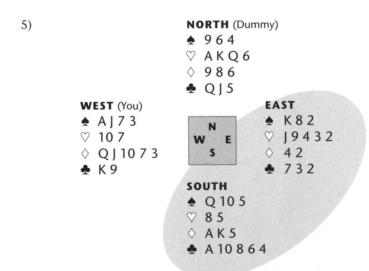

**NORTH** (Dummy)
♠ 9 6 4
♡ A K Q 6
◇ 9 8 6
♣ Q J 5

**WEST** (You)
♠ A J 7 3
♡ 10 7
◇ Q J 10 7 3
♣ K 9

**EAST**
♠ K 8 2
♡ J 9 4 3 2
◇ 4 2
♣ 7 3 2

**SOUTH**
♠ Q 10 5
♡ 8 5
◇ A K 5
♣ A 10 8 6 4

1) If partner plays the ♣2 suggesting three clubs, declarer has five clubs and nine tricks ready to rumble: three heart tricks (partner

should have five hearts judging from the ♡2), four club tricks plus the ◇AK. Your play is to shift to a low spade hoping partner has ♠Kxx.

2) If partner plays the ♣7 suggesting four clubs, declarer's trick count is only eight: three hearts, three clubs and two diamonds. Now the winning defense is to continue with a high diamond establishing your suit with the ♠A as the eventual entry.

6)

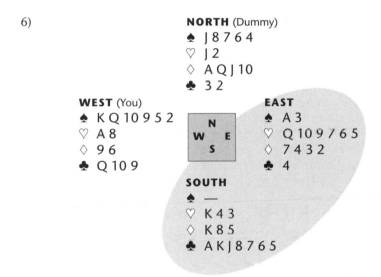

**NORTH** (Dummy)
♠ J 8 7 6 4
♡ J 2
◇ A Q J 10
♣ 3 2

**WEST** (You)
♠ K Q 10 9 5 2
♡ A 8
◇ 9 6
♣ Q 10 9

**EAST**
♠ A 3
♡ Q 10 9 7 6 5
◇ 7 4 3 2
♣ 4

**SOUTH**
♠ —
♡ K 4 3
◇ K 8 5
♣ A K J 8 7 6 5

| BOTH VUL. | | DEALER SOUTH | |
| **West** | **North** | **East** | **South** |
| | | | 1♣ |
| 1♠ | 1NT | 2♡ | 5♣ (!) |
| dbl | all pass | | |

**Trick 1:** ♠K ♠4 ♠A ♣5
**Trick 2:** ♣A ♣9 ♣2 ♣4
**Trick 3:** ◇K ♣10 ♣3 ◇2
**Trick 4:** ♣6 ♣Q ♠6 ♡5
**Trick 5:** ?

This is a good exercise in trick counting and passive defense application. Declarer has six club tricks and partner's discouraging diamond discard tells you that declarer has four more tricks available in diamonds for a total of ten. But where is trick eleven coming from?

Nowhere, if you don't panic. Declarer's distribution must be 0-3-3-7 or 0-2-4-7. In the first case declarer can discard one heart on the fourth diamond but is still left with two hearts. In the second case there is no discard coming on dummy's diamonds and declarer again is left with two hearts. As long as declarer is left with two hearts, there is no rush to cash your ♡A. If you panic and play the ♡A and find declarer with ♡Kx and partner with the ♡Q10, declarer will think you are Santa Claus come to life.

## Key ideas from Chapter 4

- Counting your defensive tricks and declarer's offensive tricks is the key to most defensive problems.
- There are five major sources of information to determine declarer's trick count: the bidding, the lead (and partner's return of your lead), the dummy, partner's count signals, and declarer's line of play.
- If declarer doesn't attack a strong suit in dummy missing one high honor, assume declarer has the missing honor and count tricks accordingly.
- After you lead one suit and switch to another, a switch to a low card in the second suit asks partner to return that suit; a switch to a high card in the second suit asks partner to return the original suit.
- If partner leads a suit and dummy plays the queen or a lower card that you cannot top, give count. This helps partner count declarer's tricks in the suit.
- When you know that declarer has enough tricks in three suits to make the contract, switch to the fourth suit.  Do it!
- Ask yourself how many tricks you need to defeat the contract and project the least amount of honor strength necessary in partner's hand to do it — then assume partner has what you need!
- Conventional leads of the 9, 10, and J help the defending side count declarer's tricks (and the declaring side count defenders' tricks!).
- Forcing the dummy to ruff is one way of killing a dummy entry to a soon-to-be-established side suit.

# Counting High Card Points

*All the powerful kings and queens...*

JOHN DONNE

*Who's got that missing queen of hearts?*

We've discussed two kinds of counting that help you to figure out what is going on during the play of a hand, and to determine your appropriate defensive strategy: counting distribution and counting tricks. Implicit in both of these, but definitely worth inclusion in this book, is a third kind of counting — counting the high card points around the table.

It goes without saying that once you know who has the missing honors, you can defend like a demon. It all starts with analyzing the bidding.

# Notrump sequences

## Opener rebids notrump

Most opening notrump bids are limit bids, typically with a three-point range. You must keep in mind, however, that not everyone uses the same ranges as you do!

As an example, for many years 16-18 HCP was the biblically prescribed point count range for an opening bid of 1NT; in the modern style this has been shaded down to 15-17. However many players play a 'weak notrump', swearing by a 12-14 range; players who play the Precision Club system opt for a 13-15 range; and let's not forget the 'mini'-notrumpers who rejoice with 10-12, or the 'Kamikaze' fringe group who are out to get you with an 8-10 range!

The opening bid of 2NT has undergone the same metamorphosis. It used to be 22-24 in the good old Goren days. Nowadays it is more like 20-21 or 20-22. The stronger hands are shown by opening an artificial 1♣ or 2♣ and rebidding 2NT.

The idea here is not to determine which is the best range, but rather to know which range your opponents are using, and to try to work out where the missing honors are early in the play.

In tournament bridge, the opponents' convention cards are supposed to be marked telling you what their ranges are on the most common notrump sequences. But there are too many notrump sequences for any convention card to include them all. What you might have to do is ask if you are not sure. Besides, you may not be playing in a tournament, and there may not be any convention cards lying around. *Ask!*

We're assuming a strong notrump system in all the bidding sequences in this chapter. If your opponents are using a different range for the opening 1NT, then their rebids will also show different ranges from 'standard'.

Now let's look at a few bidding sequences where opener is limited by a notrump rebid (assume a 1NT opening would be 15-17 HCP):

| Opener | Responder |
|--------|-----------|
| 1♣     | 1♠        |
| 1NT    |           |

Opener shows a hand too weak to open 1NT; play opener for 12-14.

| Opener | Responder |
|--------|-----------|
| 1♣ | 1♠ |
| 2NT | 3NT |
| pass | |

Opener describes a hand that is too strong to open 1NT and not strong enough to open 2NT. Play opener for 18-19.

| Opener | Responder |
|--------|-----------|
| 1♣ | 1♠ |
| 3NT | pass |

This is an atypical case where opener describes a hand with a long, solid minor suit, not necessarily balanced. This is more of a trick-taking rebid. Play opener for about 15-17 HCP but expect a six- or seven-card running suit to come showering down upon you once opener gets in.

| Opener | Responder |
|--------|-----------|
| 1♠ | 2◇ |
| 2NT | 3NT |
| pass | |

This is one you may have to ask about. Some play that it shows a minimum, 12-14, others play it shows the range of a strong notrump, 15-17. Ask.

| Opener | Responder |
|--------|-----------|
| 1♠ | 2◇ |
| 3NT | 6NT |
| pass | |

If a 2NT rebid shows 12-14, then a 3NT rebid shows 15-17; if a 2NT rebid shows 15-17, then a 3NT rebid shows 18-19. Ask.

| Opener | Responder |
|--------|-----------|
| 1◇ | 2♣ |
| 2NT | 4NT |
| pass | |

In this 2NT sequence, most play that opener has the equivalent of a 1NT rebid after a one-level response — 12-14. 'Most' doesn't mean 'all'. Check it out.

| Opener | Responder |
|--------|-----------|
| 1◇ | 2♣ |
| 3NT | pass |

Opener should have 18-19. With 15-17, opener begins with 1NT.

| Opener | Responder |
|--------|-----------|
| 1♣ | 2♣ |
| 2NT | 3♣ |
| pass | |

This is a strong rebid showing 18-19, the equivalent of a jump rebid of 2NT. It does *not* mean that opener has a 'short club' and is running away from his suit.

Every so often, opener will have a six-card suit with 15-17 HCP.

**Fourth-suit forcing** is a popular and useful convention in which a bid of the only unbid suit by responder at his second turn is an artificial waiting bid. It promises nothing about the suit bid, but simply gives opener another chance to describe his hand. Some pairs play FSF as creating a game force, particularly after an original two-level response.

Sometimes opener doesn't bid notrump until the third round of bidding. No matter; notrump bids are still limit bids and you want to get a handle on the range. The following 'third-round' notrump rebids come after responder has bid the fourth suit, an artificial force asking opener to limit her hand. Once she does, it makes it much easier for you on defense.

| Opener | Responder |
|--------|-----------|
| 1♠ | 2♣ |
| 2◇ | 2♡ |
| 2NT | 3NT |
| pass | |

After the 'fourth suit' is bid, look for opener to limit her hand. When opener bids the cheapest notrump bid available, assume a minimum, 12-14.

| Opener | Responder |
|--------|-----------|
| 1♠ | 2♣ |
| 2◇ | 2♡ |
| 3NT | 4NT |
| pass | |

This one shows 15-17 HCP. Once again opener is limiting her hand. Responder's 4NT is natural, inviting opener to bid slam with a maximum hand.

| Opener | Responder |
|--------|-----------|
| 1♠ | 2♣ |
| 2◇ | 2♡ |
| 4NT | 6NT |
| pass | |

After the 'fourth suit', 4NT is natural. Opener should have 18-19 HCP.

Opener may also rebid 3NT after responder's invitational rebid:

| Opener | Responder |
|--------|-----------|
| 1♣ | 1◇ |
| 1♡ | 3◇[1] |
| 3NT | pass |

1) Invitational

This time opener's range is a mystery. If opener has a fitting diamond honor, opener will gamble 3NT on a wing and a prayer; with a misfit for diamonds opener, unless a loony-tune, should have extras.

| Opener | Responder |
|--------|-----------|
| 1♣ | 1♡ |
| 1♠ | 3♣[1] |
| 3NT | pass |

1) Invitational

Again, not so easy to determine. If opener has five clubs, opener is more apt to gamble 3NT with a minimum hand. With a four card club suit, opener should have extras, perhaps 14-17. With 15-17, opener starts with 1NT.

# Responder bids notrump

Responder can also bid notrump naturally and wind up being the declarer. Again, the notrump bid must have a range; it's your job to know the range.

| Opener | Responder |
|--------|-----------|
| 1♣ | 1NT |
| pass | |

After a 1♣ opening, a 1NT response usually shows 8-10 HCP.

| Opener | Responder |
|--------|-----------|
| 1◇ | 1NT |
| 3NT | pass |

This one is a bit different as responder may have long clubs and may not be strong enough to bid them. Figure responder for 6-10, a wide range.

| Opener | Responder |
|--------|-----------|
| 1♡ or 1♠ | 1NT |

The typical range is 6-10. However, if the opponents play the 1NT response as forcing, the range is 6-11.

Many five-card major systems use a **forcing 1NT** response to 1♡ and 1♠ as part of their structure. It is especially common in Two-over-One methods, where a two-level response to an opening bid is usually game-forcing.

| Opener | Responder |
|--------|-----------|
| 1♣ or 1◇ | 2NT |

There are two possible ranges. Some play this sequence to show 10-12, others 13-15. Ask.

| Opener | Responder |
|--------|-----------|
| 1♣ or 1◇ | 3NT |
| 6NT | pass |

The most common range is 16-17, possibly a 'bad' 18 if there is such an animal. However, some play 13-15. Ask.

| Opener | Responder |
|--------|-----------|
| 1♡ or 1♠ | 2NT |

If not artificial, this shows 13-15, balanced; some play it as 11-12.

Many pairs use the 2NT and 3NT responses to major-suit openings as conventional bids that show specific kinds of strong raises.

| Opener | Responder |
|--------|-----------|
| 1♡ or 1♠ | 3NT |

If not artificial, 16-17, balanced; some play it as 13-15.

## Responder rebids notrump

When the responder rebids notrump, the defenders should have a good idea of the range.

| Opener | Responder |
|--------|-----------|
| 1♣ | 1♡ |
| 1♠ | 1NT |
| pass | |

The 1NT rebid is similar to a 1NT response excluding 6-point hands which sometimes pass the 1♠ rebid. Figure responder for 7-10.

| Opener | Responder |
|--------|-----------|
| 1♣ | 1♡ |
| 1♠ | 2NT |
| pass | |

This is one you want to be familiar with. The range is 11-12 (at times a 'good' 10). The bid is not forcing.

| Opener | Responder |
|--------|-----------|
| 1♠ | 2♢[1] |
| 2♡ | 2NT |
| 3NT | pass |

1) Not a game force

11-12. It doesn't matter whether the 2NT rebid is a jump or not, the range remains constant. If 2♢ is a game force, play responder for 12-14/15.

| Opener | Responder |
|--------|-----------|
| 1♣ | 1♢ |
| 1♡ | 3NT |
| pass | |

Responder shows 13-15, perhaps 16.

| Opener | Responder |
|--------|-----------|
| | pass |
| 1♡ | 2NT |

A passed-hand jump response of 2NT shows 11-12; more often than not, 11.

It is easier to determine responder's range after opener shows a minimum opening bid. However, when opener jumps and responder bids notrump, don't look for any easy answers — or ranges!

| Opener | Responder |
|--------|-----------|
| 1♣ | 1♡ |
| 3♣ | 3NT |
| pass | |

God alone knows what responder has. Responder can be gambling or can have a pretty good hand just short of a slam try.

| Opener | Responder |
|--------|-----------|
| 1♡ | 1♠ |
| 3♣ | 3NT |
| pass | |

This one is even worse than the previous one. In the previous example, opener made a non-forcing jump which responder

| Opener | Responder |
|--------|-----------|
| 1♡ | 1♠ |
| 3♣ | 3NT |
| pass | |

was at liberty to pass. In this sequence, if responder passes 3♣, it may be the last call he ever makes! Responder's range in this sequence is something like 6-11.

In sequences where opener begs to be let off the hook, but responder persists to game, play responder for a full opening bid:

| Opener | Responder |
|--------|-----------|
| 1♢ | 1♠ |
| 2♢ | 2♡ |
| 3♢ | 3NT |
| pass | |

Opener shows a minimum hand with long, long, diamonds. Responder figures to have 13-16.

Whatever the range, the overriding objective of the defense is to defeat the contract. However, at tournament play, when beating the contract is clearly out of the question, holding down the overtricks becomes the main goal.

# Suit sequences

If opener becomes the declarer in a suit contract, opener's hand figures to fall into one of these ranges:

| | |
|--------|-----------|
| 6-9 | Preemptive opening bid |
| 11-14/15 | Minimum opening bid |
| 15-17/18 | Intermediate opening bid |
| 18-21 | Powerhouse opening bid |
| 22+ | Rock Crusher |

Notice the overlaps, particularly the 15- and 18-point hands. With these counts, opener has to decide which way to go on the rebid. Distribution, system, and whether he has any kind of fit with partner's suit, all enter into the picture.

Hands in all groups except preempts and rock crushers are opened with one of a suit. Therefore you have to wait for opener's rebid, or even opener's third bid (if the first rebid doesn't limit opener's hand), to get a handle on opener's range.

Here are some of the easy sequences:

| Opener | Responder |
|--------|-----------|
| 1◇ | 1♡ |
| 2◇ | |

Opener has a minimum hand (11-14/15).

| Opener | Responder |
|--------|-----------|
| 1◇ | 1♡ |
| 3◇ | |

Opener has an intermediate hand (15-18).

| Opener | Responder |
|--------|-----------|
| 1◇ | 1♡ |
| 2♠ | |

Opener has a powerhouse (18-21).

| Opener | Responder |
|--------|-----------|
| 1◇ | 1♠ |
| 2♡ | |

Opener has reversed after a one-level response, showing a minimum of 17 HCP.

| Opener | Responder |
|--------|-----------|
| 1◇ | 1♠ |
| 2♡ | 3♡ |
| 4♡ | |

Opener has reversed, but has made no move toward slam. Play opener for 17-18

The toughest sequences are those where the opener bids a second suit without reversing or jump-shifting. The range can vary from an unlikely 11 all the way up to 18. What you have to do is wait for opener to clarify on her next bid... if there is a next bid.

| Opener | Responder |
|--------|-----------|
| 1♡ | 1♠ |
| 2♣ | pass |

There is no way of knowing (unless opener groans), whether opener has a minimum or an intermediate type hand; with a powerhouse, opener jump shifts.

| Opener | Responder |
|--------|-----------|
| 1♡ | 1♠ |
| 2♣ | 3♣ |
| pass | |

Opener has a minimum in the face of an invitational bid.

This last sequence raises the point of 'narrowing' the range. When a bid shows a range, any range, and the bidder's partner makes an invitational bid which is passed, the defenders can assume that the player who passes is at the low end of the range; a player who accepts is at the high end of the range. In this case, opener figures to be at the low end: play opener for 11-13 HCP.

| Opener | Responder |
|--------|-----------|
| 1♦ | 1♥ |
| 1♠ | 3♠ |
| pass | |

Figure opener for trash.

| Opener | Responder |
|--------|-----------|
| 1♦ | 1♥ |
| 1♠ | 3♠ |
| 4♠ | pass |

This one isn't as easy as it looks. The reason is that opener's range for the 1♠ bid was 11-18. The fact that opener has bid 4♠ simply means that opener doesn't have cheese.

| Opener | Responder |
|--------|-----------|
| 1♠ | 2♣ |
| 2♠ | 3♠ |
| 4♠ | pass |

A limited opener has accepted an invitational bid and should have more than a bare minimum.

Here's one where you have to know your customers:

| Opener | Responder |
|--------|-----------|
| 1♥ | 2♦ |
| 2♠ | |

Opener has reversed after a *two-level* response. Some play that a reverse after a two-level response can show a minimum; others insist that it shows at least an intermediate type hand.

In Two-over-One methods, a two-level response is a game-force and reverses over them usually need not show extras.

## Sequences where responder becomes declarer

Responder often times becomes the declarer. Responder's hands can usually be classified by range:

| | |
|--------|-----------|
| 6-9/10 | Minimum |
| 10-12 | Invitational |
| 12-15 | Game-going |
| 16-19 | Slam try |
| 19+ | Usually on to a slam |

Again, there are overlaps due to distribution, intermediate spot cards, fit for partner, etc.

| Opener | Responder |
|--------|-----------|
| 1◇ | 1♡ |
| 2♣ | 2♡ |
| 3♡ | pass |

Minimum, minimum, minimum (5 to an ugly 8). With 9-10, responder accepts the invitation.

| Opener | Responder |
|--------|-----------|
| 1◇ | 1♡ |
| 2♣ | 3♡ |
| pass | |

Invitational (10-12). Responder might have as few as 9 HCP with a healthy-looking six-card suit or perhaps a seven-card suit.

| Opener | Responder |
|--------|-----------|
| 1◇ | 1♡ |
| 2♣ | 4♡ |
| pass | |

Game-going values (12-15). (Possibly 10-11 HCP with a seven-card suit.)

| Opener | Responder |
|--------|-----------|
| 1◇ | 2♡ |
| 3◇ | 3♡ |
| 4♡ | pass |

Responder has slam try values, 16-18. The days of the 19-point-plus jump shift are long gone. If responder had a powerhouse, it is unlikely he would pass 4♡.

# Other techniques for counting declarer's points

Assuming you have an idea of declarer's range, once you see dummy you should be able to determine how many of the 40 HCP in the deck partner has. Here's how it works:

NEITHER VUL.  DEALER SOUTH

| West | North | East | South |
|------|-------|------|-------|
| | | | 1NT[1] |
| pass | 3NT | all pass | |

1) 15-17 HCP

**NORTH** (Dummy)
♠ A 6 4
♡ K 3
◇ Q 10 7 3 2
♣ 9 5 4

**WEST** (You)
♠ Q J 10 5
♡ A 8 5
◇ K 6 4
♣ Q 8 3

You lead the ♠Q and dummy tables with a 9-count. Take declarer's middle count, 16, and add it to dummy's count giving you a total of 25. That figure represents (within one point) the number of points declarer is playing with. If the opponents hold 25 HCP, you and your partner have 15. You have 12 so partner has about 3. If partner happens to have the ♠K, you've just seen Paris.

When declarer is known to have a weak hand and turns up with an ace and a king early in the play, you may have seen all declarer has:

**NORTH** (Dummy)
♠ K Q J 10 6
♡ A K Q
◇ 4 3
♣ Q 10 8

**WEST** (You)
♠ A 4 3 2
♡ J 10 4
◇ Q J 10 9
♣ K 6

```
      N
  W       E
      S
```

| NEITHER VUL. | | DEALER NORTH | |
|---|---|---|---|
| **West** | **North** | **East** | **South** |
| | 1♠ | pass | 1NT |
| pass | 2NT | all pass | |

You lead the ◇Q, partner plays the ◇2, and declarer the ◇K. The clues are rolling in. South, with an original range of 6-10, has passed an invitational bid; play South for 6-7. Partner's discouraging play of the ◇2 tells you that declarer has the ◇AK for a total of 7 HCP. Putting this all together tells you that partner has the ♣AJ.

When declarer leads a spade, take the ace and shift to the king and a club. On a good day partner will have five clubs and the contract will be defeated a trick. Making the lazy continuation of a diamond can't be right — it presents declarer with nine sure tricks: four spades, three hearts and two diamonds. This kind of ongoing tracking is vital to good defense.

Declarer's hand: ♠ 98 ♡ 7632 ◇ AK76 ♣ 954
Partner's hand: ♠ 75 ♡ 985 ◇ 852 ♣ AJ732

Slam bidding sequences, particularly where there has been a Blackwood bid, can lead you in the right direction:

| BOTH VUL. | | DEALER SOUTH | |
|-----------|-------|--------------|--------|
| **West** | **North** | **East** | **South** |
| | | | 2♣¹ |
| pass | 3♣ | pass | 3♠ |
| pass | 4♠ | pass | 4NT |
| pass | 5♣ | pass | 6♠ |
| all pass | | | |

1) Strong (a rock crusher) and artificial

**NORTH** (Dummy)
♠ Q 9 7
♡ K 6
◇ 10 6 4
♣ K Q 8 7 5

**EAST** (You)
♠ 8 4 3
♡ Q J 10 8 7
◇ A 7 5 3
♣ 3

Partner leads the ◇9 to your ace and declarer's jack. Where is your second trick coming from? If partner has the ♡A, you had better return a heart; if partner has the ♣A, you can return a club and even get a ruff. Dreamer. How can partner have an ace? Declarer has used Blackwood, discovered his partner doesn't have an ace, and has bid slam anyway. Declarer must have three aces. Your only chance is to return a diamond and hope partner ruffs.

| | |
|---|---|
| Declarer's hand: | ♠ AKJ1062 ♡ A ◇ KQJ82 ♣ A |
| Partner's hand: | ♠ 5 ♡ 95432 ◇ 9 ♣ J109642 |

Try this one from the West vantage point:

| BOTH VUL. | | DEALER NORTH | |
|-----------|-------|--------------|--------|
| **West** | **North** | **East** | **South** |
| | 1◇ | pass | 1♡ |
| pass | 3♡ | all pass | |

**NORTH** (Dummy)
♠ 5 2
♡ A K 8 6
◇ K Q J 10
♣ K 9 5

**WEST** (You)
♠ K 8 5 3
♡ 7 4
◇ A 4 3 2
♣ Q 8 2

You lead the ♠3 and partner's ♠Q falls to declarer's ace. Already you know of 5HCP in declarer's hand, the ♠AJ. Declarer continues with the ♡AK, partner turning up with ♡Qx. Next comes the ◇K from dummy, partner playing the ◇5. What do you make of all of this?

Declarer is known to have five hearts headed by the J10 and the ♠AJ. Declarer doesn't need much more to bid 4♡. Certainly partner has the ♣A.  Counting tricks can also be helpful.  Declarer is known to have five heart tricks, three diamonds, a spade and a likely spade ruff in dummy for nine or ten tricks.  In order to defeat this contract, partner not only needs the ♣A, a card he is known to hold, but the ♣J10 as well!  Might as well go for it; shift to the ♣Q after winning the ◇A.

| | |
|---|---|
| Declarer's hand: | ♠ AJ4  ♡ J10532  ◇ 98  ♣ 643 |
| Partner's hand: | ♠ Q1096  ♡ Q9  ◇ 765  ♣ AJ107 |

Are you a genius, or what?

The lead of an honor card usually tells third hand where the missing honors are in that suit.  Third hand can use this information to pinpoint the location of other missing honors.

**NORTH** (Dummy)
♠  Q 10 2
♡  J 7
◇  K Q J 8
♣  A K Q J

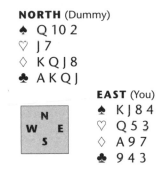

**EAST** (You)
♠  K J 8 4
♡  Q 5 3
◇  A 9 7
♣  9 4 3

| EAST-WEST VUL. | | DEALER NORTH | |
|---|---|---|---|
| **West** | **North** | **East** | **South** |
| | 1◇ | pass | 1NT |
| pass | 3NT | all pass | |

Opening lead:  ♡10 (shows 0 or 2 higher, one of which must be the jack)

Dummy plays the ♡J, you cover with the ♡Q, and declarer wins the ♡K.  At trick two declarer leads a diamond to dummy, partner playing the ◇2.

You should organize your thinking like this: partner's lead tells me that declarer has the ♡AK for 7 HCP.  No way South can have more than 10 HCP, so partner must have the ♠A.  Forget returning partner's suit, it is a waste of time.  Declarer will run home with four clubs, three diamonds, and two hearts.  Switch to a low spade and take four spade tricks.

| | |
|---|---|
| Declarer's hand: | ♠ 965  ♡ AK4  ◇ 1043  ♣ 10852 |
| Partner's hand: | ♠ A73  ♡ 109862  ◇ 652  ♣ 76 |

# When partner bids

There's more than one way of skinning a cat (counting declarer's points) in this game. You can also use your partner's bidding to tell you what declarer has!

EAST-WEST VUL.    DEALER WEST

| West | North | East | South |
|------|-------|------|-------|
| 1♡ | pass | 2♡ | 2♠ |
| all pass | | | |

**NORTH** (Dummy)
- ♠ 4 2
- ♡ Q 9 3
- ◇ K Q 5
- ♣ Q 10 4 3 2

**WEST** (You)
- ♠ A Q 8
- ♡ J 10 8 7 6
- ◇ J 9
- ♣ A J 6

```
      N
  W       E
      S
```

You lead the ♡J, covered by the queen and taken by partner's king. Partner continues with the ace and another heart, declarer ruffing the third round. You should be thinking that partner, a known weak hand, has already shown up with the ♡AK and cannot realistically have any other ace or king. Partner is not a favorite to have a side-suit queen either.

This type of play in the trump suit, called an **uppercut**, is discussed in more detail in Chapter 6: Trump Tricks.

Declarer crosses to dummy with a diamond and leads a spade to the jack and your queen. If your analysis is right, declarer has the ◇A, the ♣K, and likely a spade suit headed by the KJ10. If you are right, you can see five defensive tricks, but where is the sixth defensive trick coming from? Don't forget the trump suit! Cash the ♣A to see whether partner starts a high-low to show a doubleton. If he does, continue a club and give him a club ruff on getting in with the ♠A. If partner plays his lowest club, give up on the club ruff, and go for the 'uppercut' instead. Lead a fourth heart and hope partner can ruff with the ♠9, promoting your ♠8 to the setting trick.

| | |
|---|---|
| Declarer's hand: | ♠ KJ10763  ♡ 42  ◇ A104  ♣ K5 |
| Partner's hand: | ♠ 95  ♡ AK5  ◇ 87632  ♣ 987 |

Even when partner's bidding shows strength, the opponents may wind up playing the hand.

**NORTH** (Dummy)
♠ 6 2
♡ Q 6 5
◇ J 4 3 2
♣ A Q 10 7

**WEST** (You)
♠ Q 9 4
♡ K J 9 2
◇ 9 8 7
♣ 4 3 2

|   | N |   |
|---|---|---|
| W |   | E |
|   | S |   |

| NORTH-SOUTH VUL. DEALER WEST | | | |
|---|---|---|---|
| **West** | **North** | **East** | **South** |
| pass | pass | 1NT[1] | 2♠ |
| all pass | | | |

1) 15-17 HCP

You would like to compete, but given your methods, you can't bid a natural 2NT over 2♠ so you pass. You begin with the ◇9 ducked in dummy and won by partner's queen, declarer furnishing the ten. Partner continues with the ◇A which declarer ruffs.

Even now you should be counting points. Partner has between 15 and 17, so assume 16 and go from there. If partner has 16 (you've already seen 9), the good guys have 22 HCP and the bad guys 18. Looks good, but nine of partner's points are only going to take one trick. Back to business. Dummy has 9 HCP, so figure declarer for 9 as well. Remember, your calculations can never be off by more than 1 point.

Declarer leads the ♣J to the queen, partner playing the ♣5, and then a spade to the jack and queen. You're in! Given the vulnerability and the weakness of declarer's hand pointwise, declarer must be credited with six spades. If declarer's spades are headed by the AKJ, partner must have both the ♡A and the ♣K. Is that possible? Not really. Now a negative inference: with two small spades and a 16-count, partner would have reopened with a takeout double. Since partner didn't, play partner for a spade honor and not two small spades. If partner has a spade honor, partner can't have both the ♡A and the ♣K. If partner has the ♣K and declarer the ♡A, you are not going to defeat this contract, so play partner for the ♡A and declarer for the ♣K. Besides, partner's second diamond play, the ace instead of the king, told you of heart, rather than club strength.

Your marked play at this point is the ♡J, a **surrounding play**, in case declarer has the ♡10. It is now time to look at the entire hand so you can bask in your brilliance:

Partner's play of the ◇A is a subtle suit-preference signal: partner had a choice of cards to play, so his selection of one rather than the other can be used to send a message.

**Surrounding plays** are discussed in detail in Chapter 8.

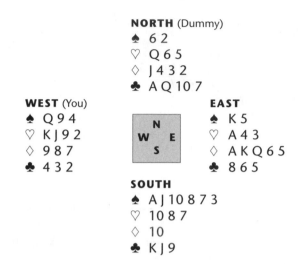

**NORTH** (Dummy)
♠ 6 2
♡ Q 6 5
♢ J 4 3 2
♣ A Q 10 7

**WEST** (You)
♠ Q 9 4
♡ K J 9 2
♢ 9 8 7
♣ 4 3 2

**EAST**
♠ K 5
♡ A 4 3
♢ A K Q 6 5
♣ 8 6 5

**SOUTH**
♠ A J 10 8 7 3
♡ 10 8 7
♢ 10
♣ K J 9

After your heart switch, your side collects three quick heart tricks and you wind up on lead. Lead your last heart allowing partner to trump with the ♠K. Your ♠9 now becomes the setting trick.

When partner makes a non-vulnerable preempt and turns up with a strong suit, don't look for much else on the side — you will be disappointed:

NORTH-SOUTH VUL. DEALER WEST

| West | North | East | South |
|------|-------|------|-------|
| pass | pass | 3♠ | 4♡ |
| all pass | | | |

**NORTH** (Dummy)
♠ 7 6 3
♡ 5 3
♢ K Q 10 8 4
♣ A 10 5

**WEST** (You)
♠ 2
♡ A 10 6
♢ A J 6 2
♣ Q 8 4 3 2

You are close to doubling, but you have seen your partner's preempts at favorable vulnerability before. In any case you lead your spade and partner's jack drives out declarer's ace. At trick two declarer exits with the ♡J. Any thoughts?

Partner has six or seven spades headed by the KQJ. With a six-card suit, partner might have opted to open 2♠, so play partner for seven. Declarer surely has the ♡KQJ, and the ♠A you know about, so the only key honor unaccounted for is the ♣K. Partner could just barely have it, but declarer is more likely to have it given that vulnerable 4♡ overcall. But if declarer has it, is there any chance of defeating this contract? Yes. If partner has a singleton diamond. If you win the ♡A and bang down the ace and a diamond. On a good day partner will ruff, cash a spade, and play another spade. Don't look now but your ♡10 has just turned into the second undertrick. Doubling 4♡ was right all along!

| | |
|---|---|
| Declarer's hand: | ♠ A10  ♡ KQJ984  ◇ 753  ♣ K9 |
| Partner's hand: | ♠ KQJ9854  ♡ 72  ◇ 9  ♣ J76 |

# Notrump ranges in competition

Ranges change in competitive auctions. These are the most common notrump bids in a competitive auction.

| West | North | East | South |
|---|---|---|---|
| | 1♡ | 1♠ | 1NT |

South shows 8-10 with one or two spade stoppers.

| West | North | East | South |
|---|---|---|---|
| | 1♡ | 1♠ | 2NT |

Some play this shows 13-15, balanced, game forcing. Some play this shows 11-12, balanced, invitational. (Ask.)

| West | North | East | South |
|---|---|---|---|
| | 1♡ | 2♣ | 2NT |

Most everyone plays this as 10-12, not forcing.

| West | North | East | South |
|------|-------|------|-------|
| 1♡ | 1♠ | pass | 1NT, 2NT, or 3NT |

The 1NT response to an overcall typically shows 9 to a bad 12. A bad 12 usually means a singleton in partner's suit. The 2NT response shows 12 to a bad 15 and is invitational. The 3NT response shows 15+.

| West | North | East | South |
|------|-------|------|-------|
| 1♠ | 2◇ | pass | 2NT or 3NT |

After a two-level overcall, a response of 2NT shows 10-12; a 3NT response shows 12+. Again, the overlap occurs when you have a fitting honor in partner's suit. Bid 'em up with those fitting honors!

| West | North | East | South |
|------|-------|------|-------|
|  |  | 3◇ | 3NT |

Would you believe 16-22? Well, that is the range.

| West | North | East | South |
|------|-------|------|-------|
|  |  | 2♠ | 2NT or 3NT |

The 2NT overcall shows the strength of a strong notrump, typically 15 to a bad 18. The 3NT overcall, if a balanced hand, shows upwards of 18 HCP. However, if South has a long running suit, forget the points: South is basing her overcall on tricks.

| West | North | East | South |
|------|-------|------|-------|
| 1♡ | dbl | pass | 1NT, 2NT, or 3NT |

The 1NT response has a wide range: 5-9 HCP. The 2NT response shows 10 to a bad 13. The 3NT response shows 13-16. These ranges are based to a certain extent on how light North can be to make a takeout double. If North can double with as few as 11 HCP (4-1-4-4 pattern), then responder has to exercise a little caution when jumping to game!

# Practice Hands

**Hand 1**

**NORTH** (Dummy)
♠ K Q
♡ Q 8 7 6
♢ Q J 6 5
♣ A 5 2

**WEST** (You)
♠ 10 9 8 6 4
♡ A 10
♢ K 3
♣ 10 9 6 4

```
    N
  W   E
    S
```

**EAST**
♠ 5 3 2
♡ 4 2
♢ A 8 7 4
♣ Q J 7 3

**SOUTH**
♠ A J 7
♡ K J 9 5 3
♢ 10 9 2
♣ K 8

| EAST-WEST VUL. | | DEALER NORTH | |
|------|------|------|------|
| **West** | **North** | **East** | **South** |
| | 1♢ | pass | 1♡ |
| pass | 2♡ | pass | 4♡ |
| all pass | | | |

Opening lead: ♠10

It is likely that South has at least five hearts — unless the raise to 2♡ has promised four-card support, in which case South could have only four hearts (ask about stuff like that).

Dummy's queen takes the first trick, partner playing the deuce, and a low heart goes to the king and your ace. The play in spades tells you that declarer has at least the ace and possibly the jack. The play in hearts suggests that declarer has the ♡KJ. If declarer has the ♢A and partner the ♣K, the most you can get is a trick in each minor. However, if partner has the ♢A and declarer at least three diamonds, a diamond ruff is in your future. Switch to the ♢K at trick three. It is far and away your best shot to defeat this contract.

The missing important cards are the ♢A and the ♣K and declarer could well have both, but then defeating the contract is impossible. However, declarer would be strong enough to leap to game with just one of those cards.

**Hand 2**

**NORTH** (Dummy)
♠ J 8 4
♡ 6 3 2
♢ A 7 5
♣ K Q J 9

**WEST**
♠ A 6
♡ J 10 9 8
♢ 8 6 3
♣ 10 8 4 2

```
    N
  W   E
    S
```

**EAST** (You)
♠ K Q 10 5
♡ 7 5 4
♢ K 10 2
♣ 7 6 5

**SOUTH**
♠ 9 7 3 2
♡ A K Q
♢ Q J 9 4
♣ A 3

| BOTH VUL. | | DEALER SOUTH | |
|------|------|------|------|
| **West** | **North** | **East** | **South** |
| | | | 1NT[1] |
| pass | 3NT | all pass | |

1) 15-17 HCP

Opening lead: ♡J (denies a higher honor)

Declarer wins the ♡Q and exits with the ◊Q, to partner's three and your king. What do you know?

You know declarer has the ♡AKQ for three tricks and 9 HCP. Declarer would have knocked out the ♣A right away if he didn't have it, so play declarer for the ♣A. That little inference brings declarer up to 13 HCP and seven tricks. The play in diamonds strongly suggests the ◊QJ in declarer's hand; partner's ◊3 is a count card, probably showing three, leaving declarer with ◊QJxx. If all this is true, declarer has already shown up with 16 HCP and ten tricks. Partner must have the ♠A. Shift to a *low* spade in order not to block the suit in case partner has ♠Ax, and collect four tricks before it is too late.

| NORTH-SOUTH VUL. DEALER NORTH | | | |
|------|------|------|------|
| **West** | **North** | **East** | **South** |
| | 1♣ | pass | 1♠ |
| pass | 1NT | pass | 4♠ |
| all pass | | | |

**Hand 3**

**NORTH** (Dummy)
♠ Q 2
♡ J 8 6
◊ K 6 5
♣ A K 9 7 5

**WEST**
♠ 8 4
♡ A K 2
◊ 10 8 7 4 3
♣ 4 3 2

**EAST** (You)
♠ J 10 9
♡ Q 9 5 3
◊ Q J 9 2
♣ Q J

**SOUTH**
♠ A K 7 6 5 3
♡ 10 7 4
◊ A
♣ 10 8 6

Partner starts with the ace, king, and a heart to your queen after you encourage a continuation. You are off to a great start with three quick tricks, but where is the fourth coming from?

What do you know? You know declarer has at least six spades plus opening-bid or near-opening-bid values to justify the leap to game facing a minimum opener. The missing honors are the ♠AK and the ◊A. It's hard to imagine that any sane declarer doesn't have them all. Furthermore, you know declarer has at most four minor-suit cards so no trick can possibly be coming from the minors with the opponents holding the ace-king of both suits.

When there are no tricks coming from the side suits, look to the trump suit to defeat the contract (the gist of the next chapter). Think ruff-sluff. If you lead a fourth round of hearts and partner uppercuts that ♠Q off dummy, your spade holding will produce the setting trick.

**Hand 4**

**NORTH** (Dummy)
♠ Q 7 2
♡ Q J 2
♢ K Q J 10 5
♣ 7 5

**WEST** (You)
♠ J 10 9 8
♡ A 6 3
♢ 4 3
♣ A Q 10 2

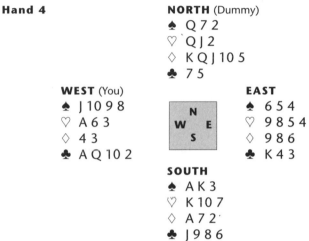

**EAST**
♠ 6 5 4
♡ 9 8 5 4
♢ 9 8 6
♣ K 4 3

**SOUTH**
♠ A K 3
♡ K 10 7
♢ A 7 2
♣ J 9 8 6

| NEITHER VUL. | | DEALER EAST | |
|---|---|---|---|
| **West** | **North** | **East** | **South** |
| | | pass | 1NT[1] |
| pass | 3NT | all pass | |

1) 15-17 HCP

Your ♠J floats around to declarer's king, partner playing the ♠4. At trick two declarer leads a low heart towards dummy. What do you know? You know declarer has the ♢A (4 HCP), because without that card, driving it out would be the first order of business. What about the ♠A? Can partner have the ♠A43? Count points. Between you and dummy there are 22 HCP. If declarer has 15, the very least she can have, partner has at most 3 HCP. Cancel partner's having the ♠A. Let's go further. Can partner have the ♡K? Yes, but then declarer has the ♣KJ. If you play a low heart, and partner wins and shifts to a club, you can still only take two clubs (unless declarer has ♣KJ doubleton) and two hearts without setting up a ninth trick for declarer.

Since you can't realistically defeat the contract if partner has the ♡K, why not play partner for the ♣K instead? Win the ♡A (don't let declarer steal her ninth trick right out from under your nose!), and shift to a low club. A good partner will produce the ♣K, return a club, and you can watch another contract bite the dust. Sometimes, the suit you want partner to lead so badly is the very suit you should be leading yourself!

# Test Yourself

Estimate declarer's point range and distribution on each auction.

1)
| North | South |
|-------|-------|
| 1♡ | 1♠ |
| 2♡ | 4♡ |
| pass | |

2)
| North | South |
|-------|-------|
| 1♡ | 1♠ |
| 3♡ | 4♡ |
| pass | |

3)
| North | South |
|-------|-------|
| 1♣ | 1♡ |
| 2NT | 3♢ |
| 3NT | pass |

4)
| North | South |
|-------|-------|
| 2♣ | 2♢ |
| 2NT | 3NT |
| pass | |

5)
| North | South |
|-------|-------|
| 2♡[1] | 4♡ |
| pass | |

1) Weak

6)
| North | South |
|-------|-------|
| 1♣ | 1♠ |
| 2♡ | 2♠ |
| 3NT | pass |

7)
| North | South |
|-------|-------|
| pass | 1♠ |
| 2♢ | pass |

8)
| North | South |
|-------|-------|
| pass | 1♢ |
| 1♠ | 2♠ |
| 2NT | pass |

9)
| North | South |
|-------|-------|
| 1♣ | 1♡ |
| 1♠ | 2♡ |
| 2NT | pass |

10)
| North | South |
|-------|-------|
| 1♢ | 1♡ |
| 3NT | pass |

11)
| North | South |
|-------|-------|
| 1♠ | 2♡ |
| 3♢ | 3♠ |
| 4♠ | pass |

12)
| North | South |
|-------|-------|
| 1♣ | 1♡ |
| 1NT | 4♡ |
| pass | |

13)
| North | South |
|-------|-------|
| 1♢ | 2NT |
| 3NT | pass |

14)
| North | South |
|-------|-------|
| 1♣ | 1♡ |
| 1♠ | 2NT |
| 3NT | pass |

15)
| North | South |
|-------|-------|
| 1♢ | 1♠ |
| 3♠ | 4♠ |
| pass | |

16)
| North | South |
|-------|-------|
| 1♡ | 2♣ |
| 2♢ | 3♣ |
| pass | |

17)
| North | South |
|-------|-------|
| 1♡ | 1♠ |
| 2♣ | 3♠ |
| pass | |

18)
| North | South |
|-------|-------|
| 1NT[1] | 4NT |
| pass | pass |

1) 15-17 HCP

19)
| North | South |
|-------|-------|
| 1♡ | 1♠ |
| 3♣ | 3♠ |
| 3NT | pass |

20)
| North | South |
|-------|-------|
| 1♡ | 1♠ |
| 4♡ | pass |

21)
| North | South |
|-------|-------|
| 2NT | 3♣ |
| 3♠ | 4♠ |
| pass | |

22)
| North | South |
|-------|-------|
| 1♠ | 2♣ |
| 2♢ | 3♣ |
| 3NT | pass |

23)
| North | South |
|-------|-------|
| 1♠ | 1NT |
| 2♢ | 2NT |
| pass | |

24)
| North | South |
|-------|-------|
| 1♢ | 1NT |
| 2NT | 3NT |
| pass | |

# Test Yourself — Solutions

1) 11-14 At least six hearts.

2) 15-18 At least six hearts; 18 HCP would be the exception.

3) 18-19 Fewer than three hearts, and very unlikely to have four diamonds.

4) 22-24 Balanced.

5) 6-9 Six hearts — unlikely to have four spades.

6) 19-21 Five clubs, four hearts, fewer than three spades. With 17-18, opener rebids 2NT over 2♠.

7) 10-11 Five or six diamonds. A passed hand response at the two-level, which can be passed, promises a five-card suit, minimum.

8) 10-12 Exactly four spades. If responder has exactly 10 HCP, an exception, she should have good intermediates plus a fitting diamond honor. Assume 11-12.

9) 16-18 Responder signed off: opener must have serious extras.

10) 15-17 Solid diamonds; usually a seven-bagger. It is a trick-taking bid, not a point-count bid. It can be made with a singleton or void in partner's suit.

11) 15-17 At least five spades. With a stronger hand, opener makes a slam try over 3♠. (Some play the 3◊ rebid does not show extras. Ask.)

12) 11-14 At least six hearts.

13) 13-15 Flat, typically no four-card major. Some play this as 10-12. Ask.

14) 10-12 With 10 responder should have either a good five-card suit, a fitting honor in opener's first suit, or great inter-mediates. With 10 HCP you can also make a 1NT rebid. Assume 11-12.

15) 8+ All you know is that responder was strong enough to try for game, but not strong enough to make a slam try.

16) 9-11 With six or seven clubs.

17) 9-11 With at least six spades. With only 9 HCP responder figures to have a side four-card suit or a seven-bagger.

18) 15-16 With 17 opener bids on; with 15 opener passes; with 16 opener usually bids on unless he's exactly 4-3-3-3.

19) 18-20 Fewer than three spades. Opener's most likely distribu-tion is 1-5-3-4.

20) 16-19 At least six hearts, maybe more. The more hearts, the fewer high card points needed.

21) 20-21 Four spades and fewer than four hearts. Check your opponents' range: not everyone plays 20-21.

22) 15-18  Responder's 3♣ rebid is not forcing, therefore opener needs extras (or a club fit) to go on.

23) 9-10  Usually 10.  If the 1NT response is forcing, 10-11.

24) 8-10  No four-card major.  In this sequence, responder's long suit is usually clubs.  Beware of a club lead!

## Key ideas from Chapter 5

• Notrump bids have ranges.  If the bidder has a 3-point range, assume the middle count until it proves otherwise.

• When a limited hand passes an invitational sequence, assume it is at the bottom of the range;  if the invitation is accepted, assume it is at the top or near top of the range.

• When an unlimited hand accepts an invitational bid, all you know is that the hand is not a bare minimum and not strong enough to make a slam try.

• When opener declares a suit contract, you should have some idea (within three or four) how many HCP declarer has. Add dummy's HCP to declarer's estimated HCP to determine how many HCP you and partner have. Start by taking declarer's middle count unless you need declarer to be minimum to defeat the contract.

• Use partner's bidding to help determine declarer's point count.  If you know within a point or two how strong partner is, you know the same about declarer's hand.

• After you determine partner's point count, assume those points that you haven't already seen are where you need them in order to defeat the contract.

• If declarer is known to be weak and turns up with beaucoup high-card strength early in the play, assume partner has what's left.

• When partner leads an honor card, you usually know how many points (and tricks) declarer has in that suit.

• Partner's signal can give you information about declarer's high-card strength in that suit.

• If all else fails, look to the trump suit for the setting trick; perhaps an uppercut or an overruff possibility exists.

• Keep track of declarer's strength as the hand progresses. It's how you know who has what near the end of a hand.

# Tricks With Trumps

*A wise man will make more opportunities
than he finds*

FRANCIS BACON

When a hand is played at a suit contract, it is harder for the defenders to figure out what declarer is going to do, and how close he is to making his contract. This is because declarer can use trumps to ruff losers, establish side suits, and ruff the defenders' winners, none of which he can do in notrump contracts. The good news is that the defenders can make use of the trump suit too. In the first place, defensive winners in the trump suit aren't going to go away: the ace of trumps is always a trick, for example. In the second place, there are a host of stratagems that the defenders can employ to squeeze extra tricks out of their trump holdings. We're going to look at some of them in this chapter

# Getting your ruff

A relatively simple way to get a ruff is to lead a short suit. It's important, of course, that declarer cannot draw trumps, and that partner can get in to return your suit. This strategy works well when partner has the ace of your suit, or when he has an outside ace and you have a trump entry.

| NORTH-SOUTH VUL. | DEALER SOUTH | | |
|---|---|---|---|
| **West** | **North** | **East** | **South** |
| | | | 1♡ |
| 1♠ | 2♣ | 3♠ | 4♣ |
| 4♠ | 5♡ | all pass | |

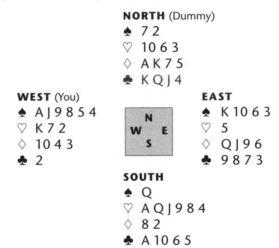

**NORTH** (Dummy)
♠ 7 2
♡ 10 6 3
◇ A K 7 5
♣ K Q J 4

**WEST** (You)
♠ A J 9 8 5 4
♡ K 7 2
◇ 10 4 3
♣ 2

**EAST**
♠ K 10 6 3
♡ 5
◇ Q J 9 6
♣ 9 8 7 3

**SOUTH**
♠ Q
♡ A Q J 9 8 4
◇ 8 2
♣ A 10 6 5

Holding trump control (♡Kxx), you lead your singleton club which is taken in dummy with the jack, partner playing the ♣9 (more about that in a moment). Fearing a club ruff and willing to give up on a trump finesse, declarer plays the ace and a heart which you pounce upon with your king, partner discarding the ♠10, showing a high spade honor, typically the ace or king. Your play now is marked: lead a low spade to partner's king; ruff the club return and get on with the next hand.

That ♣9. What was that all about? Partner has made a good play. When an obvious singleton is led and third hand has nothing to speak of in the suit, third hand gives suit preference telling partner where her outside entry lies. In this case the ♣9, East's highest, is an effort to show an entry in the higher ranking-suit, spades. In case you were sleeping at trick one, partner gave you another wake-up call at trick three with that discard of the ♠10 reconfirming the original message. You don't always get two bites at the same apple.

**NORTH** (Dummy)
♠ 6 2
♡ J 10 6 4
♦ Q 9 6
♣ A K J 3

**WEST** (You)
♠ A J 9 8 5 4
♡ A 7
♦ 8 5 4 3
♣ 2

**EAST**
♠ Q 10 7 3
♡ 3
♦ A 10 7 2
♣ 9 8 5 4

**SOUTH**
♠ K
♡ K Q 9 8 5 2
♦ K J
♣ Q 10 7 6

| BOTH VUL. | | DEALER EAST | |
| **West** | **North** | **East** | **South** |
| | | pass | 1♡ |
| 1♠ | 2♣ | 3♠ | 4♣ |
| pass | 4♡ | all pass | |

Again you lead a club which everyone knows is a singleton. When dummy takes the trick with the king, you had better watch partner's card closely to see where her outside entry lies. In this case, partner's entry is in the *lower*-ranking side suit, diamonds, so partner plays her lowest club. When declarer floats the ♡J to your ace, you can make things *really* easy for partner. Cash the ♠A (denying the king), and shift to the ♦8, showing weakness in diamonds. Partner will surely win the ♦A and give you a club ruff.

Besides giving suit preference when partner leads an obvious singleton, third hand has other responsibilities. At times third hand has to take charge of the defense early on to secure a ruff of her own.

After trick one, the king is *always* led from ace-king. In addition, when leading a suit partner has supported, the king is also led from ace-king. Finally, in case partner has forgotten, declarer's king appears when you lead your ace.

**NORTH** (Dummy)
♠ J 7 4 2
♡ K Q J 6 3
♦ 5 2
♣ A Q

**WEST**
♠ 6
♡ 9 7 4 2
♦ Q J 10 7
♣ K J 10 7

**EAST** (You)
♠ A 8
♡ 5
♦ A K 9 6 4
♣ 9 8 5 4 3

**SOUTH**
♠ K Q 10 9 5 3
♡ A 10 8
♦ 8 3
♣ 6 2

| EAST-WEST VUL. | | DEALER EAST | |
| **West** | **North** | **East** | **South** |
| | | 1♦ | 1♠ |
| 2♦ | 4♠ | all pass | |

Notice that in all these examples, you have trump control, so that you are certain of getting the lead early on. When you're trying to get a ruff in the opponents' long, strong side suit, trump control is the name of the game.

When partner leads the ◇Q, overtake and shift to your singleton heart keeping partner's known ◇J for a *later* re-entry. Declarer can do no better than win in dummy and fake a spade finesse by leading the jack. You've been around too long to fall for that one. Win the ♠A; underlead your ◇A to partner's jack, and get your heart ruff. One in the soup!

# Giving partner a ruff

Nothing makes partner happier than getting a ruff — unless it is getting two ruffs!

| EAST-WEST VUL. | | DEALER SOUTH | |
| --- | --- | --- | --- |
| **West** | **North** | **East** | **South** |
| | | | 2NT |
| pass | 3♣ | pass | 3♡ |
| pass | 4♡ | all pass | |

Opening lead: ♠5

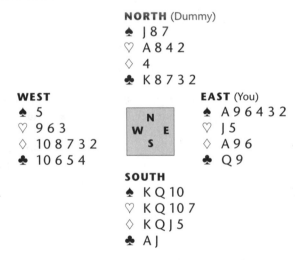

**NORTH** (Dummy)
♠ J 8 7
♡ A 8 4 2
◇ 4
♣ K 8 7 3 2

**WEST**
♠ 5
♡ 9 6 3
◇ 10 8 7 3 2
♣ 10 6 5 4

**EAST** (You)
♠ A 9 6 4 3 2
♡ J 5
◇ A 9 6
♣ Q 9

**SOUTH**
♠ K Q 10
♡ K Q 10 7
◇ K Q J 5
♣ A J

Partner has led an obvious singleton (if it is from three to an honor, declarer has opened 2NT with a singleton!), so hasten to win the ♠A and give partner a ruff. But don't hasten so much that partner doesn't know how to get you back in for a second ruff! The spade you play, a suit preference return, tells partner where your outside entry lies. Of course you don't always have an outside entry, but for the moment, let's assume you do. Your outside entry is in diamonds, the higher-ranking of the two remaining side suits, so return the *highest* spade you can afford, the ♠9, to let partner in on that little secret. Partner ruffs, returns a diamond to your ace, and ruffs a second spade. Down one. If your entry were in clubs (the ♣A instead of the ◇A), you would return your *lowest* spade asking partner to return the lower-ranking side suit.

What if you don't have an outside ace for a sure re-entry, but have an outside king? Sometimes you have to make do.

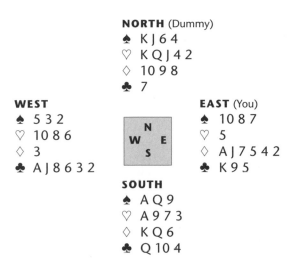

**NORTH** (Dummy)
♠ K J 6 4
♡ K Q J 4 2
♢ 10 9 8
♣ 7

**WEST**
♠ 5 3 2
♡ 10 8 6
♢ 3
♣ A J 8 6 3 2

**EAST** (You)
♠ 10 8 7
♡ 5
♢ A J 7 5 4 2
♣ K 9 5

**SOUTH**
♠ A Q 9
♡ A 9 7 3
♢ K Q 6
♣ Q 10 4

| BOTH VUL. | | DEALER SOUTH | |
| **West** | **North** | **East** | **South** |
| | | | 1NT |
| pass | 2♣ | pass | 2♡ |
| pass | 4♡ | all pass | |

Opening lead: ♢3

You seem to have found a partner who always has a singleton to lead. Even though you do not have an outside ace for a re-entry, you do have a king. Win the ♢A and return the ♢2, a suit preference play for clubs. Partner ruffs and underleads his ♣A to your ♣K to get another diamond ruff. Down one again.

Again, you can tell the lead is a singleton from the bidding.

Well, you are probably thinking, in these lovely examples that Kantar makes up I always have the ace of the suit partner leads *and* an outside king or ace too. In real life I seldom have the ace of partner's suit, or if I do, I never seem to have an outside ace or king. What should I do then? Hold the fort. If you have the ace of partner's singleton suit, and no outside entry, signal for the side suit that you think is the safer for partner to return — the lesser of evils.

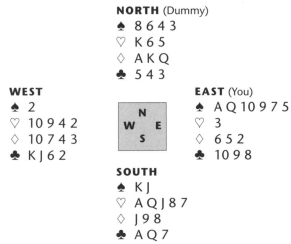

**NORTH** (Dummy)
♠ 8 6 4 3
♡ K 6 5
♢ A K Q
♣ 5 4 3

**WEST**
♠ 2
♡ 10 9 4 2
♢ 10 7 4 3
♣ K J 6 2

**EAST** (You)
♠ A Q 10 9 7 5
♡ 3
♢ 6 5 2
♣ 10 9 8

**SOUTH**
♠ K J
♡ A Q J 8 7
♢ J 9 8
♣ A Q 7

| NORTH-SOUTH VUL. | | DEALER EAST | |
| **West** | **North** | **East** | **South** |
| | | 2♠ | 3♡ |
| pass | 4♡ | all pass | |

Next time North has that hand he might cuebid 3♠ looking for a 3NT rebid from South, thus arriving at a makable game contract.

Opening lead: ♠2

After you win the opening lead, an obvious singleton, you have nothing you want partner to return. However, you *know* you don't want partner to shift to a club, so return the ♠10 asking for a diamond shift. Once partner sees you want a diamond shift, she will reason you have zilch in clubs. Of course, South realizes this too, but there is nothing South can do about those two club losers.

Now try one from the West seat:

| EAST-WEST VUL. | | DEALER NORTH | |
|---|---|---|---|
| **West** | **North** | **East** | **South** |
| | 1♣ | pass | 1♡ |
| pass | 2♡ | pass | 4♡ |
| all pass | | | |

**NORTH** (Dummy)
♠ 6 4 3
♡ A K J
♢ 6 4
♣ A K Q 10 9

**WEST** (You)
♠ A 5
♡ 5 4 3 2
♢ K 9 8 5
♣ 8 3 2

You decide desperate measures are needed and go straight away for a spade ruff by leading the ♠A. Your lead is greeted by the ♠8 from partner and the ♠10 from declarer. You continue with a spade to partner's king and declarer's ♠9. At trick three partner returns the ♠2, declarer plays the ♠Q, and you ruff. What do you play now? Can partner really be asking for a club switch? You better believe it.

This is the entire hand:

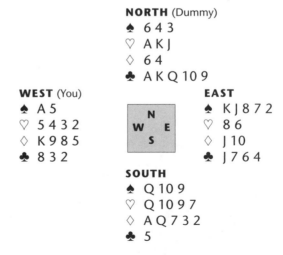

**NORTH** (Dummy)
♠ 6 4 3
♡ A K J
♢ 6 4
♣ A K Q 10 9

**WEST** (You)
♠ A 5
♡ 5 4 3 2
♢ K 9 8 5
♣ 8 3 2

**EAST**
♠ K J 8 7 2
♡ 8 6
♢ J 10
♣ J 7 6 4

**SOUTH**
♠ Q 10 9
♡ Q 10 9 7
♢ A Q 7 3 2
♣ 5

You may not agree with the bidding, but your job is to follow partner's defense unless you have an overriding reason not to (like cashing the setting trick partner may not know you have, etc.). If you
return a club (or a trump), you will eventually take a trick with your
◇K. Even if declarer establishes the clubs for three discards, it's not
enough. She still needs the diamond finesse.

Then there are hands where you can give partner an immediate ruff
while still holding the ace of trumps as a further outside entry.
Suddenly there are new considerations: how many trumps does
partner have? If partner has *more* than two trumps, you may be
able to give partner two ruffs, but if partner only has two trumps,
you can only give partner one ruff. After partner ruffs and declarer
plays a trump, partner will not be ruffing anything until the next
hand.

By delaying the ruff (when partner can only get one ruff anyway),
you might be able to arrange getting a ruff of your own, or possibly
set up a side-suit trick *before* giving partner her beloved ruff. Of
course, this means watching partner squirm a bit when she doesn't
immediately get that ruff she is expecting.

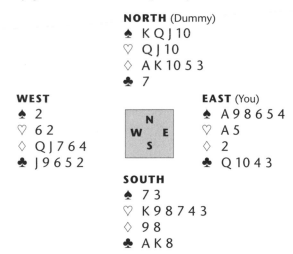

**NORTH** (Dummy)
♠ K Q J 10
♡ Q J 10
◇ A K 10 5 3
♣ 7

**WEST**
♠ 2
♡ 6 2
◇ Q J 7 6 4
♣ J 9 6 5 2

**EAST** (You)
♠ A 9 8 6 5 4
♡ A 5
◇ 2
♣ Q 10 4 3

**SOUTH**
♠ 7 3
♡ K 9 8 7 4 3
◇ 9 8
♣ A K 8

| NORTH-SOUTH VUL. DEALER NORTH | | | |
|------|-------|------|-------|
| **West** | **North** | **East** | **South** |
| | 1◇ | 1♠ | 2♡ |
| pass | 4♡ | all pass | |

Opening lead: ♠2

You play your ♠A and when declarer doesn't ruff, you know partner
has led a singleton. Restrain yourself from giving partner an immediate ruff. See that singleton diamond in your hand? See that ace
of trumps in your hand? Those are signals that are supposed to
alert you to an alternate defense. Shift to your singleton at trick

two; win the first round of hearts, return the ♠9, suit preference for diamonds, and ruff partner's diamond return. Don't look now, but that's four tricks. It takes *two* ruffs to defeat this contract.

And you don't necessarily need a singleton to make it right to delay giving partner a ruff; a doubleton might do quite nicely, thank you.

NORTH-SOUTH VUL.  DEALER WEST

| West | North | East | South |
|------|-------|------|-------|
| pass | pass | pass | 1♠ |
| 2♠[1] | 3♠ | all pass | |

1) **Michaels**: 5 hearts with an unknown five- or six-card minor.

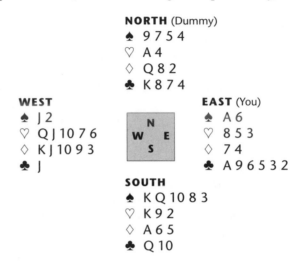

**NORTH** (Dummy)
- ♠ 9 7 5 4
- ♡ A 4
- ◇ Q 8 2
- ♣ K 8 7 4

**WEST**
- ♠ J 2
- ♡ Q J 10 7 6
- ◇ K J 10 9 3
- ♣ J

**EAST** (You)
- ♠ A 6
- ♡ 8 5 3
- ◇ 7 4
- ♣ A 9 6 5 3 2

**SOUTH**
- ♠ K Q 10 8 3
- ♡ K 9 2
- ◇ A 6 5
- ♣ Q 10

Partner leads the ♣J which has the aura of a singleton. You win the ace and declarer falsecards correctly with the queen, a card she is known to hold.

If you decide to play partner for 2-5-5-1 distribution, your best defense is to shift to a high diamond at trick two. Declarer has no winning options. If declarer wins the ace, crosses to dummy with a heart and leads a trump, you fly ace and give your partner a club ruff; after partner cashes the ◇K you get a diamond ruff. Nor does it help declarer to duck your diamond return. Partner wins and returns a diamond to dummy's queen. You win the first spade, give partner a club ruff, get a diamond ruff, etc. Down one.

A trusting partner has to realize that when you don't give her an immediate ruff, it's not because you have misread the lead, it is because you are trying to develop an outside trick *before* giving the ruff. That outside trick doesn't necessarily have to be in the form of a return ruff; it may involve setting up a winner in another suit first.

**NORTH** (Dummy)
♠ K Q 6 5
♡ Q J 8
♢ 6
♣ K Q J 10 8

**WEST**
♠ 9 3
♡ K 7 4 3
♢ K 9 7 4 3 2
♣ 6

**EAST** (You)
♠ A 8
♡ 10 9 5
♢ Q J 8
♣ A 7 5 3 2

**SOUTH**
♠ J 10 7 4 2
♡ A 6 2
♢ A 10 5
♣ 9 4

| EAST-WEST VUL. | | DEALER NORTH | |
| **West** | **North** | **East** | **South** |
|---|---|---|---|
| | 1♣ | pass | 1♠ |
| pass | 3♠ | pass | 4♠ |
| all pass | | | |

Partner leads the ♣6. When a good player leads dummy's first-bid suit, chances are that it is a singleton lead as opposed to a doubleton. You win the ace and declarer plays the inevitable ♣9, trying to sow the seeds of doubt in your mind.

If partner has specifically ♠Jxx, you can give partner a club ruff and then when you get in with the ♠A give partner a second club ruff, partner overruffing declarer. However, that's a long shot. Partner may not have three spades and partner may not have the ♠J.

A better shot is to play partner for the ♡K and shift to a heart at trick two intending to give partner a club ruff when in with the trump ace. This defense nets you four tricks: the ♣A, the ♠A, the ♡K and a club ruff.

If you give partner a club ruff at trick two, partner's ♡K vanishes on dummy's clubs. Follow the play: you give partner an immediate club ruff and partner exits with a diamond to declarer's ace. Declarer leads a spade to your ace, and if you make a belated heart shift, declarer rises with the ace, draws trumps, and discards both hearts on dummy's clubs.

Then there are hands where you have a void and therefore can't lead the suit. The trick is to get partner to lead it.

BOTH VUL.      DEALER WEST

| West | North | East | South |
|------|-------|------|-------|
| 4♠ | dbl | 5♠ | 6♡ |
| all pass | | | |

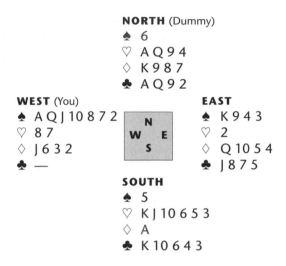

**NORTH** (Dummy)
♠ 6
♡ A Q 9 4
♢ K 9 8 7
♣ A Q 9 2

**WEST** (You)
♠ A Q J 10 8 7 2
♡ 8 7
♢ J 6 3 2
♣ —

**EAST**
♠ K 9 4 3
♡ 2
♢ Q 10 5 4
♣ J 8 7 5

**SOUTH**
♠ 5
♡ K J 10 6 5 3
♢ A
♣ K 10 6 4 3

Partner likely has the ♠K and you have one spade trick, max. Lead the ♠2, surely suit preference on the bidding! Partner wins the ♠K and gives you a club ruff. Any time you lead an 'impossible' card from known length, it should be considered a suit preference lead.

Furthermore, whenever you underlead an ace in a supported suit, there is a strong inference you have a desire for some switch, as the ace is the normal lead in a supported suit. And let's not forget those hands where you can determine from *their* bidding that partner has a side-suit void.

EAST-WEST VUL.      DEALER SOUTH

| West | North | East | South |
|------|-------|------|-------|
| | | | 1♠ |
| pass | 2♣ | pass | 3♣ |
| pass | 3♠ | pass | 4♠ |
| all pass | | | |

Opening lead: ♢4

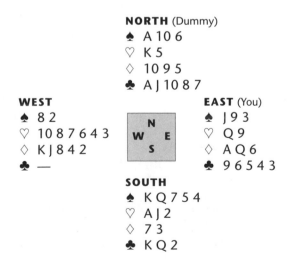

**NORTH** (Dummy)
♠ A 10 6
♡ K 5
♢ 10 9 5
♣ A J 10 8 7

**WEST**
♠ 8 2
♡ 10 8 7 6 4 3
♢ K J 8 4 2
♣ —

**EAST** (You)
♠ J 9 3
♡ Q 9
♢ A Q 6
♣ 9 6 5 4 3

**SOUTH**
♠ K Q 7 5 4
♡ A J 2
♢ 7 3
♣ K Q 2

It doesn't take a genius to work out that your partner is void in clubs. The easiest defense is to play the ◊Q at trick one (if partner doesn't have the ◊K, you are unlikely to defeat this contract), and return the ♣3, suit preference for diamonds. Partner ruffs, leads a diamond, and voila, you give partner a second club ruff.

Say you play the ◊A at trick one and return the ♣3 asking partner for a diamond return after ruffing. Now partner has to underlead the ◊K to get you in again for a second club ruff. Only you know whether your partner is up to such a play. When you are the better player, which of course you always are, do not expect partner to come up with difficult plays. It's not gonna happen.

# Overruffing positions

Anytime partner is in a position to overruff declarer or dummy, chances are your side is in pretty good shape. Even if declarer ruffs high enough to prevent an overruff, that too can cost him a trick.

**NORTH** (Dummy)
♠ A 7 4
♡ J 5 4
◊ Q 10
♣ Q J 9 6 5

**WEST**
♠ J 10 9
♡ K 7
◊ J 7 6 5 4
♣ A 7 3

**EAST** (You)
♠ 8
♡ A Q 10 8 6 3
◊ 9 8 3
♣ 8 4 2

**SOUTH**
♠ K Q 6 5 3 2
♡ 9 2
◊ A K 2
♣ K 10

NORTH-SOUTH VUL. DEALER EAST

| West | North | East | South |
|------|-------|------|-------|
|      |       | 2♡   | 2♠    |
| pass | 3♠    | pass | 4♠    |
| all pass |    |      |       |

Your weak two-bid gets partner off to the right lead on this hand, the ♡K. You signal happily with the ♡8, and partner plays a second heart to your ace. Now watch what happens if you play a third round of hearts. Declarer is ruffing, of course, but so is partner. If declarer ruffs with a low spot, partner simply overruffs; but if declarer ruffs with the king or queen, then partner suddenly has a trump trick to go with the ♣A and your two heart tricks.

I might suggest that while reading this section and the following one on the **uppercut** you remove a suit from a deck of cards and follow the promotion of the lower spot cards in the trump suit as described.

At times partner leads a suit that allows you to overruff declarer or dummy, yet, it may be in your best interest *not* to overruff.

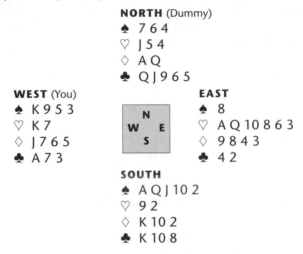

| EAST-WEST VUL. | | DEALER EAST | |
|---|---|---|---|
| **West** | **North** | **East** | **South** |
| | | 2♡ | 2♠ |
| 3♡ | 3♠ | all pass | |

**NORTH** (Dummy)
♠ 7 6 4
♡ J 5 4
◇ A Q
♣ Q J 9 6 5

**WEST** (You)
♠ K 9 5 3
♡ K 7
◇ J 7 6 5
♣ A 7 3

**EAST**
♠ 8
♡ A Q 10 8 6 3
◇ 9 8 4 3
♣ 4 2

**SOUTH**
♠ A Q J 10 2
♡ 9 2
◇ K 10 2
♣ K 10 8

You lead the ♡K and continue the suit. Partner wins the second heart, plays a third, declarer ruffing with the ♠Q. If you overruff, the ♣A is your only other defensive trick as declarer can easily draw your remaining three trumps with the ♠AJ10. But if you discard, your ♠9 promotes to a second defensive trump trick and you defeat the contract one trick.

There is yet another consideration when giving partner an overruff: declarer may decline to ruff, discarding a loser instead. Now dummy's trumps may protect declarer from further overruffs.

| BOTH VUL. | | DEALER SOUTH | |
|---|---|---|---|
| **West** | **North** | **East** | **South** |
| | | | 1♡ |
| pass | 2♣ | 2♠ | 3♡ |
| pass | 4♡ | all pass | |

**NORTH** (Dummy)
♠ J 7 3
♡ Q 7 3
◇ K Q
♣ K Q J 3 2

**WEST**
♠ A 2
♡ J 9 4
◇ 10 9 6 5
♣ 10 8 6 5

**EAST** (You)
♠ K Q 10 9 8 5
♡ 6
◇ 8 7 2
♣ A 9 7

**SOUTH**
♠ 6 4
♡ A K 10 8 5 2
◇ A J 4 3
♣ 4

Partner leads the ace and a spade and it seems right to play a third high spade, but it isn't!  Declarer, fearing an overruff promotion if she ruffs high or a simple overruff if she ruffs low, discards a club instead.  Now you are fixed.  Both dummy and declarer are out of spades, and dummy has a high enough trump card, the queen, to protect declarer from any possible overruffs.  If you play a fourth spade, declarer will discard a diamond and no matter what partner does, declarer has the rest... easily.

The mistake came at trick three. Instead of playing a high spade, cash the ♣A first and then lead a high spade.  Now let's see declarer make this hand!

# The uppercut

Once you get the knack of *not* overruffing a declarer who has a known strong trump suit (your trump holding will typically be J8xx, Q8x(x), K8x(x), A8x(x) Q9x(x) K9x(x), A9x(x), K10x(x) or A10x(x), it's only a skip and a jump to understand the **uppercut**, another play that can destroy declarer's trump holding.  The uppercut is a form of trump promotion — in reverse.  In this scenario you lead some suit in which both partner and declarer are void and partner ruffs high forcing out a trump honor.  This, in turn, promotes one of your lower trump cards to eventual top rank.

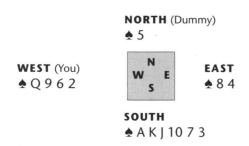

**NORTH** (Dummy)
♠ 5

**WEST** (You)
♠ Q 9 6 2

**EAST**
♠ 8 4

**SOUTH**
♠ A K J 10 7 3

In this position if partner leads a side suit in which both you and declarer are void, and declarer ruffs with the ten or jack, you gain a trick by *not* overruffing.  Now consider this scenario: you lead a suit in which both your partner and declarer are void and partner trumps with the ♠8 driving out the ♠10.  Once again, with the ten removed, you have two trump tricks just as you did when you did not overruff the ten.  This maneuver is called an **uppercut**.

Now look at this one:

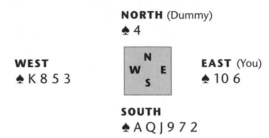

**NORTH** (Dummy)
♠ 4

**WEST**
♠ K 8 5 3

**EAST** (You)
♠ 10 6

**SOUTH**
♠ A Q J 9 7 2

Say partner leads a suit which neither you nor declarer have and declarer ruffs with the ♠9. If you overruff, that is your last trump trick; if you discard, your ♠8 promotes to a second trick. Let's turn it around again. You lead a suit that neither your partner nor declarer has; partner ruffs with the ♠10 and declarer overruffs with the jack or queen. Your ♠8 becomes an eventual second trump trick.

Another example:

| BOTH VUL. | | DEALER WEST | |
| **West** | **North** | **East** | **South** |
| 2♠[1] | pass | pass | dbl |
| pass | 3♣ | pass | 3♡ |
| pass | 4♡ | all pass | |

1) Weak

**NORTH** (Dummy)
♠ Q 8 4
♡ 9 6 4
◇ Q 4
♣ K Q 10 8 7

**WEST**
♠ A K J 7 5 3
♡ J 7 2
◇ 6 3
♣ 5 2

**EAST** (You)
♠ 6 2
♡ 10 3
◇ J 10 9 8 7 2
♣ A 4 3

**SOUTH**
♠ 10 9
♡ A K Q 8 5
◇ A K 5
♣ J 9 6

Partner starts with the two top spades, and you echo to show a doubleton. A third round of spades forces you to ruff dummy's ♠Q. But if you pusillanimously trump with the ♡3, South overruffs, draws trumps, and concedes the ♣A for ten easy tricks. However, if you courageously ruff in with the ten, you perform an uppercut. South is forced to overruff with an honor, and partner's ♡J has now been promoted to trick-taking status. That along with the ♣A spells a one-trick set.

These examples showed a defender uppercutting declarer's trump holding, but it's also possible to uppercut the dummy.

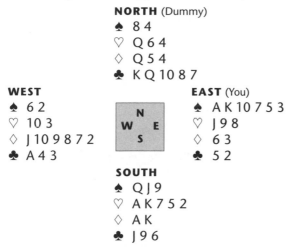

**NORTH** (Dummy)
♠ 8 4
♡ Q 6 4
♢ Q 5 4
♣ K Q 10 8 7

**WEST**
♠ 6 2
♡ 10 3
♢ J 10 9 8 7 2
♣ A 4 3

**EAST** (You)
♠ A K 10 7 5 3
♡ J 9 8
♢ 6 3
♣ 5 2

**SOUTH**
♠ Q J 9
♡ A K 7 5 2
♢ A K
♣ J 9 6

| BOTH VUL. | | DEALER EAST | |
|---|---|---|---|
| **West** | **North** | **East** | **South** |
| | | 2♠[1] | dbl |
| pass | 3♣ | pass | 3♡ |
| pass | 4♡ | all pass | |

1) Weak

Partner leads the ♠6 and the bidding tells you your best chance is to play partner for a minor-suit ace along with a trump spot that can knock out dummy's queen, perhaps promoting a trump trick for your jack. You put your plan into action and play three rounds of spades. Partner makes you look like a genius by producing the ♡10, overruffed with the queen. Your ♡J98 has blossomed into a sure trump trick and partner's ♣A is the setting trick.

You ain't seen nuttin' yet. Can you believe promoting a six-spot in the trump suit to the setting trick?

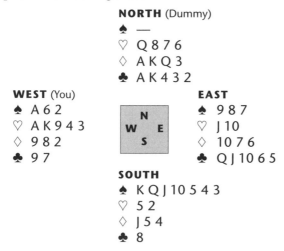

**NORTH** (Dummy)
♠ —
♡ Q 8 7 6
♢ A K Q 3
♣ A K 4 3 2

**WEST** (You)
♠ A 6 2
♡ A K 9 4 3
♢ 9 8 2
♣ 9 7

**EAST**
♠ 9 8 7
♡ J 10
♢ 10 7 6
♣ Q J 10 6 5

**SOUTH**
♠ K Q J 10 5 4 3
♡ 5 2
♢ J 5 4
♣ 8

| BOTH VUL. | | DEALER SOUTH | |
|---|---|---|---|
| **West** | **North** | **East** | **South** |
| | | | 3♠ |
| pass | 4♠ | all pass | |

You lead a high heart and admire North's gutsy 4♠ raise with a void. Obviously, North didn't know you had the ♠6!

You play a second high heart, then a third heart, partner ruffing with the ♠7, declarer overruffing with the ♠10. When declarer continues with a high spade, you win the ace and play another heart; this time partner ruffs with her last trump, the ♠9, driving out yet another spade honor from the South hand. South, having lost three tricks, remains with the ♠Q543, the shredded remains of a once glorious trump suit. You remain with the ♠62; down one.

# The forcing defense

We have seen how holding the ace of trumps gives you a lot of latitude when trying to maneuver a ruff for yourself or for your partner. When you have trump length, typically four, and are attempting to force declarer to trump, the ace of trumps is also a very important card and the defender who holds it must be careful to win it at exactly the right moment.

| BOTH VUL. | | DEALER EAST | |
|-----------|-------|------|-------|
| **West** | **North** | **East** | **South** |
| | | 1♠ | 2♡ |
| pass | 4♡ | all pass | |

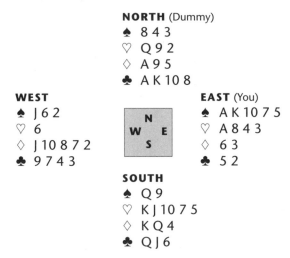

**NORTH** (Dummy)
♠ 8 4 3
♡ Q 9 2
◇ A 9 5
♣ A K 10 8

**WEST**
♠ J 6 2
♡ 6
◇ J 10 8 7 2
♣ 9 7 4 3

**EAST** (You)
♠ A K 10 7 5
♡ A 8 4 3
◇ 6 3
♣ 5 2

**SOUTH**
♠ Q 9
♡ K J 10 7 5
◇ K Q 4
♣ Q J 6

Partner leads the ♠2 and you continue with the king, ace and a third spade forcing declarer to ruff. When declarer exits with the ♡K and partner follows, you know that both you and declarer have exactly four trumps at this point. Your objective is to make *declarer* trump a spade so you can wind up with more hearts than declarer — always a good sign.

However, as long as dummy has a heart, you cannot force declarer to trump a spade; dummy will trump and declarer will remain with the same number of trumps as you — a bad sign. What you have to do (when both declarer and dummy are void in the 'force suit', spades) is take your ace of trumps when dummy is playing its *last* trump. In other words, take the third round of hearts with your ace and play a fourth spade driving out declarer's last trump. Not only do you remain with the only trump left in the game, you have a winning spade as well. Down two.

Yes, declarer can save a trick. After you duck two rounds of hearts, declarer can play her club and diamond winners allowing you to trump one of them with your low trump; down one only.

This is an example with the same theme, only a little more complex; you shouldn't have any trouble with it.

**NORTH** (Dummy)
♠ 10 4
♡ Q 10 5 2
♢ Q J 9
♣ A K 10 8

**WEST**
♠ 6 4 2
♡ 6
♢ 10 8 7 5 3
♣ 9 7 4 3

**EAST** (You)
♠ A K Q 7 5
♡ A 8 4 3
♢ 6 2
♣ 5 2

**SOUTH**
♠ J 9 3
♡ K J 9 7
♢ A K 4
♣ Q J 6

| BOTH VUL. | | DEALER EAST | |
|-----------|-------|-------------|-------|
| **West** | **North** | **East** | **South** |
| | | 1♠ | dbl |
| pass | 2♠ | pass | 3♡ |
| pass | 4♡ | all pass | |

This time you are defending against a 4-4 trump fit; on the previous hand it was a 5-3 trump fit. On the previous hand, once you forced declarer to trump you were defending against a 4-3 trump fit. When defending against a 4-4 trump fit, if either declarer or dummy trumps something you are once again defending against a 4-3 trump fit; with Axxx of trumps, you can go into your same act.

Partner leads the ♠2 and you play three rounds of spades forcing dummy to ruff. Voila, they are playing a 4-3 trump fit and you have four trumps headed by the ace. You know what you must do when declarer begins to draw trumps: take the third round of trumps, the one that exhausts dummy, and play a fourth spade removing declarer's last trump; down two. If declarer does not play a third round of trumps, you will eventually ruff a minor-suit winner for down one.

When declarer and dummy are both void in the force suit but dummy only has two trumps, win the second round of trumps, again the one that exhausts dummy. Piece of cake.

| NEITHER VUL. | | DEALER SOUTH | |
|---|---|---|---|
| **West** | **North** | **East** | **South** |
| | | | 1♠ |
| pass | 2♣ | pass | 2♠ |
| pass | 3◇ | pass | 4♣ |
| pass | 4♠ | all pass | |

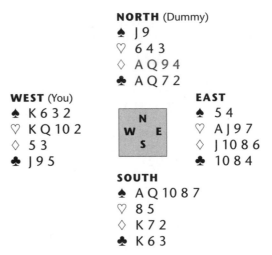

**NORTH** (Dummy)
♠ J 9
♡ 6 4 3
◇ A Q 9 4
♣ A Q 7 2

**WEST** (You)
♠ K 6 3 2
♡ K Q 10 2
◇ 5 3
♣ J 9 5

**EAST**
♠ 5 4
♡ A J 9 7
◇ J 10 8 6
♣ 10 8 4

**SOUTH**
♠ A Q 10 8 7
♡ 8 5
◇ K 7 2
♣ K 6 3

Having a keen ear for the bidding, you lead a high heart eventually forcing declarer to ruff the third round. Say declarer crosses to dummy with a minor-suit winner and runs the ♠J; *duck*! Don't even think of winning this trick. Your play with four trumps is to wait until dummy's *last* trump is played. Say declarer continues by taking a second spade finesse. This time you pounce upon the trick with your king and play a fourth heart forcing declarer to ruff again, reducing declarer to one trump while you remain with two. Down goes declarer again... but only if you take the *second* round of spades.

One last reminder about taking dummy's last trump. This play is only necessary when dummy and declarer are *both* void in the force suit. If declarer is void and dummy isn't, you don't have to wait until dummy is exhausted of trumps to continue the force; you can do it earlier.

# The dreaded ruff-sluff

No defensive play in bridge has a worse rep than giving the opponents a ruff and a sluff (letting declarer trump in one hand while discarding a loser from the other). But what if neither declarer nor dummy has a meaningful side-suit loser to discard? Now giving declarer a ruff and sluff may promote an extra trump trick(s) for you or your partner. The following examples illustrate how extra trump tricks can be promoted. But first, this repeat warning: giving a ruff and a sluff can be dangerous to your health if declarer or dummy has a certain loser that can be discarded while ruffing in the other hand. Forewarned is forearmed.

One common application of the ruff and sluff occurs when a defender leads a suit through declarer allowing partner to trump higher than dummy or forcing declarer to ruff so high that partner's trump holding promotes to a trick anyway.

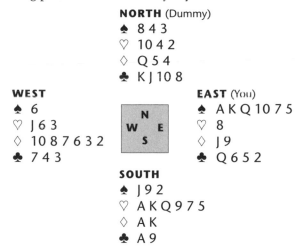

**NORTH** (Dummy)
♠ 8 4 3
♡ 10 4 2
◇ Q 5 4
♣ K J 10 8

**WEST**
♠ 6
♡ J 6 3
◇ 10 8 7 6 3 2
♣ 7 4 3

**EAST** (You)
♠ A K Q 10 7 5
♡ 8
◇ J 9
♣ Q 6 5 2

**SOUTH**
♠ J 9 2
♡ A K Q 9 7 5
◇ A K
♣ A 9

NORTH-SOUTH VUL. DEALER WEST

| West | North | East | South |
|------|-------|------|-------|
| pass | pass | 1♠ | dbl |
| pass | 2♣ | 2♠ | 4♡ |
| all pass | | | |

Opening lead. ♣6

You begin by cashing three spades, partner discarding a low diamond and a low club. Declarer figures to have eight or, more likely, nine major-suit cards. Partner's negative discards have indicated that declarer has the ◇AK and the ♣A. Therefore, declarer cannot have a side-suit loser. When you arrive at such a conclusion, *think ruff-sluff*. Lead a fourth spade hoping to promote a possible ♡Jxx in partner's hand. If declarer discards, partner's ♡J becomes the setting trick. If declarer ruffs high, partner's ♡J still becomes the setting trick.

Sometimes one of these ruff-sluff trump promotion plays will be combined with partner declining to overruff. Say these were the hearts on the previous hand:

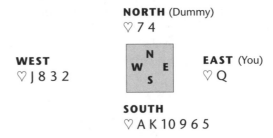

**NORTH** (Dummy)
♡ 7 4

**WEST**
♡ J 8 3 2

**EAST** (You)
♡ Q

**SOUTH**
♡ A K 10 9 6 5

When you lead a fourth spade declarer ruffs with the ♡10. If partner discards, partner winds up with two trump tricks; if partner overtrumps, one trump trick is the limit. While we're at it, notice that if partner leads something that allows you to uppercut with the ♡Q driving out a high honor, partner wins the same two heart tricks with the ♡J832.

Sometimes giving the opponents a ruff and a sluff gives partner a chance for an uppercut, promoting a trump trick for you.

NORTH-SOUTH VUL. DEALER EAST

| West | North | East | South |
|------|-------|------|-------|
|      |       | pass | 1♡ |
| 1♠[1] | 2◇ | pass | 2♡ |
| pass | 4♡ | all pass | |

1) Most experts would overcall 1♠ with such a strong suit, even though it is only a four-carder. Certainly West wants a spade lead if North becomes declarer. There is a second advantage: it is close to impossible for the opponents to arrive at 3NT now, which may be the only game they can make, as is the case here.

**NORTH** (Dummy)
♠ 9 7 2
♡ 8 7 6
◇ A K Q 8 5
♣ K Q

**WEST** (You)
♠ A K Q J
♡ 10 4 2
◇ 6 3
♣ J 9 8 2

**EAST**
♠ 10 5 3
♡ K
◇ 10 9 7 2
♣ 10 7 5 4 3

**SOUTH**
♠ 8 6 4
♡ A Q J 9 5 3
◇ J 4
♣ A 6

Most West players would cash three spades and shift to a club hoping partner has the ace. After that soft defense declarer has easy sailing, particularly when the ♡K appears the first time the suit is led from dummy.

A sharper West defender realizes that South is a heavy favorite to own the ♣A and that a far better chance to defeat this contract is to play partner to have a heart honor, any heart honor. If so, playing a fourth spade allows partner to uppercut declarer with that presumed honor, promoting your ♡10 to the setting trick.

Another time a ruff and a sluff can be used to the defender's advantage is when declarer is playing a known 4-3 trump fit and one defender has four trumps, preferably headed by an honor. In this case, trumping in either hand can hurt declarer.

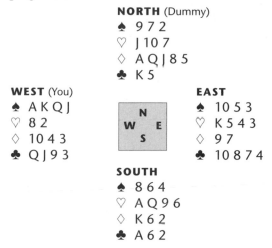

**NORTH** (Dummy)
♠ 9 7 2
♡ J 10 7
♢ A Q J 8 5
♣ K 5

**WEST** (You)
♠ A K Q J
♡ 8 2
♢ 10 4 3
♣ Q J 9 3

**EAST**
♠ 10 5 3
♡ K 5 4 3
♢ 9 7
♣ 10 8 7 4

**SOUTH**
♠ 8 6 4
♡ A Q 9 6
♢ K 6 2
♣ A 6 2

| NORTH-SOUTH VUL. | DEALER EAST | | |
|---|---|---|---|
| **West** | **North** | **East** | **South** |
| | | pass | 1♣ |
| 1♠ | 2♢ | pass | 2♡ |
| pass | 2♠ | pass | 3♢ |
| pass | 3♡ | pass | 4♡ |
| all pass | | | |

You did it again with one of your four-card overcalls; you scared them away from 3NT into a 4-3 heart fit. Now you have a chance to beat them!

You start with three rounds of spades, but where, oh where is the fourth trick coming from? Think about declarer's hand. Declarer has three spades and four hearts and has given partner a diamond preference after opening 1♣. Clearly South has a balanced hand. What about point count? There are 16 HCP missing and declarer cannot have as many as 15 or else she would have opened 1NT. Ergo partner has something like a king over there. If the king is in diamonds, it won't go away, but if it is in hearts, it may because it is finessable. But it won't be finessable if you play a fourth spade. If declarer ruffs in her hand, partner's fourth trump becomes a long trump winner. If declarer ruffs in dummy, partner pitches a diamond. When declarer leads the ♡J and ♡10 partner plays low, retaining the ♡K5, and eventually takes the setting trick.

If a ruff and a sluff can turn a 4-3 trump fit into a 4-2 trump fit, it can also turn a 4-4 trump fit into a 4-3 trump fit. Then if one defender has Axxx of trumps plus a forcing card, the declarer is in trouble and the defenders are in business.

| NEITHER VUL. | | DEALER SOUTH | |
|------|-------|------|--------|
| **West** | **North** | **East** | **South** |
| | | | 1♣ |
| 1♠ | dbl[1] | 3♠[2] | pass |
| pass | dbl | 4♡ | all pass |

1) Negative
2) Preemptive — very preemptive!

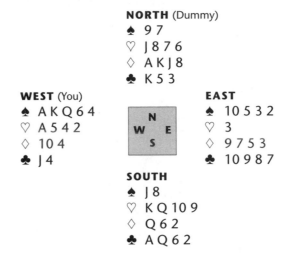

**NORTH** (Dummy)
♠ 9 7
♡ J 8 7 6
♢ A K J 8
♣ K 5 3

**WEST** (You)
♠ A K Q 6 4
♡ A 5 4 2
♢ 10 4
♣ J 4

**EAST**
♠ 10 5 3 2
♡ 3
♢ 9 7 5 3
♣ 10 9 8 7

**SOUTH**
♠ J 8
♡ K Q 10 9
♢ Q 6 2
♣ A Q 6 2

You begin with two rounds of spades and it is quite clear that neither dummy nor declarer remain with any more spades. However, your trump holding suggests giving the opponents a ruff and a sluff. In fact, it guarantees defeating the contract!

You know from the bidding that the defenders are playing a 4-4 fit. When you play a third spade, declarer has to ruff in one hand or the other. Once that happens, the opponents are playing a 4-3 and you have Axxx of trumps. You are in charge. If declarer tries to draw trumps, you know to win the third round and play another spade; down two. If declarer draws only two rounds of trumps and plays minor-suit winners, you ruff at the appropriate time; down one. If you don't play a third spade at trick three, you can't promote a second trump trick for yourself.

# Ruffing air

A defensive no-no (most of the time) is 'ruffing air'. What does that mean? An example is the best teacher:

**NORTH** (Dummy)
♠ 10 8 7
♡ A 9 8 7 4
♢ Q 6
♣ J 10 4

**WEST**
♠ 6 2
♡ J 10 5
♢ J 10 7 5 2
♣ A K 8

**EAST** (You)
♠ J 9 5
♡ K Q 6 3
♢ 4
♣ Q 9 7 6 5

**SOUTH**
♠ A K Q 4 3
♡ 2
♢ A K 9 8 3
♣ 3 2

| | | NEITHER VUL. | DEALER EAST | |
|---|---|---|---|---|
| **West** | **North** | **East** | **South** | |
| | | pass | 1♠ | |
| pass | 2♠ | pass | 4♠ | |
| all pass | | | | |

Partner leads the ace, king, and a third club, declarer ruffing. Declarer leads a diamond to the queen and a diamond from dummy. If you ruff, you are ruffing air. You are ruffing a loser with a winner! How do you know you are ruffing a loser? If declarer's diamonds were all high, declarer would be drawing trumps, not playing diamonds. But why is your ♠5 a winner?

The easiest way to explain this is to notice the difference between ruffing that diamond and not ruffing.

Say you ruff and return a high heart to the ace. Declarer, with only one diamond loser remaining, can afford to draw two rounds of trumps and then trump her diamond loser. You can't overtrump because you don't have any trumps left. It's one of the rules of the game. So declarer winds up losing two clubs and your ♠5.

Now let's see what happens when you don't trump. Declarer wins the ◇A and ruffs a diamond. You overtrump and exit with a high heart to dummy's ace. Declarer re-enters her hand with a trump and tries to ruff her last diamond with the ♠10. No good. You overtrump to defeat the contract one trick.

By not ruffing with the five you were able to overtrump dummy twice with the ♠9 and the ♠J because you hadn't shortened yourself by ruffing 'air' with the ♠5. But what about ruffing air when you can't overtrump dummy? That's a horse of a different color. Look at this example:

| EAST-WEST VUL. | | DEALER NORTH | |
|---|---|---|---|
| **West** | **North** | **East** | **South** |
| | 1◇ | pass | 1♠ |
| pass | 2♠ | pass | 4♠ |
| all pass | | | |

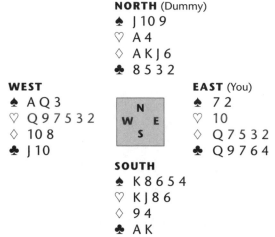

**NORTH** (Dummy)
♠ J 10 9
♡ A 4
◇ A K J 6
♣ 8 5 3 2

**WEST**
♠ A Q 3
♡ Q 9 7 5 3 2
◇ 10 8
♣ J 10

**EAST** (You)
♠ 7 2
♡ 10
◇ Q 7 5 3 2
♣ Q 9 7 6 4

**SOUTH**
♠ K 8 6 5 4
♡ K J 8 6
◇ 9 4
♣ A K

Partner leads the ♣J to declarer's ace. Declarer starts by leading a heart to the ace and a low heart off dummy. *Ruff*! True, you are ruffing air, but look at your trump holding and look at dummy's. You can't overruff dummy. Ruff, and return a trump. Partner clears trumps and declarer winds up one trick short. If you don't ruff air in this case, declarer wins the ♡K, ruffs a heart, returns to her hand via a club, ruffs her last heart, and winds up making an overtrick!

# Holding the master trump

Consider this diagram (spades are trumps):

**NORTH** (Dummy)
♠ K 6 3 2

**WEST** (You)
♠ Q J 9

**EAST**
♠ 10 8

**SOUTH**
♠ A 7 5 4

Early in the play declarer cashes the ♠AK, leaving you with the ♠Q and partner fresh out. At this moment your spade is the highest outstanding trump and is called the master trump.

When you hold the master trump and wind up taking a side-suit trick, it is almost always right to cash the master trump, taking a trump from both declarer and dummy with you.

**NORTH** (Dummy)
♠ K 6 3 2
♡ 5 3 2
◇ A K 8 4
♣ 9 4

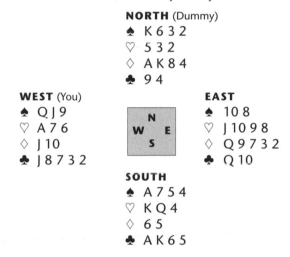

**WEST** (You)
♠ Q J 9
♡ A 7 6
◇ J 10
♣ J 8 7 3 2

**EAST**
♠ 10 8
♡ J 10 9 8
◇ Q 9 7 3 2
♣ Q 10

**SOUTH**
♠ A 7 5 4
♡ K Q 4
◇ 6 5
♣ A K 6 5

| BOTH VUL. | | DEALER SOUTH | |
|---|---|---|---|
| **West** | **North** | **East** | **South** |
| | | | 1NT |
| pass | 2♣ | pass | 2♠ |
| pass | 4♠ | all pass | |

You lead the ◇J and the play develops like this: dummy wins the opening lead and declarer continues (incorrectly) by playing the ♠AK and then a heart from dummy to the jack, king, and ace. Partner's play of the ♡J shows a sequence headed by the jack. At this point you hold the master trump. Take it, taking a trump from both declarer and dummy, leaving them with one trump each.

Declarer is now one trick short of her contract. She has nine tricks: four spades (the ♠AK, plus a small spade in each hand which can be used separately), the AK of both minors and one heart trick. Had you not cashed the master trump, declarer could make at least five tricks in spades, ruffing twice in one hand and at *least* once in the other.

Declarer made a common error by not developing a heart trick *before* cashing the ♠AK. If she had, she would have removed your fangs (the ♡A) and made the contract easily.

Say declarer begins by playing the ♠AK at tricks two and three followed by a high diamond and a diamond ruff. Should you over-ruff? *No!* You have the master trump plus an outside entry. Discard a heart and wait until you get in with the ♡A so you can take two trumps with your master trump. If you overtrump, you only get one.

Is it ever right not to cash the master trump? You don't think there's a rule without an exception, do you? The following hand demonstrates when *not* to cash the master trump.

| EAST-WEST VUL. | | DEALER SOUTH | |
|---|---|---|---|
| **West** | **North** | **East** | **South** |
| | | | 1♠ |
| pass | 1NT | pass | 3♠ |
| all pass | | | |

**NORTH** (Dummy)
♠ 6
♡ J 9 5 4
◇ K Q 10 8 7
♣ J 5 4

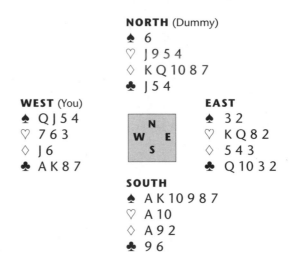

**WEST** (You)
♠ Q J 5 4
♡ 7 6 3
◇ J 6
♣ A K 8 7

**EAST**
♠ 3 2
♡ K Q 8 2
◇ 5 4 3
♣ Q 10 3 2

**SOUTH**
♠ A K 10 9 8 7
♡ A 10
◇ A 9 2
♣ 9 6

Somehow the opponents always seem to stop short when trumps aren't breaking. You begin with three rounds of clubs, declarer ruffing. Declarer continues with the ♠AK and ♠10 to your ♠J, partner discarding the ♡8. You are on lead with the ♠J and you have the master trump, the ♠Q, but you should not take it. Why?

*Because dummy has a side suit that is likely to run.* As long as you retain your master trump, declarer cannot use dummy's diamonds. Follow partner's encouraging heart signal and exit a heart to the queen and ace. When declarer begins to play diamonds, ruff the third round, and collect the setting trick in hearts. Had you cashed the master trump and then shifted to a heart, you would not get a heart trick; the heart loser would go off on a winning diamond.

# Practice Hands

**Hand 1**

**NORTH** (Dummy)
♠ 8 4 3
♡ Q 10 2
◊ A Q 5
♣ K 10 8 7

**WEST**
♠ A K Q 6
♡ 6
◊ J 10 8 7
♣ 9 6 4 3

```
  N
W   E
  S
```

**EAST** (You)
♠ J 7 5 2
♡ A 8 4 3
◊ 9 4 3
♣ 5 2

**SOUTH**
♠ 10 9
♡ K J 9 7 5
◊ K 6 2
♣ A Q J

| EAST-WEST VUL. | | DEALER EAST | |
|---|---|---|---|
| **West** | **North** | **East** | **South** |
| | | pass | 1♡ |
| 1♠ | 2♣ | 2♠ | 3♣ |
| pass | 3♡ | pass | 4♡ |
| all pass | | | |

Partner leads the ♠Q, and continues with the ♠K and ♠A when you signal to show an even number. Declarer ruffs and plays on hearts. You have to win the *third* round of hearts in order to force South to ruff when you play your last spade. Your ♡8 is the setting trick.

**Hand 2**

**NORTH** (Dummy)
♠ K Q 4 2
♡ J 7 6
◊ —
♣ A K J 8 7 6

**WEST** (You)
♠ 9
♡ A K Q 9 8 4
◊ J 5 3
♣ Q 4 2

```
  N
W   E
  S
```

**EAST**
♠ 10 8 7 5 3
♡ 5 2
◊ 10 8
♣ 10 9 5 3

**SOUTH**
♠ A J 6
♡ 10 3
◊ A K Q 9 7 6 4 2
♣ —

| BOTH VUL. | | DEALER SOUTH | |
|---|---|---|---|
| **West** | **North** | **East** | **South** |
| | | | 1◊ |
| 1♡ | 2♣ | pass | 3◊ |
| pass | 3♠ | pass | 5◊ |
| all pass | | | |

You play two high hearts and partner plays high-low. Now what? Don't even think of switching to your singleton spade! Declarer must have the ♠A for all that jumping around as well as solid diamonds. So what chance do you have? One small one. If partner has the ◊10 you can beat this contract. Play a low heart. If partner comes up with the ◊10, your ◊J will be the setting trick. Would I let you down? Of course partner comes up with the ◊10.

| EAST-WEST VUL. | | DEALER EAST | |
|---|---|---|---|
| **West** | **North** | **East** | **South** |
| | | 1♢ | 1♠ |
| pass | 2♢ | dbl | pass |
| pass | 3♠ | all pass | |

**Hand 3**

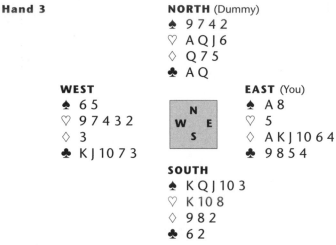

NORTH (Dummy)
♠ 9 7 4 2
♡ A Q J 6
♢ Q 7 5
♣ A Q

WEST
♠ 6 5
♡ 9 7 4 3 2
♢ 3
♣ K J 10 7 3

EAST (You)
♠ A 8
♡ 5
♢ A K J 10 6 4
♣ 9 8 5 4

SOUTH
♠ K Q J 10 3
♡ K 10 8
♢ 9 8 2
♣ 6 2

Your double emphasized a good diamond suit, and partner leads it. You win the ◇10 and continue diamonds, partner discarding a club. Now that you know partner has a singleton, you can do some planning. Shift to your singleton heart, and upon winning the ♠A lead a diamond for partner to ruff. Partner returns a heart for you to ruff. Down one. Masterful.

| BOTH VUL. | | DEALER NORTH | |
|---|---|---|---|
| **West** | **North** | **East** | **South** |
| | pass | 2♡ | dbl |
| pass | 3♣ | pass | 3♠ |
| pass | 4♠ | all pass | |

**Hand 4**

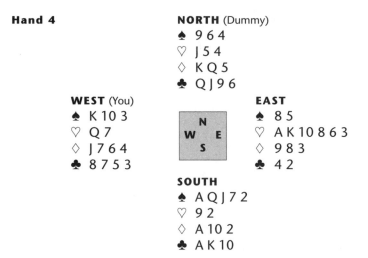

NORTH (Dummy)
♠ 9 6 4
♡ J 5 4
♢ K Q 5
♣ Q J 9 6

WEST (You)
♠ K 10 3
♡ Q 7
♢ J 7 6 4
♣ 8 7 5 3

EAST
♠ 8 5
♡ A K 10 8 6 3
♢ 9 8 3
♣ 4 2

SOUTH
♠ A Q J 7 2
♡ 9 2
♢ A 10 2
♣ A K 10

You lead the ♡Q, which holds, and continue when partner encourages. Partner leads a third heart, which declarer ruffs with the ♠Q. Don't fall for it: you must not overruff! Later, you'll be rewarded with two spade tricks, not one. Play it out.

# Test Yourself

1)

**NORTH** (Dummy)
♠ A Q 6 2
♡ J 5
◇ A Q J 5 3
♣ K Q

**EAST** (You)
♠ 8 5 4
♡ A K 10 8 6 3
◇ 9 8
♣ A J

| | | BOTH VUL. | | DEALER NORTH | |
| --- | --- | --- | --- | --- | --- |
| | **West** | **North** | **East** | **South** |
| | | 1◇ | 1♡ | pass |
| | pass | dbl | 2♡ | 3♣ |
| | pass | 3♡ | pass | 4♣ |
| | all pass | | | |

Partner leads the ♡4.  You win the ♡K and cash the ♡A, partner playing the ♡7, declarer the ♡2 and ♡9.  What do you do next?

*Solution on page 184*

2)

**NORTH** (Dummy)
♠ K Q
♡ K J 10 5
◇ K Q J 5
♣ J 6 2

**EAST** (You)
♠ J 10 9 8
♡ Q 9 3
◇ 9 8
♣ A K Q 4

| | EAST-WEST VUL. | | DEALER EAST | |
| --- | --- | --- | --- | --- |
| | **West** | **North** | **East** | **South** |
| | | | 1♣ | dbl |
| | pass | 2♣ | pass | 2♡ |
| | pass | 4♡ | all pass | |

Partner leads the ♣3, and three rounds of clubs live.  What now?

*Solution on page 184*

3)

**NORTH** (Dummy)
♠ J 8 4
♡ K Q J
◇ J 7 4 3
♣ Q 4 2

**EAST** (You)
♠ Q 10 9 7
♡ 10 5
◇ K Q 10
♣ 10 8 7 5

| | NORTH-SOUTH VUL. | DEALER SOUTH | |
| --- | --- | --- | --- |
| | **West** | **North** | **East** | **South** |
| | | | | 1◇ |
| | 3♣ | 3◇ | pass | 5◇ |
| | all pass | | | |

Partner leads the ♣K (king from AK at the five- or six-level).  Declarer ruffs and plays ace and a diamond, partner discarding a club on the second diamond.  You are in with the ◇Q.  What now?

*Solution on page 185*

NORTH-SOUTH VUL. DEALER SOUTH

| West | North | East | South |
|------|-------|------|-------|
|      |       |      | 1♠    |
| 2♡   | 3♡    | pass | 3♠    |
| pass | 4♠    | all pass |   |

*Solution on page 185*

4)

**NORTH** (Dummy)
♠ K 8 7 6
♡ 9 7 6 3
◇ Q 9
♣ A K J

**WEST** (You)
♠ J 10 9
♡ K Q J 10 2
◇ A 7 5
♣ 7 5

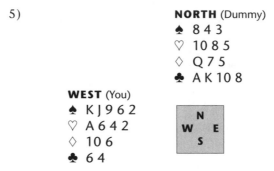

You lead the ♡K; partner overtakes and returns a heart, declarer following. What is your plan?

NORTH-SOUTH VUL. DEALER WEST

| West | North | East | South |
|------|-------|------|-------|
| pass | pass  | pass | 1♡    |
| 1♠   | 2♡    | 2♠   | 4♡    |
| all pass |   |      |       |

*Solution on page 186*

5)

**NORTH** (Dummy)
♠ 8 4 3
♡ 10 8 5
◇ Q 7 5
♣ A K 10 8

**WEST** (You)
♠ K J 9 6 2
♡ A 6 4 2
◇ 10 6
♣ 6 4

Your ♠6 goes to partner's ace, and he returns your suit. Declarer ruffs the third round with the ♡9 and plays the ♡K. What's your plan?

NORTH-SOUTH VUL. DEALER WEST

| West | North | East | South |
|------|-------|------|-------|
| pass | 1NT   | 2♡   | 4♠    |
| all pass |   |      |       |

*Solution on page 186*

6)

**NORTH** (Dummy)
♠ J 8 7 3
♡ K J 8
◇ A J 10
♣ A 10 3

**EAST** (You)
♠ —
♡ A 9 7 6 5 2
◇ K 8 4
♣ J 6 5 2

Partner leads the ♡4, and dummy puts in the ♡J. How do you plan to defend?

7)

**NORTH** (Dummy)
♠ Q 7 4 2
♡ K Q J
♢ 10 7
♣ Q 9 7 6

**EAST** (You)
♠ 8 3
♡ A 9 6 4
♢ J 9 8 4
♣ A 8 2

| NORTH-SOUTH VUL. | DEALER WEST | | |
|---|---|---|---|
| **West** | **North** | **East** | **South** |
| pass | pass | pass | 1♠ |
| pass | 3♠ | pass | 4♠ |
| all pass | | | |

Partner leads the ♣10 and dummy plays low.  What is your plan?

*Solution on page 187*

8)

**NORTH**
♠ 8 6 4
♡ 6
♢ Q 4 2
♣ A K Q 10 8 7

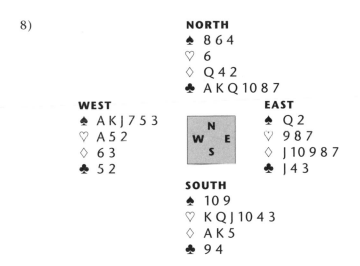

**WEST**
♠ A K J 7 5 3
♡ A 5 2
♢ 6 3
♣ 5 2

**EAST**
♠ Q 2
♡ 9 8 7
♢ J 10 9 8 7
♣ J 4 3

**SOUTH**
♠ 10 9
♡ K Q J 10 4 3
♢ A K 5
♣ 9 4

| NEITHER VUL. | DEALER EAST | | |
|---|---|---|---|
| **West** | **North** | **East** | **South** |
| | | pass | 1♡ |
| 1♠ | 2♣ | pass | 2♡ |
| pass | 2♠[1] | pass | 4♡ |
| all pass | | | |

1)  Looking for a spade stopper

This one is a little different.  Looking at all four hands, can you see any way for the defenders to beat 4♡, if South plays properly?

*Solution on page 187*

# Test Yourself — Solutions

BOTH VUL.          DEALER NORTH

| West | North | East | South |
|------|-------|------|-------|
|      | 1◇    | 1♡   | pass  |
| pass | dbl   | 2♡   | 3♣    |
| pass | 3♡    | pass | 4♣    |
| all pass |    |      |       |

**Trick 1:** ♡4 ♡5 ♡K ♡2
**Trick 2:** ♡A ♡9 ♡7 ♡J
**Trick 3:** ?

1)

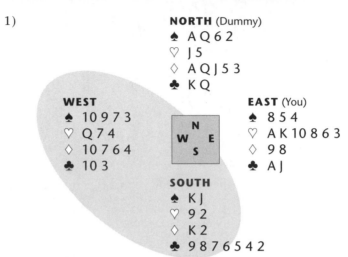

NORTH (Dummy)
♠ A Q 6 2
♡ J 5
◇ A Q J 5 3
♣ K Q

WEST
♠ 10 9 7 3
♡ Q 7 4
◇ 10 7 6 4
♣ 10 3

EAST (You)
♠ 8 5 4
♡ A K 10 8 6 3
◇ 9 8
♣ A J

SOUTH
♠ K J
♡ 9 2
◇ K 2
♣ 9 8 7 6 5 4 2

Partner started with ♡Q74 and didn't raise. Partner must be near flat broke on the outside, so look to the trump suit. Play three rounds of hearts voiding partner, win the first club and play a fourth heart. Partner may be able to uppercut dummy and promote your ♣J to the setting trick. Partner needs the ♣10x or the ♣9xx.

EAST-WEST VUL.          DEALER EAST

| West | North | East | South |
|------|-------|------|-------|
|      |       | 1♣   | dbl   |
| pass | 2♣    | pass | 2♡    |
| pass | 4♡    | all pass |    |

**Trick 1:** ♣3 ♣2 ♣Q ♣5
**Trick 2:** ♣9 ♣6 ♣K ♣8
**Trick 3:** ♣7 ♣J ♣A ♣10
**Trick 4:** ?

2)

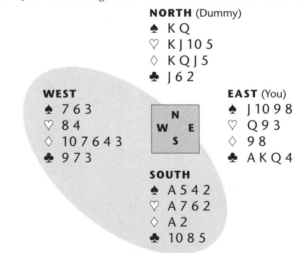

NORTH (Dummy)
♠ K Q
♡ K J 10 5
◇ K Q J 5
♣ J 6 2

WEST
♠ 7 6 3
♡ 8 4
◇ 10 7 6 4 3
♣ 9 7 3

EAST (You)
♠ J 10 9 8
♡ Q 9 3
◇ 9 8
♣ A K Q 4

SOUTH
♠ A 5 4 2
♡ A 7 6 2
◇ A 2
♣ 10 8 5

You know that declarer has the missing aces for his takeout double. Declarer knows you have all the missing points for your opening bid. In other words, declarer knows you have the ♡Q! No matter. If you play a fourth club and partner can force a heart honor from dummy, your ♡9 becomes the setting trick. It is your best chance.

3)

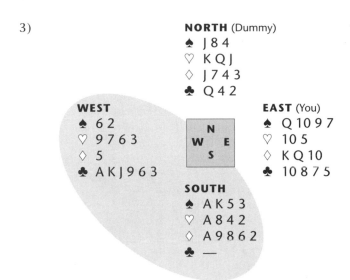

**NORTH** (Dummy)
♠ J 8 4
♡ K Q J
♢ J 7 4 3
♣ Q 4 2

**WEST**
♠ 6 2
♡ 9 7 6 3
♢ 5
♣ A K J 9 6 3

**EAST** (You)
♠ Q 10 9 7
♡ 10 5
♢ K Q 10
♣ 10 8 7 5

**SOUTH**
♠ A K 5 3
♡ A 8 4 2
♢ A 9 8 6 2
♣ —

| West | North | East | South |
|------|-------|------|-------|

NORTH-SOUTH VUL. DEALER SOUTH

| West | North | East | South |
|------|-------|------|-------|
|      |       |      | 1♢    |
| 3♣   | 3♢    | pass | 5♢    |
| all pass |    |      |       |

**Trick 1:** ♣K ♣2 ♣8 ♢2
**Trick 2:** ♢A ♢5 ♢3 ♢10
**Trick 3:** ♢6 ♣3 ♢J ♢Q
**Trick 4:** ?

Declarer is known to hold five diamonds and no clubs, therefore he is 4-4 in the majors and he holds all the missing honors. In order to ensure one more trick, cash the master trump and exit a club or a heart. With one trump remaining in each hand, declarer can neither ruff two spades in dummy (after discarding one on the ♡A) nor ruff two clubs in the closed hand. Down one.

Declarer misplayed the hand badly. After cashing the ♢A, declarer should go about his business cashing heart and spade winners, discarding a spade from dummy on the fourth heart. All you can take will be your two trump tricks, as declarer will be able to ruff two spades in dummy.

4)

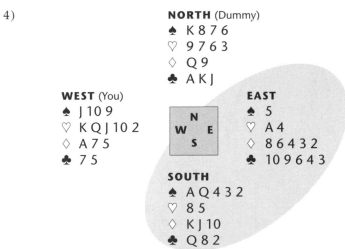

**NORTH** (Dummy)
♠ K 8 7 6
♡ 9 7 6 3
♢ Q 9
♣ A K J

**WEST** (You)
♠ J 10 9
♡ K Q J 10 2
♢ A 7 5
♣ 7 5

**EAST**
♠ 5
♡ A 4
♢ 8 6 4 3 2
♣ 10 9 6 4 3

**SOUTH**
♠ A Q 4 3 2
♡ 8 5
♢ K J 10
♣ Q 8 2

NORTH-SOUTH VUL. DEALER SOUTH

| West | North | East | South |
|------|-------|------|-------|
|      |       |      | 1♠    |
| 2♡   | 3♡    | pass | 3♠    |
| pass | 4♠    | all pass |    |

**Trick 1:** ♡K ♡3 ♡A ♡5
**Trick 2:** ♡10 ♡6 ♡4 ♡8
**Trick 3:** ?

Declarer must have the 12 missing high card points: the ♠AQ, ♢K and ♣Q. So where does that leave you? It leaves you needing to find partner with the ♠5! Cash the ♢A and lead a low heart. If partner has that little gem and plays it, it forces an honor from South and promotes your trump holding to the setting trick. Far out.

NORTH-SOUTH VUL. DEALER WEST

| West | North | East | South |
|------|-------|------|-------|
| pass | pass | pass | 1♡ |
| 1♠ | 2♡ | 2♠ | 4♡ |
| all pass | | | |

**Trick 1:** ♠6 ♠3 ♠A ♠7
**Trick 2:** ♠10 ♠Q ♠K ♠4
**Trick 3:** ♠J ♠8 ♠5 ♡9
**Trick 4:** ♡K ?

5)

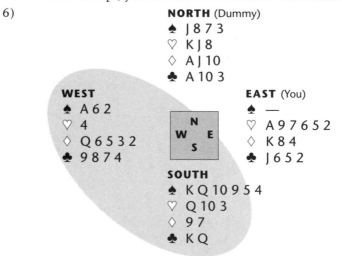

**NORTH** (Dummy)
♠ 8 4 3
♡ 10 8 5
◇ Q 7 5
♣ A K 10 8

**WEST** (You)
♠ K J 9 6 2
♡ A 6 4 2
◇ 10 6
♣ 6 4

**EAST**
♠ A 10 5
♡ 3
◇ J 9 3 2
♣ J 7 5 3 2

**SOUTH**
♠ Q 7
♡ K Q J 9 7
◇ A K 8 4
♣ Q 9

Don't win this trick! You want to force declarer, but you can't while dummy still has a trump. You must win the *third* round of trumps and play a spade, leaving you with the last trump after he ruffs. If he abandons trumps, you ruff the third round of either minor.

NORTH-SOUTH VUL. DEALER WEST

| West | North | East | South |
|------|-------|------|-------|
| pass | 1NT | 2♡ | 4♠ |
| all pass | | | |

**Trick 1:** ♡4 ♡J  ?

6)

**NORTH** (Dummy)
♠ J 8 7 3
♡ K J 8
◇ A J 10
♣ A 10 3

**WEST**
♠ A 6 2
♡ 4
◇ Q 6 5 3 2
♣ 9 8 7 4

**EAST** (You)
♠ —
♡ A 9 7 6 5 2
◇ K 8 4
♣ J 6 5 2

**SOUTH**
♠ K Q 10 9 5 4
♡ Q 10 3
◇ 9 7
♣ K Q

Take the ♡A and return the ♡9, suit preference for diamonds, hoping that the ♡4 was singleton. Partner ruffs, and returns a diamond. Declarer can't avoid a diamond loser now, as well as the two tricks already lost and the ♠A. If partner plays back anything else at trick three, the diamond loser goes on the ♣A. The diamond switch removes dummy's entry while the club suit is still blocked. Declarer is going two down. When partner gets in with the ♠A, she'll put you back in with a diamond and ruff another heart.

7)

**NORTH** (Dummy)
- ♠ Q 7 4 2
- ♡ K Q J
- ◇ 10 7
- ♣ Q 9 7 6

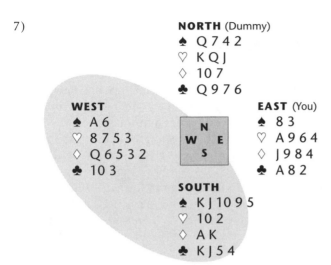

**WEST**
- ♠ A 6
- ♡ 8 7 5 3
- ◇ Q 6 5 3 2
- ♣ 10 3

**EAST** (You)
- ♠ 8 3
- ♡ A 9 6 4
- ◇ J 9 8 4
- ♣ A 8 2

**SOUTH**
- ♠ K J 10 9 5
- ♡ 10 2
- ◇ A K
- ♣ K J 5 4

| NORTH-SOUTH VUL. | DEALER WEST | | |
|---|---|---|---|
| **West** | **North** | **East** | **South** |
| pass | pass | pass | 1♠ |
| pass | 3♠ | pass | 4♠ |
| all pass | | | |

**Trick 1:** ♣10 ♣6?

This a hand where you don't need to work out whether the ♣10 is singleton or doubleton — it doesn't matter, since you have the ♡A. Win the ♣A and return the ♣8, suit preference showing partner where your entry lies. If the club lead is a singleton, partner gets two quick ruffs. If it is a doubleton, partner needs a quick trump entry.

8)

**NORTH**
- ♠ 8 6 4
- ♡ 6
- ◇ Q 4 2
- ♣ A K Q 10 8 7

**WEST**
- ♠ A K J 7 5 3
- ♡ A 5 2
- ◇ 6 3
- ♣ 5 2

**EAST**
- ♠ Q 2
- ♡ 9 8 7
- ◇ J 10 9 8 7
- ♣ J 4 3

**SOUTH**
- ♠ 10 9
- ♡ K Q J 10 4 3
- ◇ A K 5
- ♣ 9 6

| NEITHER VUL. | DEALER EAST | | |
|---|---|---|---|
| **West** | **North** | **East** | **South** |
| | | pass | 1♡ |
| 1♠ | 2♣ | pass | 2♡ |
| pass | 2♠[1] | pass | 4♡ |
| all pass | | | |

1) Looking for a spade stopper

West leads three rounds of spades; East ruffs with the ♡7, forcing declarer to overruff. South leads a high trump; West wins the ♡A and plays yet another spade. East ruffs in with his last heart, the ♡9, forcing South to overruff again with an honor. Don't look now, but the ♡5 just became the setting trick. Wow — a double uppercut!

## Key ideas from Chapter 6

- If partner is leading from a likely doubleton and you have the ace in that suit with no outside entry, signal encouragement; don't play the ace. If you have a sure outside entry, win the ace and return the suit giving suit preference.
- If you think partner has led a singleton and you have the ace, win the trick and return the suit giving suit preference.
- If partner leads a singleton and you have that ace plus the ace of trumps, but you can only give partner one ruff, you have two options available before giving partner a ruff:
    1) Shift to your own short suit. When you get in with the ace of trumps, give partner a ruff and get one in return.
    2) Build up an outside trick first, partner's ruff can come later. Timing in these two cases can be critical.
- Refusing an overruff of a known strong trump holding can generate extra trump tricks when holding intermediate spot cards.
- Uppercutting declarer or dummy often promotes a trump trick for partner.
- When you are playing the forcing game and both declarer and dummy are void in the force suit, take your trump winner when the short hand's *last* trump is played.
- Don't ruff air if you can later overruff dummy in that suit.
- When holding the master trump, cash it unless it can be used to prevent declarer from running a long suit.
- When holding the master trump plus an outside entry, and there is no danger of losing any side-suit tricks, do not overruff declarer or dummy. Wait until you get in with your outside trick and then cash the master trump, taking a trump from each of their hands.
- A ruff-sluff is a wonderful play when declarer has no side-suit losers, an ugly play otherwise.
- Giving a ruff and a sluff while voiding yourself or your partner at the same time, allows for later uppercut or over-ruff possibilities — particularly if either you or partner has a trump entry.

# Doubling for the Lead

*Double, double, toil and trouble.*

SHAKESPEARE, 'MACBETH'

Bidding methods in the modern game of contract bridge are constantly evolving, and nowhere is this more obvious than in the proliferation of the various uses for 'double' that have entered the arena. For years players were content with just two doubles — the takeout double (asking partner to bid), and the penalty double (asking partner to shut up). But that's history. Theoreticians have come up with the negative double, the responsive double, the support double, the balancing double, the competitive double, the game-try double, and even the 'snapdragon' double. Help!

And guess what? This chapter is about yet another double, the **lead-directing double**. This is a big-time double, because hundreds, possibly thousands, of points can be riding on the opening lead after you or your partner make a lead-directing double.

A major advantage of using lead-directing doubles in the sequences discussed in this chapter (as well as some not discussed), is the **negative inference** factor. When partner does *not* double an artificial bid or cuebid, you can rule out that suit as an opening lead choice if it's a close call.

A lead-directing double has two outstanding characteristics: (1) it is a penalty double so partner is expected to pass; (2) it strongly suggests a particular lead. Partner had better be listening!

Most lead-directing doubles fall into these categories:

1. Doubles of voluntarily-bid suit slams
2. Doubles of artificial bids (Stayman etc.) and cuebids (usually at the four level or higher)
3. Doubles of 3NT
4. Miscellaneous lead-directing doubles

See page 202 for a discussion of doubles of 6NT.

# Doubles of voluntarily-bid suit slams

Notice that word 'voluntarily'. The opponents may bid a slam as a sacrifice; doubling a sacrifice does not call for any particular lead, it is a penalty double pure and simple.

Doubling a voluntarily-bid slam asks for a particular lead. Of course, if you can beat the slam regardless of what lead your doubles calls for, double anyway. However, most slams require a specific lead to ensure defeat. There are two main situations:

1. Doubling a slam, with neither defender having bid.
2. Doubling a slam, with one or both defenders having bid.

| West | North | East | South |
|------|-------|------|-------|
|      |       | (You) |      |
|      |       |      | 1♠ |
| pass | 2♡ | pass | 3♢ |
| pass | 4♠ | pass | 6♣ |
| pass | pass | dbl | all pass |

When you double a slam without having previously bid, you are telling partner in no uncertain terms not to lead an unbid suit, the expected lead, and not to lead a trump. In this example clubs would be the expected lead and your double says *don't* lead that suit and don't lead a trump.

Basically partner is reduced to leading one of the suits they have bid, a heart or a diamond. You could be void in one of those suits or you could have the AK of one of those suits. Partner has to look at her hand and decide. If it's a close call, partner leads dummy's first-bid suit.

If you (or partner) have bid a suit and then double a slam, the rules are a bit different. The double forbids the lead of any suit the partnership has bid, as well as, of course, a trump. Doubles of suit slams call for unexpected leads, usually dummy's first-bid suit.

| West | North | East | South |
|------|-------|------|-------|
|      |       | (You) |      |
|      |       |      | 1♠    |
| pass | 2♣    | 2♡   | 3♠    |
| pass | 4♠    | pass | 4NT   |
| pass | 5♡    | pass | 6♠    |
| pass | pass  | dbl  | all pass |

What lead are you asking for this time? Well, it can't be a heart, the suit you have bid, or a spade, a trump. Already partner has a 50-50 shot of getting it right. You probably want a club lead as it doesn't seem possible that you could hold the ◇AK — South would be bidding a slam with no diamond control.

The most common application of a Lightner Double takes place when a preemptive bidder doubles a slam contract. This double usually shows a side-suit void. The opening leader has to figure out where it is. For example, if you open 4♡ holding

♠ 63   ♡ AKJ9843   ◇ —   ♣ J1032

and the opponents arrive at 6♠, partner on lead, lash them with a double. Your double forbids a heart or a spade lead and alerts your partner to the likelihood of a minor-suit void.

For the record the lead-directing double of a voluntarily-bid suit slam is called a **Lightner Double**, after bridge legend Theodore Lightner, who devised all of this in 1929 — an idea that has stood the test of time.

# Doubles of artificial bids

An artificial bid doesn't necessarily show length in the suit being bid, it has an altogether different meaning. The most common example is the Stayman response of 2♣ to a 1NT opening bid (or 3♣ to a 2NT opening bid). A double of an artificial bid is both a penalty double and a lead-directing double. What does that mean? It means that the double has to be made with high honors as well as length in the suit at the lower levels. After you double an artificial bid, the opponents usually move on to some other contract. If your partner is on lead, he usually leads the suit you doubled. Therefore, you have to be able to stand the lead against other contracts.

| West | North | East | South |
|------|-------|------|-------|
|      |       | (You) |      |
|      |       |      | 1NT  |
| pass | 2♣    | ?    |      |

Say you hold either of these hands:

(a) ♠ A2  ♡ 654  ◇ 642  ♣ KQJ104
(b) ♠ A2  ♡ K4  ◇ J43  ♣ J97643

With hand (a) double; you can stand a club lead against any contract. With hand (b) pass; you can't stand a club lead against a suit contract.

Jacoby Transfer responses to notrump openings are all the rage these days. They are a valuable tool because they allow the hand to be played from the notrump bidder's side of the table, a decided advantage; however, they are vulnerable to lead-directing doubles.

| West | North | East | South |
|------|-------|------|-------|
|      |       | (You) |      |
|      |       |      | 1NT  |
| pass | 2♡[1] | ?    |      |

1) Transfer

Say you hold:

(a) ♠ 32  ♡ AQJ87  ◇ K43  ♣ J98
(b) ♠ J87  ♡ Q97643  ◇ QJ3  ♣ 2

With hand (a), double 2♡; you can stand a heart lead against a spade or a notrump contract. Also, your double may allow your side to compete in hearts. With hand (b), pass 2♡. Your heart suit is too weak to direct a lead against a likely spade contract.

Doubling a two-level Stayman or Jacoby response typically shows a five-card suit headed by three or more honor cards, or a six-card suit headed by two of the top three or three of the top five honors. It can be compared to the strength of a suit necessary for a vulnerable overcall. (Playing matchpoints it is not a bad idea to double a Stayman response with something like ♣KQJ10 of the suit. Even though everyone expects you to have a five- or six-card suit and things may backfire, it is well worth the risk to get the lead at that form of scoring.)

## When the opponents go through Blackwood

Another great opportunity to make a lead-directing double arises when the opponents go through Blackwood giving you an opportunity to double a Blackwood response (partner on lead, of course).

| West | North | East | South |
|------|-------|------|-------|
|      |       | (You) |      |
|      |       |      | 1♠ |
| pass | 3♠ | pass | 4NT |
| pass | 5♡ | ? | 5NT |
| pass | 6♣ | ? | 6♠ |
| all pass |  |  |  |

Say you hold one of these hands:

(a) ♠ 65  ♡ J54  ◇ J43  ♣ KQ764
(b) ♠ 65  ♡ KJ108  ◇ 976  ♣ J432
(c) ♠ 65  ♡ 9542  ◇ KQ94  ♣ 853

With hand (a), double 6♣; with hand (b), double 5♡; with hand (c), pass everything. Partner will work out to lead a club if you double 6♣, a heart if you double 5♡, and if you pass throughout he will assume that if you have anything at all, it must be in diamonds.

## Doubling for the fourth suit

This one is a little touchy. Consider this sequence:

| West | North | East | South |
|------|-------|------|-------|
|      |       | (You) |      |
|      |       |      | 1◇ |
| pass | 1♠ | pass | 2♣ |
| pass | 2♡ | ? | 2NT |
| pass | 3NT | all pass |  |

Does responder have hearts? Sometimes. But North may hold:

♠ AK764  ♡ 86  ◇ A72  ♣ J108

and have no intelligent forcing rebid available over 2♣. 2♡, the fourth suit, is the answer — at least it's forcing. Be on the alert to double fourth-suit auctions holding five or six cards in the suit headed by two or three top honors.

## Doubling a splinter jump

Another artificial bid now appearing with startling frequency is the splinter jump:

| West | North | East | South |
|------|-------|------|-------|
|      |       | (You)|       |
|      |       |      | 1♡    |
| pass | 4♣    | ?    |       |

This leap to 4♣, as most play, shows a singleton (or void) in clubs with heart support plus slam interest. A double of 4♣ says, 'Partner, my strength is in clubs, so from my point of view, even though dummy is going to have a singleton or void in clubs, that is still the safest lead'.

Say you hold:

> (a) ♠ 876  ♡ 54  ◇ 976  ♣ AQ1076
> (b) ♠ QJ5  ♡ 54  ◇ KQ10  ♣ QJ986

With hand (a), double 4♣; you can't stand any other lead. With hand (b), pass 4♣. The normal lead in this sequence is either a spade or a diamond and you can stand either. Don't throw your partner off the scent by doubling 4♣.

Sometimes an opponent makes a four-level splinter jump in a suit your partner has bid:

| West | North | East | South |
|------|-------|------|-------|
|      |       | (You)|       |
|      |       |      | 1◇    |
| 2♣   | 4♣    | ?    |       |

North has a singleton club, a strong hand, and five or six diamonds. If you want a club lead against a diamond contract, double.

The double of a splinter jump in partner's suit at the *three*-level carries a different message; it is not lead-directing, it says the opponents have stolen your bid!

There are other ways to play this double, too. Some play it not as lead-directing, but suggesting a sacrifice at appropriate vulnerability. Others, regarding it as unlikely that you will want the lead of dummy's short suit, play it to ask for the lead of the lower-ranking of the remaining two side suits.

| West | North | East | South |
|------|-------|------|-------|
|      |       | (You) |      |
|      |       |      | 1♣ |
| 1♠ | 3♠ | ? | |

Say you have:

♠ K1087  ♡ A843  ◇ Q103  ♣ 92

Double 3♠ telling partner you have enough to compete to 3♠.

## Doubling an artificial opening bid or an artificial response to an opening bid

The most common artificial opening bid is 2♣, used as a forcing opening bid by players who play Weak Two-bids. In response to 2♣, the response of 2◇ is also artificial, either a waiting response or perhaps some other artificial control-showing or denying response. In any case, lead-directing doubles are available.

| West | North | East | South |
|------|-------|------|-------|
|      |       | (You) |      |
|      | 2♣ | dbl | |

This double shows a hand with long, strong, clubs.

Some players assign more complex conventional meanings to doubles of 2♣ and 2◇, using them to show two-suited hands

| West | North | East | South |
|------|-------|------|-------|
|      |       | (You) |      |
|      |       |      | 2♣ |
| pass | 2◇ | dbl | |

And this shows a hand with long, strong, diamonds.

Similarly, if the opponents are playing a method such as Precision Club, where 1♣ is the forcing opening bid and 1◇ is the negative response, lead-directing doubles of these two bids are in effect. However, most play the double of a strong 1♣ or of a negative 1◇ response to show some two-suited hand.

### Doubling a cuebid

Doubles of most cuebids, in particular those at the four-level or higher, are lead-directing. Just make sure you are not the one that is going to be on lead when you double a cuebid. There are no 'reminder' lead-directing doubles.

| West | North | East | South |
|------|-------|------|-------|
|      |       | (You) |      |
|      | 1♠ | pass | 3♠ |
| pass | 4♣ | ? | 4♢ |
| ? |  |  |  |

Do *not* double 4♣ with strong clubs; you are going to be on lead against a spade contract. However, if partner has a suitable diamond holding such as KQx(x) or KJ10(x), she is expected to double 4♢ to help you out on opening lead.

# Doubles of 3NT contracts

We start with the most difficult of all, the lead-directing double of 3NT. These are the five sticklers and they all presume that the partner of the player who is on opening lead has doubled.

  a)  No suits have been bid by either side.
  b)  Neither defender has bid, but dummy has bid one or two suits.
  c)  A defender opens or overcalls at the *one*-level and then doubles.
  d)  One defender bids a suit and partner doubles.
  e)  Each defender bids a different suit.

### No suits have been bid by either side

| West | North | East | South |
|------|-------|------|-------|
|      |       | (You) |      |
|      |       |       | 1NT |
| pass | 3NT | dbl | all pass |

Your double announces a solid suit, and asks partner to lead it. Partner would love to, of course, if she only knew which one it was!

Given that your double shows a solid suit, she should lead a suit in which she has no honor card(s). If West has two suits without honor cards, the shorter one is usually the winner. Say partner is gazing at:

> ♠ 4  ♡ 107632  ◇ Q543  ♣ J76

Your suit could be spades, hearts, or even clubs (♣AKQ109), but the smart money is riding on the singleton spade lead.

## Neither defender has bid, but dummy has bid one or two suits

| West | North | East | South |
|------|-------|------|-------|
|      |       | (You) |      |
|      |       |      | 1◇ |
| pass | 1♡ | pass | 1NT |
| pass | 2NT | pass | 3NT |
| pass | pass | dbl | all pass |

Your double calls for a heart lead, dummy's first bid suit. Partner better have a good reason handy if a heart isn't led.

You might have:

> ♠ 54  ♡ AKJ10  ◇ 54  ♣ Q9743

| West | North | East | South |
|------|-------|------|-------|
|      |       | (You) |      |
|      | 1♣ | pass | 1♡ |
| pass | 1♠ | pass | 2◇ |
| pass | 2NT | pass | 3NT |
| dbl | all pass |      |      |

As most play, the double still asks for a heart lead, dummy's first-bid suit. However, there is something to be said for allowing East at least the option of leading a diamond if East's hearts seem to preclude partner's wanting that lead.

Say you, East, are looking at either of these hands:

> (a) ♠ K8743  ♡ 104  ◇ J1042  ♣ 109
> (b) ♠ 9874  ♡ KQ954  ◇ 52  ♣ 98

With hand (a), lead the ♡10. With hand (b), common sense tells you that partner is asking for a diamond. This is one sequence you might discuss with your partner. One other point: if partner had great diamonds, he might have doubled 2◇, the fourth suit. Since he didn't, a heart lead is indicated in all but the most obvious cases.

In the remaining sequences, you, partner, or both you and partner have bid before the 'dreaded' double.

## A defender opens or overcalls a major suit at the one-level

| West | North | East | South |
|------|-------|------|-------|
|      |       | (You) |      |
|      |       | 1♠ | 1NT |
| pass | 3NT | dbl | all pass |

Consider these two East hands before jumping to any conclusions as to the lead-directing implications of your double.

(a) ♠ KQJ104  ♡ 3  ◇ KJ874  ♣ A9
(b) ♠ KJ874  ♡ 3  ◇ KQJ104  ♣ A9

With hand (a), you are almost certain to set the contract with a spade lead. With hand (b), you may or may not set the contract with a spade lead, but you are a heavy favorite to do so with a diamond lead.

Before discussing what lead this double asks for, let it be known that partner is likely to lead a spade if you pass. After all, as most play, a major-suit opening bid shows a five-card suit, minimum, as does a one-level major-suit overcall. A spade is the expected lead, double or no double.

Assuming partner is likely to lead a spade, why use the double to ask for a spade lead, the suit partner is going to lead anyway? My (minority) feeling is that this double should be used to alert partner that you have a powerful, hidden, lower-ranking suit — a suit you were not able to mention at the two-level — hand (b).

Whichever way you decide to play this double, make sure your partner is playing the same way!

| West | North | East | South |
|------|-------|------|-------|
|      |       | (You) |       |
|      |       |      | 1◇    |
| pass | 1♡    | 1♠   | 1NT   |
| pass | 2NT   | pass | 3NT   |
| pass | pass  | ?    |       |

This minority reasoning can also be applied after a one-level major suit overcall. Say you are looking at either of these hands:

(a) ♠ KQJ107 ♡ 94 ◇ A1076 ♣ 92
(b) ♠ Q10764 ♡ 5 ◇ A10 ♣ KQJ102

With hand (a) you want a spade lead. With hand (b) you want a club lead. If you play 'standard' methods, you will double with (a) to ensure getting a spade lead, and pass with (b). If you believe otherwise as I do, you will pass with (a) expecting a spade lead, and double with (b) to tell your partner *not* to lead a spade.

## A defender opens 1♣ or 1◇

However, after you open 1♣ or 1◇, a *minor* suit, and later double 3NT, your double should call for the lead of the suit you have bid. Why? Because after a minor-suit opening bid followed by a notrump overcall, partner is apt to think you have opened a short club or a short diamond or perhaps have opened the bidding with a weak four-card suit and will look elsewhere for tricks.

| West | North | East | South |
|------|-------|------|-------|
|      |       | (You) |       |
|      |       | 1♣   | 1♡    |
| pass | 2◇    | pass | 2NT   |
| pass | 3NT   | dbl  | all pass |

Your hand:

♠ A10 ♡ A75 ◇ QJ3 ♣ QJ1095

With that club suit and your certain outside entries, you want a club lead; 'double' is the way to get it.

Overcalls at the two- or three-level normally show one-suited hands. Therefore, you seldom have any surprise hidden suits when you make one of these overcalls. Consequently a double of 3NT following a two- or three-level overcall asks partner to lead your suit. The opponents have overstepped themselves and it's time to make them pay.

| West | North | East | South |
|------|-------|------|-------|
|      |       | (You) |      |
|      |       |      | 1♡ |
| pass | 2♣ | 2♢ | pass |
| pass | 2♠ | pass | 2NT |
| pass | 3NT | dbl | all pass |

West should lead a diamond because you have overcalled at the two-level.

## Partner bids a suit and you double 3NT

| West | North | East | South |
|------|-------|------|-------|
|      |       | (You) |      |
|      |       |      | 1♢ |
| 1♡ | 1♠ | pass | 1NT |
| pass | 2NT | pass | 3NT |
| pass | pass | dbl | all pass |

What tortuous meaning does your double have this time? Some play that it asks partner to lead a heart, the suit he has bid, period. I don't like it.

My feeling is that if you want a heart lead so badly, you would already have bid 2♡. When you don't support partner's suit at the two-level when you could have, a double by you should ask for dummy's first-bid suit.

Contrast the previous sequence with this one:

| West | North | East | South |
|------|-------|------|-------|
|      |       | (You) |      |
|      |       |      | 1♣ |
| 1♢ | 3♣ | pass | 3NT |
| pass | pass | dbl | all pass |

In this sequence you did *not* have a chance to support partner's suit at the two-level, so the double asks partner to lead her suit, diamonds.

## You and partner each overcall at the one-level, and dummy has bid a suit

| West | North | East | South |
|------|-------|------|-------|
|      |       | (You) |       |
|      |       |      | 1♣ |
| 1◇ | 1♡ | 1♠ | 1NT |
| pass | 2NT | pass | 3NT |
| pass | pass | dbl | all pass |

Again, there is some disagreement here. Some think this double calls for a spade lead, others think a diamond; still others (moi included) think it calls for a heart lead!

The reason I don't think it calls for a diamond lead is this: the **snapdragon double** has now entered the scene. What is it? A snapdragon double would find you doubling 1♡ in this sequence to show length in the unbid suit, spades, plus diamond support. In other words, if you were looking at:

♠ A10876  ♡ J943  ◇ K65  ♣ 5

you would double 1♡ getting two messages across with one bid. If you and your partner play snapdragon doubles, it is clear that your double of 3NT in the above example cannot be asking for a diamond lead. So partner's choice is now between a spade and a heart. As a spade is the expected lead, I think the double should ask for a heart lead. Maybe you have:

♠ J10943  ♡ AK108  ◇ 103  ♣ 96

Anyway, that's my feeling if you play snapdragon doubles. If you don't, the double calls for a diamond lead as a spade is the expected lead.

## You and partner each make an overcall, and dummy is silent

| West | North | East | South |
|------|-------|------|-------|
|      |       | (You) |       |
|      |       |      | 1◇ |
| 1♡ | pass | 2♣ | 2NT |
| pass | 3NT | dbl | all pass |

The expected lead is a club so the double asks for a heart lead.

# Miscellaneous lead-directing doubles

## Doubling 6NT

A double of 6NT asks for dummy's first-bid suit. Therefore, if you have the AK of the suit you have bid, or the AK of some other suit, don't double 6NT unless you can stand the lead of dummy's first-bid suit, because that's what you're gonna get.

## Doubling a 1NT response in the balancing seat

| West | North | East | South |
|------|-------|------|-------|
|      |       | (You) |      |
|      | 1♠    | pass | 1NT   |
| pass | pass  | dbl  | pass  |
| ?    |       |      |       |

Your double is *not* for takeout. It is penalty-oriented describing a hand with strong spades. You might have:

♠ AQ1054  ♡ 5  ◇ AQ105  ♣ K52

How should partner react to this double? She should be reluctant to pull the double to some random suit because you have *not* promised support for the unbid suits. You could have a side-suit singleton! Unless partner has a weak distributional hand with a six-card suit, partner does best to pass, pray, and lead a spade.

What if you actually want to make a takeout double of 1NT with short spades? What if you have:

♠ 5  ♡ A874  ◇ K543  ♣ Q843

You have to reason like this: South's 1NT response typically denies three spades. If South has one or two spades, your partner has five or six spades! Partner may not even have a four-card suit to bid. Why look for trouble? Pass.

The situation is a little different if the opening bid is in a minor:

| West | North | East | South |
|------|-------|------|-------|
|      |       | (You) |      |
|      | 1♣    | pass | 1NT   |
| pass | pass  | ?    |       |

A 1NT response to a 1♣ opening typically shows 8-10 HCP, so there is less reason to compete. However, you can still compete by:
1) Doubling to show a good hand with clubs.
2) Bidding 2♣ as a light takeout double with club shortness.
3) Bidding 2◇ as a light takeout double for the majors.
4) Bidding 2♡ or 2♠ — natural, but weaker than an original overcall.

Let's look at four possible reopening hands you might hold:
(a) ♠ AJ10 ♡ 43 ◇ KJ4 ♣ KQ1087
(b) ♠ KJ65 ♡ A1054 ◇ 10543 ♣ 2
(c) ♠ A1043 ♡ QJ54 ◇ A ♣ 10542
(d) ♠ K98432 ♡ 3 ◇ QJ4 ♣ 965

With (a), double — penalty-oriented. With (b), bid 2♣ — a light takeout double of clubs. With (c), bid 2◇ — a light major-suit takeout. With (d), bid 2♠, natural.

| West | North | East | South |
|------|-------|------|-------|
|      |       | (You) |      |
|      | 1◇ | pass | 1NT |
| pass | pass | ? |  |

Here, South can have as few as 6 HCP, so it is safer to compete. Furthermore, since South seldom has a four-card major, his long suit figures to be *clubs*. Beware of bidding clubs!

Your reopening possibilities are the same:
1) Doubling to show an opening hand with good diamonds.
2) Bidding 2♣ as a light takeout double with short diamonds.
3) Bidding 2◇ as a light takeout double for the majors.
4) Bidding 2♡ or 2♠ — natural, but weaker than an original overcall.

Let's look at four possible reopening hands you might hold:
(a) ♠ AK ♡ 943 ◇ AQ108 ♣ J1093
(b) ♠ AJ43 ♡ K1087 ◇ Q875 ♣ 3
(c) ♠ K4 ♡ K4 ◇ 943 ♣ K97543
(d) ♠ 432 ♡ A108643 ◇ 3 ♣ Q108

With (a), double — penalty-oriented. With (b), bid 2◇ — a light major-suit takeout double. With (c), pass — a reopening bid of 2♣ is played as a light takeout double of diamonds (*South* has clubs). With (d), bid 2♡, natural.

Talk this stuff over with your partner: not everyone plays this way.

You cannot, of course, reopen with a natural 2◇ playing this method. No big loss — you could have overcalled 1◇ already.

# Practice Hands

| BOTH VUL. | | DEALER NORTH | |
|---|---|---|---|
| **West** | **North** | **East** | **South** |
| | 1♣ | pass | 1♠ |
| pass | 3♠ | pass | 4NT |
| pass | 5♡ | dbl | 5NT |
| pass | 6♢ | pass | 6♠ |
| all pass | | | |

Opening lead: ♡3

**Hand 1**

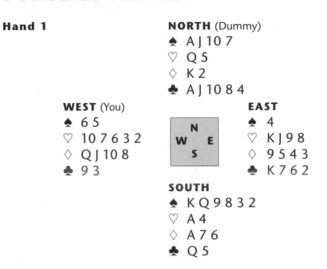

**NORTH** (Dummy)
♠ A J 10 7
♡ Q 5
♢ K 2
♣ A J 10 8 4

**WEST** (You)
♠ 6 5
♡ 10 7 6 3 2
♢ Q J 10 8
♣ 9 3

**EAST**
♠ 4
♡ K J 9 8
♢ 9 5 4 3
♣ K 7 6 2

**SOUTH**
♠ K Q 9 8 3 2
♡ A 4
♢ A 7 6
♣ Q 5

Partner has seized the opportunity to make a lead-directing double of the artificial 5♡ response to Blackwood. You would normally lead a diamond, but you comply by leading a heart.

The ball is now in South's court. South knows from the double that East must have the ♡K, so South must plan a strip and endplay to overcome this killing lead. South plays *low* from dummy at trick one, wins the ace, draws trumps and strips the diamonds, finally exiting with a heart to the queen and king. What can East do? If East exits a club, South has no club loser; if East exits with a red card, conceding a ruff and a sluff, South ruffs in dummy and discards a club from the closed hand.

However, even though South can still make the hand with a heart lead, South has to play it well. If South plays the ♡Q at trick one, for example, the hand can no longer be made. After the stripping process, West can win the heart exit and fire a club through dummy promoting the ♣K to the setting trick.

Also, a finessaholic sitting South might take the club finesse after the heart lead instead of playing for the strip and endplay, even though the latter is a near 100% line requiring only that East has the ♡K.

**Hand 2**

**NORTH** (Dummy)
♠ A 7 6 2
♡ A 8 6
♢ A J 5
♣ 7 5 3

**WEST** (You)
♠ 10 3
♡ J 10 9 7 2
♢ K 8 4 3
♣ 9 2

```
    N
  W   E
    S
```

**EAST**
♠ K Q J 9 5
♡ 5 3
♢ 9 6 2
♣ A 6 4

**SOUTH**
♠ 8 4
♡ K Q 4
♢ Q 10 7
♣ K Q J 10 8

| NEITHER VUL. | | DEALER SOUTH | |
| West | North | East | South |
| --- | --- | --- | --- |
| | | | 1♣ |
| pass | 1♠ | pass | 1NT |
| pass | 3NT | dbl | all pass |

Opening lead: ♠10

Left to your own devices you surely would have led the ♡J. However, partner's lead-directing double of 3NT asks for dummy's first-bid suit, spades. After you plunk the ♠10 on the table, South is a goner. South can do no better than to win the second or third round of spades with dummy's ace and go after clubs. No good. East is waiting with the ♣A plus the setting tricks in spades. With the normal heart lead, South has no trouble at all making three notrump by simply knocking out the ♣A.

**Hand 3**

**NORTH** (Dummy)
♠ J 10 6 5
♡ A Q 9 2
♢ Q J
♣ 10 7 5

**WEST** (You)
♠ 7 2
♡ 10 6 5 4
♢ 10 9 8 5 3 2
♣ K

```
    N
  W   E
    S
```

**EAST**
♠ Q 9 8
♡ J 7
♢ 6 4
♣ A Q J 8 4 2

**SOUTH**
♠ A K 4 3
♡ K 8 3
♢ A K 7
♣ 9 6 3

| EAST-WEST VUL. | | DEALER SOUTH | |
| West | North | East | South |
| --- | --- | --- | --- |
| | | | 1NT |
| pass | 2♣ | dbl | 2♠ |
| pass | 4♠ | all pass | |

Opening lead: ♣K

Once again partner has tipped you off to the winning lead by doubling an artificial bid. It is safe to say you would have led something else if there had been no double. Now that you have made the lead partner wanted, the rest is up to partner. For starters, partner must overtake your king in case it is a singleton. After surviving that hurdle and cashing three rounds of clubs, partner can do a little point counting. Partner has 10 HCP; dummy also has 10 HCP for a total of 20. If declarer has 15 HCP, you can have no more than 5 HCP and partner has already seen 3, the ♣K. That leaves you with 2 HCP, at most. But partner can see all four queens, so you can't have a queen, and partner can see all four jacks so you can't have a jack either! Conclusion: you have no more high card points. Still, there is no law saying you can't hold the ♠7!

If partner plays a fourth club and you uppercut dummy with the ♠7 driving out the ♠10, partner's ♠Q98 is now a natural trump trick. Down one. Without the fourth club play, declarer takes a simple spade finesse and racks up the game.

| BOTH VUL. | | DEALER SOUTH | |
|------|-------|------|----------|
| **West** | **North** | **East** | **South** |
| | | | 1NT |
| pass | 2NT | pass | 3NT |
| pass | pass | dbl | all pass |

**Hand 4**

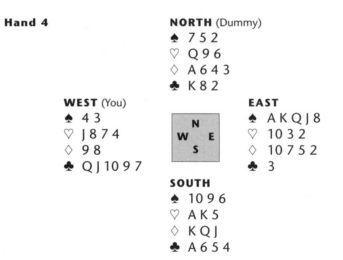

**NORTH** (Dummy)
♠ 7 5 2
♡ Q 9 6
♢ A 6 4 3
♣ K 8 2

**WEST** (You)
♠ 4 3
♡ J 8 7 4
♢ 9 8
♣ Q J 10 9 7

**EAST**
♠ A K Q J 8
♡ 10 3 2
♢ 10 7 5 2
♣ 3

**SOUTH**
♠ 10 9 6
♡ A K 5
♢ K Q J
♣ A 6 5 4

This time partner's double announces a solid suit, so don't even think about leading the ♣Q; partner's suit can't be clubs! It doesn't figure to be hearts, either, with you holding ♡Jxxx. You have now narrowed down your choices to a top diamond or a top spade. Although it is isn't a 100% clear (what ever is?) a spade lead is the better shot. One clue is that the opponents did not use Stayman so dummy is unlikely to have four spades, increasing the chances that partner has spade length. If you found the spade lead, you are the hero, at least for the moment.

# Test Yourself

1) You are West, holding:

♠ 6 3  ♡ Q J 9 5  ◇ K 10 7 3  ♣ 6 5 2

| West | North | East | South |
|------|-------|------|-------|
|      |       |      | 1◇    |
| pass | 1♠    | pass | 2NT   |
| pass | 3NT   | dbl  | all pass |

What do you lead?

*Solution on page 210*

2) You are West, holding

♠ 6 3  ♡ Q J 9 5  ◇ K 10 7 3  ♣ 6 5 2

| West | North | East | South |
|------|-------|------|-------|
|      | 1♠    | pass | 1NT   |
| pass | pass  | dbl  | all pass |

What do you lead?

*Solution on page 210*

3) You are West, holding

♠ 6 3  ♡ Q J 9 5  ◇ K 10 7 3  ♣ 6 5 2

| West | North | East | South |
|------|-------|------|-------|
|      |       |      | 1NT   |
| pass | 2NT   | pass | 3NT   |
| pass | pass  | dbl  | all pass |

What do you lead?

*Solution on page 210*

4) You are West, holding

♠ 3  ♡ J 10 9 3  ◇ J 10 9 3  ♣ J 10 9 3

| West | North | East | South |
|------|-------|------|-------|
|      | 1◇    | pass | 1♠    |
| pass | 3♠    | pass | 4NT   |
| pass | 5♡    | pass | 5NT   |
| pass | 6◇    | pass | 6♠    |
| all pass |   |      |       |

What do you lead?

*Solution on page 210*

5) You are West, and the bidding has proceeded:

| West | North | East | South |
|------|-------|------|-------|
|      | 1NT[1] | pass | 2◊[2] |
| ?    |       |      |       |

1) 15-17 HCP
2) Transfer to hearts

What should you bid on each of the following hands:

*Solutions on page 210*
- a)  ♠ 7 4  ♡ A 6 3  ◊ J 8 6 5 3 2  ♣ K 4
- b)  ♠ 7 4  ♡ A 6 3  ◊ K Q 10 9 3  ♣ 5 4 2
- c)  ♠ 7 4  ♡ A 6 3  ◊ K Q 10 9 5 4 3 2  ♣ —

6) You are West, and the auction has been:

| West | North | East | South |
|------|-------|------|-------|
|      |       |      | 2NT   |
| pass | 3NT   | dbl  | all pass |

What should you lead from each of the following hands:

*Solutions on page 210*
- a)  ♠ J 4 2  ♡ J 10 9 8 7 6  ◊ A 7 2  ♣ 2
- b)  ♠ 3 2  ♡ 3 2  ◊ Q J 10 4  ♣ J 7 5 4 3

7) You are West, holding

♠ A K Q J 10 8 7  ♡ 5 3 2  ◊ —  ♣ J 4 2

| West | North | East | South |
|------|-------|------|-------|
|      | 2♣    | pass | 2◊    |
| 4♠   | 4NT   | pass | 5♣    |
| pass | 6♡    | pass | pass  |
| ?    |       |      |       |

*Solution on page 210*

What's your call now?

8) You are West, holding

♠ A K 8  ♡ J 10 9 8 5 3  ◊ 8 6  ♣ K 2

| West | North | East | South |
|------|-------|------|-------|
|      |       |      | 1◊    |
| 1♡   | 4♣    | pass | 6♣    |
| ?    |       |      |       |

*Solution on page 210*

What is your call now?

9) You are West, holding

♠ 9 8   ♡ Q J 10 9   ◇ 8 6 5 4   ♣ J 4 2

| West | North | East | South |
|------|-------|------|-------|
|      |       |      | 1♠    |
| pass | 2◇    | pass | 4◇    |
| pass | 4♠    | pass | 4NT   |
| pass | 5◇    | pass | 6♠    |
| pass | pass  | dbl  | all pass |

What do you lead?

*Solution on page 210*

10) This is a hand that I once defended in an important tournament. Can you find the winning lead? I was West, holding:

♠ J 9 8 7 6 4 2   ♡ 10 3   ◇ J 6 5   ♣ 2

| West | North | East | South |
|------|-------|------|-------|
|      |       |      | 3♣    |
| pass | 4NT   | 5◇   | 5♡[1] |
| pass | 6♣    | dbl  | all pass |

1) Showing an ace

What would you lead?

*Solution on page 210*

# Test Yourself — Solutions

1) ♠6     If neither you nor your partner have bid, lead dummy's first-bid suit.

2) ♠6     Partner's double says that she was trapped over the 1♠ call, and that she has spades. Do as you're told and lead her suit.

3) ♠6     This double says partner has a solid suit, and your best shot at hitting it looks like spades. After all, they didn't bother with Stayman.

4) ♣J     Partner had two shots at doubling the heart and the diamond responses to Blackwood, and didn't. Might as well try a club.

*Problem 5*

a) pass    Don't bid or double on a suit this weak.

b) dbl     You want a diamond lead, especially against notrump.

c) 4◇      Yes, you could double, but holding such a long suit it's more effective to preempt.

*Problem 6*

a) ♣2      Again, partner supposedly has a solid or near-solid suit, and this looks like the best candidate.

b) ???     Do you have a coin handy to toss? Partner has herds of either spades or hearts, and you have no way of telling which. You can't even lead your stronger doubleton!

7) dbl     When you, the preemptive bidder, double a final contract, it is typically because of a side-suit void. Partner is forbidden from leading your suit or a trump. With luck, partner will have a bushelful of diamonds and will put one on the track.

8) dbl     If you pass you will get a heart lead — not good. If you double, you forbid a heart lead (and a trump). Unlike the previous example you have not preempted, so your double does not necessarily show a void suit. Your double might include the ♠AK or it might indicate a strong diamond holding. Partner has to work that out. At least you have a better chance to set this contract if partner doesn't lead a heart.

9) any ◇   The bidding suggests that partner has a diamond void with an outside ace.

10)        Well, did you lead a spade for partner to ruff? I did, but this was the whole hand:

**NORTH** (Dummy)
♠ A K 3
♡ K J 9 8 7
♢ A
♣ Q 9 8 3

**WEST**
♠ J 9 8 7 6 4 2
♡ 10 3
♢ J 6 5
♣ 2

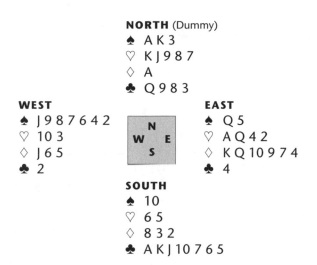

**EAST**
♠ Q 5
♡ A Q 4 2
♢ K Q 10 9 7 4
♣ 4

**SOUTH**
♠ 10
♡ 6 5
♢ 8 3 2
♣ A K J 10 7 6 5

As you can see, the spade lead didn't turn out very well. Partner knew that dummy was going to hit with the ♡K, and suspected that a diamond lead was wrong, as indeed it was. However, I wasn't clever enough to work out to lead a heart. Perhaps if he'd tapped his chest instead of doubling... just kidding.

## Key ideas from Chapter 7

- The most common lead-directing doubles are doubles of 3NT contracts, slam contracts, and artificial bids such as Stayman, transfers, splinters, high-level cuebids, the fourth suit, or Blackwood responses.
- If either you or partner has bid a suit and the opponents arrive voluntarily in a suit slam, a double expressly forbids partner from leading any suit your side has bid or a trump.
- If neither defender has bid and the opponents voluntarily bid a suit slam, a double forbids the lead of any unbid suit or a trump. It usually calls for dummy's first-bid suit.
- When partner preempts and later doubles a slam contract, assume he has a void and try to find it on opening lead!
- If you can defeat a slam contract only if partner leads the suit you have bid, don't double! The double forbids partner to lead your suit.
- If no suits have been bid, a double of 3NT shows a solid suit and asks partner to lead it. Amen.

# Card Tricks

*The art of playing cards is making the wrong move at the right time*

THE CINCINNATI KID (movie)

This chapter is a bit technical, but once you begin to recognize the positions in the diagrams, it can save you, time, trouble and many unnecessary errors at the table. Again, a key to understanding defensive play, and in particular managing certain card combinations, is to be aware *before* you lead a suit how many tricks you need in that suit, what your partner needs in that suit to take that many tricks, and the right card to lead in the suit once you have made those determinations. Keep in mind that the number of tricks you need in a suit may alter the card you lead in that suit.

Remember, too, that we are talking about attacking suits *after* the dummy comes down, not on opening lead. Rules for which card to lead can change dramatically once dummy appears. A simple example: on opening lead, the king is led from the KQxx versus a suit contract. However, if the suit wasn't led, and dummy appeared with the singleton ace, you wouldn't lead the king, you would lead low. Another example: say you have Axxxx of a suit. On opening lead versus a suit contract, if you decide to lead this suit, you start with the ace. But if you lead another suit, and you later decide to lead from your Axxxx suit, if dummy has, say, KJx, you will usually lead low, hoping partner has the queen and declarer misguesses.

In any case, that is, in part, what you have to look forward to in this chapter: card combinations where the card led after dummy is seen is not necessarily the same as the card you would lead at trick one. This chapter also touches on various techniques for telling partner what declarer already knows about your hand. For example, if partner shows out of a suit, declarer knows what *you* have in the suit. Whatever declarer knows, partner must be told! It's a rule! Finally, this chapter also includes several time-tested ruses, ruses that are practically guaranteed to manufacture tricks out of thin air.

# Leading unsupported honors

Let's start with something simple.

| BOTH VUL. | | DEALER SOUTH | |
|-----------|-------|--------------|--------|
| West | North | East | South |
| | | | 1♠ |
| pass | 4♠ | all pass | |

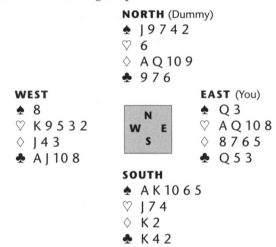

**NORTH** (Dummy)
♠ J 9 7 4 2
♡ 6
◇ A Q 10 9
♣ 9 7 6

**WEST**
♠ 8
♡ K 9 5 3 2
◇ J 4 3
♣ A J 10 8

**EAST** (You)
♠ Q 3
♡ A Q 10 8
◇ 8 7 6 5
♣ Q 5 3

**SOUTH**
♠ A K 10 6 5
♡ J 7 4
◇ K 2
♣ K 4 2

Partner leads the ♡3 to your ace as you inspect the dummy for clues. When you see a dummy with an imposing side suit (in this case, diamonds), you can anticipate that declarer is going to use that suit to discard losers — club losers (heart losers can be ruffed in dummy). Clearly it is right to shift to a club, but which one? The normal (opening) lead from Qxx is low. However, after seeing the dummy, it can be a different ball game!

Looking at this dummy, there is a strong likelihood that your side needs *three* club tricks quickly before one or two of declarer's losers go off on those diamonds. In order to take three fast club tricks, you must project the ♣AJ10 in partner's hand and lead the queen.

(Partner can't have the ♣AK — the suit would have been led.) On the other hand, defending a contract of 5♠, needing but *two* club tricks to defeat the contract, you should shift to a *low* club hoping declarer has the ♣KJ and misguesses.

# Escaping an endplay

Being forced to lead a suit you don't want to lead is a situation no defender likes to be in. Sometimes, though, it can't be avoided. We've encountered some positions earlier in the book where you could safely concede a ruff-sluff, because you knew it wouldn't actually help declarer. If that's the case, you're still OK. But what if it isn't? Now you have to break a touchy suit, and your task is to do it in a way that will still give declarer a problem, if you can.

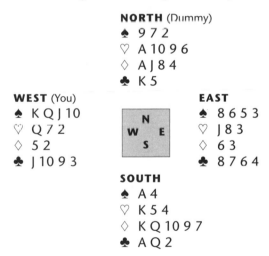

**NORTH** (Dummy)
♠ 9 7 2
♡ A 10 9 6
♢ A J 8 4
♣ K 5

**WEST** (You)
♠ K Q J 10
♡ Q 7 2
♢ 5 2
♣ J 10 9 3

**EAST**
♠ 8 6 5 3
♡ J 8 3
♢ 6 3
♣ 8 7 6 4

**SOUTH**
♠ A 4
♡ K 5 4
♢ K Q 10 9 7
♣ A Q 2

| NEITHER VUL. | | DEALER EAST | |
| West | North | East | South |
| --- | --- | --- | --- |
| | | pass | 1♢ |
| pass | 1♡ | pass | 2NT |
| pass | 4♢ | pass | 6♢ |
| all pass | | | |

Opening lead: ♠K

Once again you are going to have to make an imaginative play with the Qxx. Follow the play. Declarer wins the ♠A, draws trumps in two rounds, plays three rounds of clubs discarding a spade from dummy, and exits with a spade to your ten.

If you are counting, you know that declarer still has three hearts, including the king to justify the 2NT rebid. If declarer had ♡KJx, she would have claimed, so you must play declarer for ♡Kxx. Even so, this is not a happy position. Clearly a ruff and a sluff won't work, as declarer will ruff in dummy and discard her losing heart. Surely you can come up with something better than that!

If you lead a low heart, declarer will have little choice but to play for 'split honors'. She will play the ten from dummy, take partner's jack with the king, and lead a heart to the nine finessing you out of your queen. A better shot is to lead the ♡Q. Now at least declarer has to decide whether you started with ♡QJx(x) or the queen without the jack. If declarer plays you for the jack and wins the king and then leads low to the ten, partner's jack will be the setting trick. In any case, it is your only chance. In this same situation, lead the jack from ♡Jxx.

## Surrounding plays

Just what is a 'surrounding' play? The following hand explains all.

NORTH-SOUTH VUL. DEALER EAST

| West | North | East | South |
|------|-------|------|-------|
|      |       | 1♡   | 1NT   |
| pass | 3NT   | all pass |   |

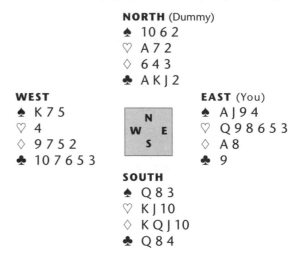

NORTH (Dummy)
♠ 10 6 2
♡ A 7 2
◇ 6 4 3
♣ A K J 2

WEST
♠ K 7 5
♡ 4
◇ 9 7 5 2
♣ 10 7 6 5 3

EAST (You)
♠ A J 9 4
♡ Q 9 8 6 5 3
◇ A 8
♣ 9

SOUTH
♠ Q 8 3
♡ K J 10
◇ K Q J 10
♣ Q 8 4

Partner leads a low heart, an obvious singleton. Declarer captures your queen and exits with the ◇K to your ace. The only hope is to grab four quickies in spades, and partner needs the king. Even so, you must attack with the *jack*, a **surrounding play**! Notice that you have dummy's ♠10 'surrounded' with the ♠J9, but you need the king or ace as well to be able to spend the jack.

Notice the difference. If you lead a low spade and declarer plays low, partner's king takes the trick. But when partner returns a spade to your ace, declarer remains with the queen. Not good. Now try it the other way, the surrounding way, by leading the jack. If declarer plays low, the jack wins and you can lead low to partner's king;

partner leads back to your ace, snapping up declarer's queen and your ♠9 is the fourth defensive spade trick. If declarer covers the jack, partner wins the king and returns the suit. You are now hovering over dummy's ♠10 with the ♠A9x and declarer has no chance to take a trick. Put that surrounding play in your memory bank.

Let's look at some other positions where a surrounding play can be made. North will be dummy and you will be East.

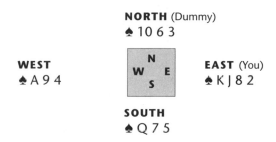

**NORTH** (Dummy)
♠ 10 6 3

**WEST**
♠ A 9 4

**EAST** (You)
♠ K J 8 2

**SOUTH**
♠ Q 7 5

This is an example of an 'imperfect' surrounding play. You would like to have the KJ92, but they dealt you the KJ82. No matter, you still lead the jack, but this time your partner needs the nine as well as the ace.

If you haven't noticed already, bridge is a diabolical game, very diabolical. Look at the following diagram:

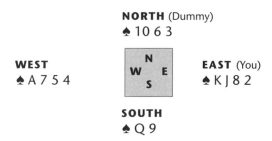

**NORTH** (Dummy)
♠ 10 6 3

**WEST**
♠ A 7 5 4

**EAST** (You)
♠ K J 8 2

**SOUTH**
♠ Q 9

This time, if you lead the jack, you're eventually going to set up dummy's ten and become one of South's favorite opponents. So if you suspect declarer has a doubleton spade, forget you ever heard of surrounding plays, and lead low.

Surrounding plays don't always require that the 10, 10x, or 10xx be on your right with you having the KJ9(8) or AJ9(x) hovering over it. They also work when the nine is on your right and you have the

Q108(x), or K108(x) lurking over it. This time you attack with the ten.

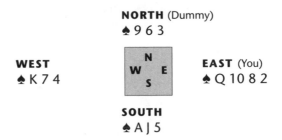

By attacking with the ten, you limit declarer to one trick. If declarer covers, partner wins and returns the suit. You remain with the ♠Q8x over dummy's guarded nine and declarer is helpless. Had you started by leading a low spade, declarer could play low forcing partner to win with the king. Then declarer remains with the ♠AJ over your queen ultimately taking two tricks.

Here's a wild one — having an eight surrounded!

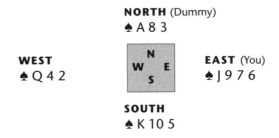

This one is rare, but it does wow the kibitzers. In order to limit declarer to two tricks in this suit, you have to start with the nine. The best declarer can do is to cover with the ten. Partner covers with the queen and dummy wins the ace. Now you have to be patient and wait for partner to return the suit through dummy's 8x with you hovering over it with the J7. Had you started with a low spade, declarer could play low; partner's queen forces out the ace, but declarer remains with the K10 over your jack. Declarer takes three tricks. Incidentally, you can make the same play holding Q97(x)(x) when the K10x or A10x is to your left.

Surrounding plays can also be made when dummy is to your left, but you have to use a little imagination because you can't see the card you are surrounding, since it is in declarer's hand, to your right. You have to assume it's there!

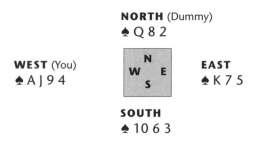

**NORTH** (Dummy)
♠ Q 8 2

**WEST** (You)
♠ A J 9 4

**EAST**
♠ K 7 5

**SOUTH**
♠ 10 6 3

This is the first example we looked at earlier, but turned around. If you decide you need a bundle of tricks from spades, you have to play your partner for the king, but partner may not have the ♠10. What you have to do is attack with the jack in case declarer has ♠10x or ♠10xx.

Sometimes you may have to imagine that the declarer has the 9x(x) when you have K108(x) or Q108(x) and dummy the AJx(x) to your left. You have to make a big play and lead the ten!

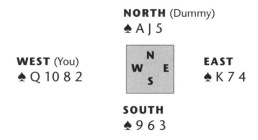

**NORTH** (Dummy)
♠ A J 5

**WEST** (You)
♠ Q 10 8 2

**EAST**
♠ K 7 4

**SOUTH**
♠ 9 6 3

Say you decide to attack spades and are pretty sure partner has the king; better attack with the ten to maintain your position in case declarer has the nine. Attacking with the ten limits declarer to one trick; attacking with the more normal fourth-best allows declarer to take two tricks. The idea, of course, is to recognize these positions when they are not laid out in front of you in a book, but at the table!

# Telling them nothing

Besides trying to work out what the declarer has, defenders have to be careful not to tell declarer too much about what they have! What follows are several techniques that every experienced defender must employ.

## Discarding from a suit where your length is known

You lead the king, ace, and a spade against 3◇. Partner ruffs and declarer overruffs. So much for spades. Not so fast. Declarer *knows* you started with six spades. If you have to discard later in the hand, it is almost always right to discard a spade. Why give declarer any extra information? Why make it easier to count your hand?

## Playing cards you are known to hold

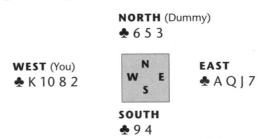

This time you lead the ♣2 in an unbid suit against a diamond contract. Partner wins the ace, continues with the queen, and then plays a third club, declarer ruffing. I hope you don't still have the ♣K in your hand! The moment partner wins the ♣A, you are marked with the ♣K. As long as it can't cost your side a trick, unload it as soon as possible. If you keep it, you are being overly friendly giving declarer GDI (gratuitous distributional information).

**NORTH** (Dummy)
♠ 6 5 3 2

**WEST** (You)
♠ Q 9 8 4

**EAST**
♠ A K 7

**SOUTH**
♠ J 10

You lead the ♠4 against a diamond contract. Partner wins the king, cashes the ace, and continues the suit, declarer ruffing. When declarer ruffs the third spade, play the queen, not the nine! Declarer knows you have the queen from partner's play of the king and ace. If you follow with the nine, once again being overly friendly, declarer knows you remain with the queen; however, if you play the queen, declarer doesn't know who has the nine. Playing the queen doesn't cost a trick — your nine is still the highest remaining spade. Is stuff like this really important? You better believe it. Declarer's play of the hand may be based partially or entirely upon knowing who has the odd spade.

Whenever declarer ruffs any suit, partner knows exactly what you have in the suit; you won't be fooling partner by playing a higher card than necessary.

## Turning two unequal honors into equal honors

**NORTH** (Dummy)
♠ A J 3

**WEST** (You)
♠ Q 10 2

**EAST**
♠ 8 7 4

**SOUTH**
♠ K 9 6 5

What does that title mean in English?

South plays the hand at suit or notrump and leads a spade to the jack which holds. At this point your queen and ten are *equals* because the jack has been played. Furthermore, South knows you have the queen but doesn't know you have the ten. When the ace is played from dummy, jettison the queen, the equal card you are known to hold. If South believes, South will lead a spade to the nine... and your ten! If you play the ten under the king, you doom your queen to an early death, because South knows you have it!

You can't always play the card you are known to hold; it may cost.

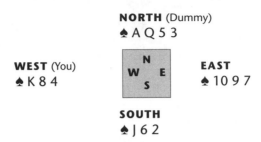

**NORTH** (Dummy)
♠ A Q 5 3

**WEST** (You)
♠ K 8 4

**EAST**
♠ 10 9 7

**SOUTH**
♠ J 6 2

South takes the spade finesse and cashes the ♠A. *Don't throw the ♠K, even though you're known to hold it!* You don't have the ♠J, and unless you know that partner does, you may be giving up a trick by dumping the ♠K.

Here, you do know it's safe:

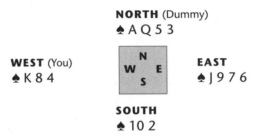

**NORTH** (Dummy)
♠ A Q 5 3

**WEST** (You)
♠ K 8 4

**EAST**
♠ J 9 7 6

**SOUTH**
♠ 10 2

Playing 3◊, declarer leads up to the ♠Q and then plays the ♠A, following with the ♠10. This time you can afford to play the king, a card you are known to hold, because partner must have the ♠J. What declarer in her right mind plays spades this way holding J10x? With this holding, declarer would start with the jack. Defenders are constantly required to make negative inferences like this; it comes with the territory.

It doesn't hurt to scare declarer out of his wits from time to time. How? By playing a card you are known to hold.

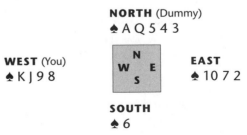

**NORTH** (Dummy)
♠ A Q 5 4 3

**WEST** (You)
♠ K J 9 8

**EAST**
♠ 10 7 2

**SOUTH**
♠ 6

South, still stuck in 3◇, takes an early spade finesse and then cashes the ace, discarding a loser. When you see South discard, you know all your spades are equals. You also know that South knows you have the ♠K. As long as you keep that ♠K, South can ruff spades back to her hand with low trumps, knowing you can't overruff. However, if you play the ♠K under the ace, South can never be sure she can ruff spades low. She might panic and ruff higher than necessary, eventually promoting a trump trick for you or partner. In any case, there is no reason on earth to hold on to that ♠K.

If, at times, you can induce declarer to ruff with a higher trump than necessary, you might also be able to induce dummy to ruff with a higher trump than necessary.

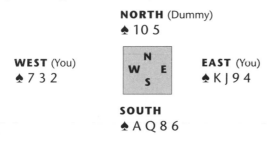

**NORTH** (Dummy)
♠ 10 5

**WEST** (You)
♠ 7 3 2

**EAST** (You)
♠ K J 9 4

**SOUTH**
♠ A Q 8 6

South (still playing 3◇!) leads a spade from dummy to the ♠Q then cashes the ♠A. If, after two rounds of spades, you still have the ♠K in your hand, I don't know you. That ♠K should be flying out on the table under the ♠A. For starters, it is a card you are known to hold; furthermore, it is the equal of your other spades. As long as you keep that ♠K, South knows he can ruff spades low in dummy.

*Do not be a friendly defender. Play the cards you are known to hold if it can't cost a trick.*

When cashing winners in a suit in which partner is void, if partner plays after declarer, cash your lower or lowest winner first, not your higher or highest.

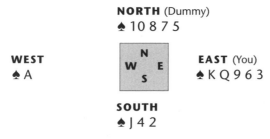

**NORTH** (Dummy)
♠ 10 8 7 5

**WEST**
♠ A

**EAST** (You)
♠ K Q 9 6 3

**SOUTH**
♠ J 4 2

Partner leads the ♠A against 2♡ and then switches, suggesting a singleton. Early in the hand you get the lead and decide to cash your

♠K and ♠Q. But don't cash the king and queen, cash the queen and king! This is not just nit-picking. If you cash the king first, partner will think declarer has the queen and will plan on making only one discard. However, if you cash the queen first, partner will know about both the king and the jack, and can plan on making two discards. It can matter. In this game, everything can matter.

## Playing your highest remaining card when you don't have to

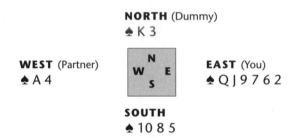

**NORTH** (Dummy)
♠ K 3

**WEST** (Partner)
♠ A 4

**EAST** (You)
♠ Q J 9 7 6 2

**SOUTH**
♠ 10 8 5

Partner leads the ♠A in your bid suit against 4◇ (you finally pushed them up a bit), then plays the ♠4 to the ♠K. Later, declarer ruffs the ♠10 in the dummy. When partner shows out of spades, declarer knows the spade count; you know the spade count, maybe dummy knows the spade count, but partner may not! When you are fourth to play and you know declarer is playing her last card in the suit being led, play your *highest* remaining card. Partner will reason that either you or declarer is now void. The bidding will tell which.

Back to the diagram. When you play the highest outstanding spade the third time the suit is led, partner figures that either you started with six spades or declarer did. If partner can't figure out from the bidding which of you started with six spades, all the signals in the world aren't going to help you.

## Discarding your highest equal honor

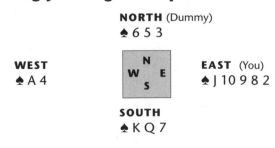

**NORTH** (Dummy)
♠ 6 5 3

**WEST**
♠ A 4

**EAST** (You)
♠ J 10 9 8 2

**SOUTH**
♠ K Q 7

You have bid spades, so partner leads the ♠A against 3◊, and continues with a spade which declarer wins with the king. At this point, you remain with the ♠J109; you know that South has the ♠Q, but your partner may not. Given the opportunity, discard the ♠J — promising the lower equals but denying anything higher. Now everyone knows where the ♠Q is.

# Stealing their underwear

Are your memory banks starting to feel full? Never mind, I'm sure we can squeeze in a few more neat positions:

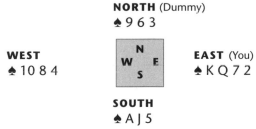

**NORTH** (Dummy)
♠ 9 6 3

**WEST**
♠ 10 8 4

**EAST** (You)
♠ K Q 7 2

**SOUTH**
♠ A J 5

If you need more than one spade trick, lead low. That nine in dummy is a huge card, because it gives declarer an option. Without it, he would probably play the jack. But with the nine he might well play low, hoping you have underled the ten. Not this time: partner wins the ten and declarer only makes one spade trick.

Here's another swindle:

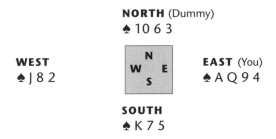

**NORTH** (Dummy)
♠ 10 6 3

**WEST**
♠ J 8 2

**EAST** (You)
♠ A Q 9 4

**SOUTH**
♠ K 7 5

This time, try leading the queen! South may think you have led from ♠QJ9. If so, he does best to play low. Now continue with the ♠2: South will almost certainly duck again, placing the ace with your partner. Surprise! Partner wins the jack and you gobble up South's king with your ace. South will not be a happy camper.

This one gives you an opportunity for another swindle play.

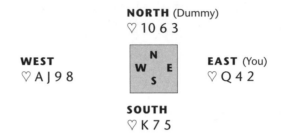

**NORTH** (Dummy)
♡ 10 6 3

**WEST**
♡ A J 9 8

**EAST** (You)
♡ Q 4 2

**SOUTH**
♡ K 7 5

If you need four heart tricks, your best shot is to attack with the queen hoping declarer has ♡Kxx and partner, ♡AJ9x. You may wonder how that is going to help as declarer can cover the queen and promote the ten to a third-round winner. True, but declarer isn't playing with mirrors.

If you actually started with the ♡QJ9(x), declarer is much better placed if he plays low under the queen, retaining control. Now, if you continue the suit, declarer is sure to take one trick. If you don't continue the suit, declarer has warded off a heart attack. That's supposed to be a joke.

This is another delicious piece of larceny:

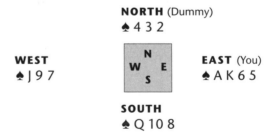

**NORTH** (Dummy)
♠ 4 3 2

**WEST**
♠ J 9 7

**EAST** (You)
♠ A K 6 5

**SOUTH**
♠ Q 10 8

As long as you think that declarer has more than two spades, you can safely lead low from your ♠AK. Typically, South will try the ten, and you'll end up with three tricks in spades (four in notrump). These swindle plays work from both sides of the table, just like surrounding plays. If you are in the West seat, holding ♠AK65 looking at dummy's ♠Q108, and you haven't touched the suit yet, think about leading a low spade. Declarer usually plays the ten, and if partner has the jack, you are the hero.

# Falsecards

Remember this play we looked at a while ago?

**NORTH** (Dummy)
♠ A J 3

**WEST** (You)
♠ Q 10 2

**EAST**
♠ 8 7 4

**SOUTH**
♠ K 9 6 5

When declarer plays a spade to the jack and then cashes the ace, you should play the queen under it, trying to look like someone with a doubleton queen. This is an example of a *mandatory false-card* — a position where you must make a falsecard to give declarer a losing option.

**Falsecard**: A card other than his lowest played by a defender in order to deceive declarer

Here's another example:

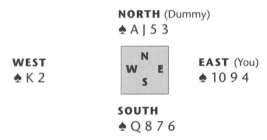

**NORTH** (Dummy)
♠ A J 5 3

**WEST**
♠ K 2

**EAST** (You)
♠ 10 9 4

**SOUTH**
♠ Q 8 7 6

This is South's trump suit, and South starts with a low spade to the jack, which holds. If both defenders have followed low, declarer has no choice now but to play the ♠A, and hope West has a doubleton king.

But suppose you cunningly drop the ♠9 under the jack. Suddenly declarer has another line available: he can play you to have started with ♠109 doubleton and return to his hand and lead the ♠Q. As the cards lie, he'll now lose a spade trick he didn't have to! Your play of the ♠9 gave declarer a losing option. Any time you have 109x, and suspect partner has a doubleton king or queen, play the 9 or 10 when you are fourth to play.

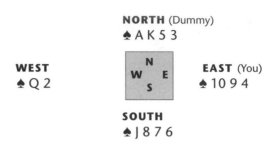

**NORTH** (Dummy)
♠ A K 5 3

**WEST**
♠ Q 2

**EAST** (You)
♠ 10 9 4

**SOUTH**
♠ J 8 7 6

Spades are trumps and South leads a low spade to the king. If you play low, South has no option other than to play the ace and hope to drop the doubleton queen. However, if you drop the nine (or ten) under the king, you give South a 'losing option'. South may think you have ♠109 doubleton or even the singleton ♠9. In either case it is better to return to the South hand and swing the ♠J. But in this case, it costs South a trick.

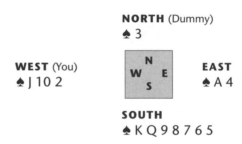

**NORTH** (Dummy)
♠ 3

**WEST** (You)
♠ J 10 2

**EAST**
♠ A 4

**SOUTH**
♠ K Q 9 8 7 6 5

Spades are trumps and declarer, who has preempted in spades, begins by leading a low spade to the king. If you play low, South has no choice but to win the king and exit with a low spade hoping your partner has ♠Ax. However, if you play the ♠10 (or ♠J), declarer now has a losing option. Declarer may decide to play you for the ♠J10 doubleton and plunk down the ♠Q. Not this time. Partner takes the ace and you make another trick with your remaining honor.

Here's one I've had a lot of luck with:

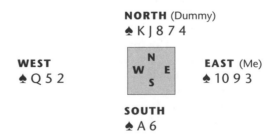

**NORTH** (Dummy)
♠ K J 8 7 4

**WEST**
♠ Q 5 2

**EAST** (Me)
♠ 10 9 3

**SOUTH**
♠ A 6

At notrump declarer starts with the ace, planning to continue by leading low to the jack. As the cards lie, declarer is entitled to five spade tricks. But it works wonders to play the nine (or ten) under the ace. Suddenly declarer thinks you might have ♠Q9 or ♠109 doubleton. In either case declarer can ensure four tricks by leading to the king. Surprise! Declarer does get those four tricks, but he had five coming all along if he finessed!

There is no end to the torment you can cause declarer once you become familiar with certain combinations.

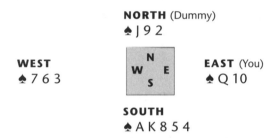

**NORTH** (Dummy)
♠ J 9 2

**WEST**
♠ 7 6 3

**EAST** (You)
♠ Q 10

**SOUTH**
♠ A K 8 5 4

Say spades are trumps and declarer plays the ♠A. If you play the ten, declarer will have no option other than laying down the ace and capturing your queen. However, if you play the *queen*, declarer will certainly place partner with ♠10xxx and lead a low spade to the nine. Ha ha.

The play works the same way when this is the position:

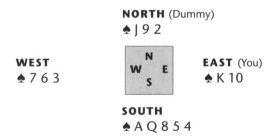

**NORTH** (Dummy)
♠ J 9 2

**WEST**
♠ 7 6 3

**EAST** (You)
♠ K 10

**SOUTH**
♠ A Q 8 5 4

This time South leads a low spade from dummy. What are you going to do? Would I be asking you if the ten was the best play? Of course not. Play the king and watch what happens. Declarer thinks you have a singleton king and partner has ♠10xxx, so confidently continues by leading low to the nine. Another ha ha. And what happens if you play the ten? Not much. Declarer plays the queen and then the ace and you get nothing.

# Practice Hands

**Hand 1**

NORTH-SOUTH VUL.  DEALER EAST

| West | North | East | South |
|------|-------|------|-------|
|      |       | pass | 1♡ |
| pass | 2♢ | pass | 2♠ |
| pass | 3♡ | pass | 4NT |
| pass | 5♢ | pass | 6♡ |
| all pass | | | |

Playing Key Card Blackwood North-South can stay out of near-hopeless slams such as this, but that's another book.

**NORTH** (Dummy)
♠ 2
♡ J 3 2
♢ A Q 4 3 2
♣ K Q 9 2

**WEST** (You)
♠ A 10 9
♡ 10 9 5
♢ 10 6 5
♣ 8 7 6 5

**EAST**
♠ 7 6 5 4 3
♡ K 4
♢ J 9 8 7
♣ 4 3

**SOUTH**
♠ K Q J 8
♡ A Q 8 7 6
♢ K
♣ A J 10

You lead the ♣8 to dummy's queen and declarer leads a low heart to the queen. Hello! Are you there? Did you remember to play the ♡9 (or ♡10)? If not, declarer has no option but to lead the ♡A and nab partner's ♡K. Had you played the ♡9 (or ♡10) you would have given declarer pause. If she plays you for the ♡109 doubleton, and returns to dummy to play the ♡J, you have just defeated a slam.

**Hand 2**

EAST-WEST VUL.  DEALER SOUTH

| West | North | East | South |
|------|-------|------|-------|
|      |       |      | 4♠ |
| all pass | | | |

**NORTH** (Dummy)
♠ A 5
♡ A 10 6 2
♢ K Q J 9
♣ 9 6 3

**WEST**
♠ 6
♡ Q 8 7 5 4
♢ 8 7 3 2
♣ A Q 10

**EAST** (You)
♠ 9 3
♡ K J 9 3
♢ A 5 4
♣ J 8 5 2

**SOUTH**
♠ K Q J 10 8 7 4 2
♡ —
♢ 10 6
♣ K 7 4

Partner leads a top diamond and you win the ace. What a depressing dummy! It looks like you need three quick club tricks, so table the ♣J, playing partner for the ♣AQ10. Oh happy day... I've been good to you again.

**Hand 3**

**NORTH** (Dummy)
- ♠ 9 6 2
- ♡ A 7 2
- ◇ K 10 9 7
- ♣ K 10 9

**WEST** (You)
- ♠ Q 7 5
- ♡ 4 3
- ◇ 5 4 3 2
- ♣ 7 6 5 3

**EAST**
- ♠ K 10 8 4
- ♡ K 9 8 6 5
- ◇ A 8
- ♣ Q 4

**SOUTH**
- ♠ A J 3
- ♡ Q J 10
- ◇ Q J 6
- ♣ A J 8 2

| | | NORTH-SOUTH VUL. DEALER EAST | |
|---|---|---|---|
| West | North | East | South |
| | | 1♡ | 1NT |
| pass | 3NT | all pass | |

Partner leads the ♡4 and declarer ducks to your king. It appears your best chance is to attack spades while you still have the ◇A. You need three spade tricks. Remember your surrounding plays? Lead the ♠10. You are hoping partner has the ♠Qxx, and if she does, you can't afford to lead a low spade: declarer may play low forcing partner to win the queen, retaining the ♠AJ over your king. But if you switch to the ♠10, declarer has no recourse; declarer loses three spades, one heart and one diamond.

**Hand 4**

**NORTH** (Dummy)
- ♠ A 5
- ♡ A K J 9
- ◇ K Q 8 2
- ♣ 10 8 3

**WEST**
- ♠ 6
- ♡ Q 8 7 5 4 3
- ◇ J 10 9
- ♣ A 6 5

**EAST** (You)
- ♠ 9 3
- ♡ 10 6 2
- ◇ A 7 4 3
- ♣ K J 9 2

**SOUTH**
- ♠ K Q J 10 8 7 4 2
- ♡ —
- ◇ 6 5
- ♣ Q 7 4

| | | EAST-WEST VUL. DEALER SOUTH | |
|---|---|---|---|
| West | North | East | South |
| | | | 4♠ |
| all pass | | | |

Partner leads the ◇J to the queen and your ace. It doesn't take an Einstein to figure out that clubs is where the money is. Holding the ♣KJ9 with the ♣10 to your right, the proper card to lead is the jack in case declarer has the queen and partner the ace. After this switch, there is no more to the story.

# Test Yourself

| BOTH VUL. | | DEALER SOUTH | |
|---|---|---|---|
| **West** | **North** | **East** | **South** |
| | | | 1♡ |
| pass | 2♣ | pass | 2♡ |
| pass | 3♡ | pass | 4♡ |
| all pass | | | |

*Solution on page 235*

1)

**NORTH** (Dummy)
♠ 7 5 2
♡ K 9 6
◇ 5
♣ A Q 10 8 7 5

**EAST** (You)
♠ A K 3
♡ 10 2
◇ K 9 6 3 2
♣ K 9 4

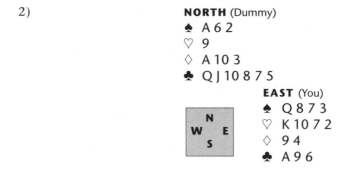

Partner leads the ◇Q, which declarer wins in the closed hand with the ace. He plays off the ace and queen of hearts, partner following with the ♡7 and ♡8. Now South leads the ♣J, partner plays the ♣3 and dummy the ♣5. Plan your defense.

| NEITHER VUL. | | DEALER WEST | |
|---|---|---|---|
| **West** | **North** | **East** | **South** |
| pass | 1♣ | pass | 1♡ |
| pass | 2♣ | pass | 2NT |
| pass | 3NT | all pass | |

*Solution on page 235*

2)

**NORTH** (Dummy)
♠ A 6 2
♡ 9
◇ A 10 3
♣ Q J 10 8 7 5

**EAST** (You)
♠ Q 8 7 3
♡ K 10 7 2
◇ 9 4
♣ A 9 6

The lead is the ◇6 which dummy's ten wins, South playing the ◇5. A low club is led to the ♣K, partner following, and a second club is led to the ♣Q, partner discarding the ◇Q. How are you going to defend?

3)

**NORTH** (Dummy)
♠ K J 10 2
♡ K 10 3
◇ 10 5 4
♣ K 5 2

                **EAST** (You)
                ♠ 8 6 5 3
   N      ♡ 9 7 5 2
W    E   ◇ K J 9 2
   S      ♣ A

| BOTH VUL. | | DEALER NORTH | |
|---|---|---|---|
| **West** | **North** | **East** | **South** |
| | pass | pass | 1NT |
| pass | 2♣ | pass | 2♡ |
| pass | 3NT | all pass | |

Partner leads the ♣J, dummy plays low and you win the ace, declarer playing the ♣3. Plan your defense from here.

*Solution on page 236*

4)

**NORTH** (Dummy)
♠ A 6
♡ 9 5 4
◇ A 10
♣ Q J 10 8 7 5

                **EAST** (You)
                ♠ Q 8 7 3
   N      ♡ K 10 8 2
W    E   ◇ 9
   S      ♣ A 9 6 4

| NEITHER VUL. | | DEALER NORTH | |
|---|---|---|---|
| **West** | **North** | **East** | **South** |
| | 1♣ | pass | 1♠ |
| 3◇ | pass | pass | 3NT |
| all pass | | | |

The lead is the ◇6 which dummy's ten wins, South contributing the ◇5. Next comes the ♣Q, which you duck as partner discards the ◇Q. When a low club is led from dummy you win the ♣A, declarer plays the ♣K, and partner discards the ◇2. Now what?

*Solution on page 236*

5)

**NORTH** (Dummy)
♠ J 5 4

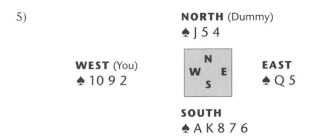

**WEST** (You)                  **EAST**
♠ 10 9 2                    ♠ Q 5

**SOUTH**
♠ A K 8 7 6

Spades are trumps. Is there a way that the defense might score a spade trick?

*Solution on page 237*

6)

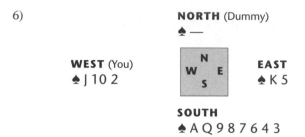

**NORTH** (Dummy)
♠ —

**WEST** (You)
♠ J 10 2

**EAST**
♠ K 5

**SOUTH**
♠ A Q 9 8 7 6 4 3

*Solution on page 237*

South opens 4♠, the closing bid. Your side takes the first two tricks, and South wins the third trick in a side suit and plays the ♠A. Can the defense do anything to garner two trump tricks?

7)

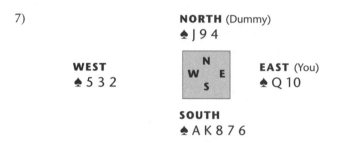

**NORTH** (Dummy)
♠ J 9 4

**WEST**
♠ 5 3 2

**EAST** (You)
♠ Q 10

**SOUTH**
♠ A K 8 7 6

*Solution on page 237*

Spades are trumps and declarer leads the ♠A. See any way of taking a spade trick?

8)

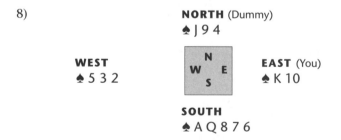

**NORTH** (Dummy)
♠ J 9 4

**WEST**
♠ 5 3 2

**EAST** (You)
♠ K 10

**SOUTH**
♠ A Q 8 7 6

*Solution on page 237*

Spades are trumps, and a low spade is led from dummy. Have any clever ideas?

# Test Yourself — Solutions

1)

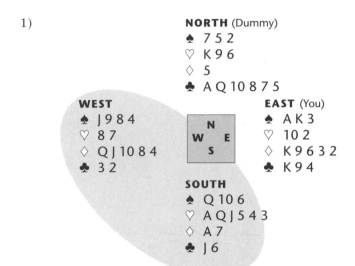

**NORTH** (Dummy)
♠ 7 5 2
♡ K 9 6
◇ 5
♣ A Q 10 8 7 5

**WEST**
♠ J 9 8 4
♡ 8 7
◇ Q J 10 8 4
♣ 3 2

**EAST** (You)
♠ A K 3
♡ 10 2
◇ K 9 6 3 2
♣ K 9 4

**SOUTH**
♠ Q 10 6
♡ A Q J 5 4 3
◇ A 7
♣ J 6

| BOTH VUL. | | DEALER SOUTH | |
|---|---|---|---|
| **West** | **North** | **East** | **South** |
| | | | 1♡ |
| pass | 2♣ | pass | 2♡ |
| pass | 3♡ | pass | 4♡ |
| all pass | | | |

**Trick 1:** ◇Q ◇5 ◇9 ◇A
**Trick 2:** ♡A ♡7 ♡6 ♡2
**Trick 3:** ♡Q ♡8 ♡9 ♡10
**Trick 4:** ♠J ♣3 ♣5 ?

Win the ♣K and shift to a low spade! You need three spade tricks to defeat this contract. If partner has the ♠Q, it doesn't matter which spade you lead, but if declarer has the ♠Q, particularly with the ♠10, you might swindle him out of his spade trick. If declarer makes the normal play of the ten, down he goes.

2)

**NORTH** (Dummy)
♠ A 6 2
♡ 9
◇ A 10 3
♣ Q J 10 8 7 5

**WEST**
♠ J 10
♡ A J 6 3
◇ Q J 8 6 5 2
♣ 2

**EAST** (You)
♠ Q 8 7 3
♡ K 10 7 2
◇ 9 4
♣ A 9 6

**SOUTH**
♠ K 9 5 4
♡ Q 8 5 4
◇ K 7
♣ K 4 3

| NEITHER VUL. | | DEALER WEST | |
|---|---|---|---|
| **West** | **North** | **East** | **South** |
| pass | 1♣ | pass | 1♡ |
| pass | 2♣ | pass | 2NT |
| pass | 3NT | all pass | |

**Trick 1:** ◇6 ◇10 ◇9 ◇5
**Trick 2:** ♣5 ♣6 ♣K ♣2
**Trick 3:** ♣3 ◇Q ♣Q ?

Partner's ◇Q tells you that declarer has the ◇K, or three diamond tricks in all. You can see that there are five club tricks once your ace is removed, and the ♠A in dummy means declarer has nine sure tricks outside of hearts. You must attack hearts and you need four tricks from the suit. You must project ♡AJ6x, ♡AQ6x or better in partner's hand and then lead the ten to silence the nine! Declarer cannot avoid the loss of four heart tricks with this diabolical switch.

3)

**NORTH** (Dummy)
♠ K J 10 2
♡ K 10 3
◇ 10 5 4
♣ K 5 2

| BOTH VUL. | | DEALER NORTH | |
|-----------|---------|--------------|---------|
| **West** | **North** | **East** | **South** |
| | pass | pass | 1NT |
| pass | 2♣ | pass | 2♡ |
| pass | 3NT | all pass | |

**Trick 1:** ♣J ♣2 ♣A ♣3
**Trick 2:** ?

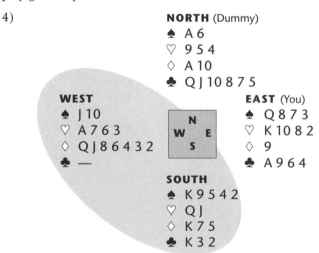

**WEST**
♠ 9 7 4
♡ 8 4
◇ A 8 3
♣ J 10 9 8 7

**EAST** (You)
♠ 8 6 5 3
♡ 9 7 5 2
◇ K J 9 2
♣ A

**SOUTH**
♠ A Q
♡ A Q J 6
◇ Q 7 6
♣ Q 6 4 3

Obviously a diamond shift has to be right; anyone who has learned as much as you from this chapter will surely play the ◇J now! Any time partner has three or four diamonds to the ace this surrounding play garners you four tricks.

4)

**NORTH** (Dummy)
♠ A 6
♡ 9 5 4
◇ A 10
♣ Q J 10 8 7 5

| NEITHER VUL. | | DEALER NORTH | |
|--------------|---------|--------------|---------|
| **West** | **North** | **East** | **South** |
| | 1♣ | pass | 1♠ |
| 3◇ | pass | pass | 3NT |
| all pass | | | |

**Trick 1:** ◇6 ◇10 ◇9 ◇5
**Trick 2:** ♣2 ◇Q ♣Q ♣6
**Trick 3:** ♣5 ♣A ♣K ◇2
**Trick 4:** ?

**WEST**
♠ J 10
♡ A 7 6 3
◇ Q J 8 6 4 3 2
♣ —

**EAST** (You)
♠ Q 8 7 3
♡ K 10 8 2
◇ 9
♣ A 9 6 4

**SOUTH**
♠ K 9 5 4 2
♡ Q J
◇ K 7 5
♣ K 3 2

This is almost a trick question! This time you need *four* heart tricks so you have to play partner for ♡AQx, ♡AJx or Axxx. In all three cases it is correct to switch to a *low* heart, particularly when partner has ♡Axxx and declarer ♡QJ. If you switch to the ten, (the normal play when declarer has *three* hearts), you set up a trick for declarer with the ♡9. Only a scoundrel would include this problem.

5) Assuming declarer starts with the ♠A or ♠K, you have a chance if you play the ♠9 or ♠10. If declarer plays you for ♠109 doubleton and crosses to dummy to lead the jack, you wind up with a spade trick. If you play low the first time, you have no chance of winning a trick if declarer needs five spade tricks; declarer is forced to play another high spade.

6) When declarer cashes the ♠A, drop the ♠J or ♠10, or else South will have no choice but to play someone for ♠Kx and lead low. However, if you play an honor, declarer may try to pin the supposed ♠J10 doubleton by playing the ♠Q next. That won't work.

7) You have a chance if you drop the ♠Q. If declarer believes, and most declarers will, a spade will be led to the ♠9... and your ♠10!

8) Here again, you should play the ♠K. It costs nothing, but if South believes you, he'll finesse the ♠9 coming back. Very tricky!

## Key ideas from Chapter 8

- The card you lead on opening lead may not be the same card you lead from that very same combination after you see the dummy.

- When dummy has an unguarded 10 (to your right) and you have the KJ9 or AJ9, it is usually right to attack with the jack. When dummy has an unguarded 9 (to your right) and you have the Q108 or K108, it is usually right to attack with the 10. These 'surrounding plays' can also be made by the player leading through dummy; that player must project the unguarded nine or ten in declarer's hand.

- Try to give partner any information about your hand that declarer already has.

- Playing the card(s) you are known to hold when it can't cost you a trick is the mark of an experienced defender.

- Be on the lookout for opportunities to create losing options for declarer by playing unnecessarily high cards in situations where it cannot cost you; situations you must learn to recognize. Amen.

# Index